Katie's
Canon

KATIE GENEVA CANNON

Katie's Canon

Womanism and the Soul
of the Black Community

CONTINUUM • NEW YORK

1995

The Continuum Publishing Company
370 Lexington Avenue, New York, NY 10017

Printed in the United States of America

Library of Congress Cataloging-in-Publication Data

Cannon, Katie G.
    Katie's canon : womanism and the soul of the Black community /
Katie Geneva Cannon.
    p. cm.
    Includes bibliographical references.
    ISBN 0-8264-0834-6
    1. American literature–Afro-American authors–History and
criticism–theory, etc. 2. American literature–Women authors–
History and criticism–Theory, etc. 3. Feminism and literature–
United States–History. 4. Women and literature–United States–
History. 5. Afro-American women in literature. 6. Womanist
theology in literature. 7. Afro-Americans in literature.
8. Community life in literature. 9. Ethics in literature.
10. Canon (Literature)   I. Title.
PS153.N5C36 1995
305.42'0973–dc20

95-33210
CIP

To
Joan Dexter Blackmer, my wise friend
Angelin Jones Simmons, my bestest friend
EttaMarie Katherine Moon, my youngblood

Contents

Foreword

For a year, Katie Cannon and I sat together locked in intense, passionate conversation: she the storyteller and sage, I the narrator and spider woman weaving her tales. Together we created Katie's life story, "The Fruit of My Labor," a penetrating portrait that opens my book *I've Known Rivers.* In *Rivers,* I was using a form of inquiry that I call "Human Archeology" — a deep examination of human relationships, development, and experience that seeks to uncover mask and persona and reveal the authentic core of a person's identity. It requires a sustained dialogue, whose success depends on extraordinary trust, empathy, symmetry, and synchrony between the storyteller and the narrator.

Katie Cannon became an enthusiastic and brave practitioner of human archeology, a creative and inspired storyteller. At first she was reluctant, understandably resistant to the exposure and vulnerability of the process. She worried about her worthiness. Were her life and experience interesting enough and exciting enough to warrant documentation and record? Were there not far more illustrious and important people whose stories deserved to be told? She worried about exposing her family and loved ones; making *their* stories public, compromising their privacy, undermining their hard-earned dignity. She worried about revisiting the trauma, the dark tunnels of her experience, and rehearsing the pain of her life. She even worried about *me.* Would I be able to tolerate the raw anguish, the bitter rage that was likely to explode in our conversations?

I, of course, assured her that when I invited her to join this project, I already knew that her life story would be rich and powerful, that she would be a courageous and provocative storyteller. I promised her that we would both be careful about honoring the dignity of her family, and that I could certainly stand the intensity and pitch of her anger and anguish. Her reluctance — having been voiced and named — was quickly discarded and Katie Cannon threw off all the shackles of caution and inhibition. She worked very hard, dug very deep, and was relentless in her pursuit of the truth. After our sessions she would feel exhausted, totally spent. She would go home, pull down the shades, sleep it off, and begin to build her energy and stamina for our next session. She even worked *between* our encounters, musing, reflecting, even acting on impulses that got ignited during our conversations. She would return to the next session with an agenda, with reminders of issues she wanted to raise, ideas and questions that deserved greater scrutiny, and emotions that needed to be voiced.

Besides the intensity and urgency of her work, Katie's stories revealed a wonderful blend of innocence and worldliness, and a fabulous, raucous sense of humor. (When she was a child, she loved doing stand-up comic routines.) She has the clear, wide-open eyes of a child and the deep, all-knowing vision of an elder. Very early in our work, I saw the power of this developmental paradox: the convergence of young and old. Katie is aware of it as well and uses it strategically in her teaching. In *I've Known Rivers,* I spoke about her mischievous wit, her youthful perspective, and her wisdom.

> [Cannon] is forty-one years old but seems to me both older and younger. Older, in the sense that she sometimes seems to be old-fashioned in her style, idiom, and connection to her roots — like someone from our mother's generation. (Katie notices that her white women colleagues often say to her, "You sound just like my mother." And, with the undergraduates she teaches at Wellesley College, "I feel like their *grandmother.*") She appears younger than her years, however, in her eagerness, her idealism, her commitments, and her irreverence.
>
> On the first day of her undergraduate course on liberation theology, Katie wanted to shatter the Wellesley "girls' " narrow image of "minister" and did it all in one swoop. She opened her first class by proclaiming, "I've already done in my life *everything* that I said I wouldn't do!" She makes a big whirling motion with her arms and spins her head around to show how "those children's minds were blown." She clearly enjoys her role as provocateur, relishes the chance to challenge the stereotype, to do the unexpected. In these moments of challenge and irreverence, she seems almost adolescent. Her eyes are mischievous, her face unlined, her body in motion. (18)

Not only was Katie's storytelling enlivened by the combination of her innocence and wisdom; she also had a unique way of seeing, naming, critiquing, and analyzing her experience, a way of dancing across the boundaries of theory and practice, a way of turning commonly held assumptions on their head. These same qualities of perception and critique also inform the essays in this volume. They are pure Katie

Cannon: provocative, irreverent, strong. As I listened to her tales and traced her life-journey, I was often treated to fascinating analyses and surprising interpretations. In the following passage from *Rivers,* Katie recalled November 1963, when John F. Kennedy was murdered, and remembered her ninth-grade classmates' response to the news of his death.

"It was a *comical* day at Carver" [George Washington Carver High School, a segregated school Katie attended in Kannapolis, North Carolina], recalls Katie. The ninth-grade civics class listened to the news of Kennedy being shot and waited for reports from the Dallas hospital emergency room about whether the doctors, with all their best efforts and fancy technology, would be able to revive the president. "Are these white people going to be able to do this resurrection thing on Kennedy? Are they going to be able to pump the life back into him?" The Carver students' questions were laced with bitter laughter and mixed with conversation about "the horrors that occurred in the colored wing of the hospital. We knew we were not first-class citizens.... Our lives were worth nothing to these white people.... In ninth grade, we were already working on organically critiquing society. We knew the country was evil and violent. None of us really mourned Kennedy's death." No one except Katie's sister Sara, who was "the *only* one who cried." Everyone else experienced the injustice, the inequalities, the white privilege of this event — even in death, Kennedy's one life was worth more than hundreds of theirs. "But my sister Sara wept. I was so embarrassed!... How could she cry?" says Katie, remembering her incredulity.

Katie characterizes the class discussion, the bitterness and attitude of deep suspicion. I ask her about this suspicion, and she replies without skipping a beat. "It means that you know danger without having to be taught.... It is what June Jordan calls 'jungle posture'... what Ntozake Shange calls 'the combat stance.'... It is like when Sojourner Truth said, 'nobody lifts me into carriages or over mud puddles, but I am a woman.' You know where the minefields are... there is wisdom.... You are in touch with the ancestors... and it is from the gut, not rationally figured out. Black women have to use this all the time, of course, the creativity is still there, but we are not fools... we call it the 'epistemological privileges of the oppressed.' How do you tap that wisdom — name it, mine it, pass it on to the next generation?"

I recognize that my eyes have widened in amazement and I'm sitting with my back straight as a rod, stretching to understand this gushing avalanche of words and feelings flowing out of Katie.

She seems to be saying so many things, and speaking on so many levels, all at once. There is the idea of the "organic" understanding African-American youngsters possess: they sense that they are second-class citizens in an unjust society, that their lives are not counted or treasured in the same ways as white lives. There is the idea that the development of this understanding is not rational — it comes from "the gut"; it is based on experience and intuition. There is the idea that this suspicion is passed down from the ancestors who teach the next generation the subtle dangers — through act and deed — who instruct their offspring in how to walk through treacherous mine fields, who show them "jungle posture." There is the idea that this suspicion is healthy, necessary for survival *and* that it can coexist with creativity — that even in creativity and expression one must always be watchful, clear-headed, not "act the fool." And finally, there is the idea that African-American women have this deep, instinctive suspicion down to a science. We use it subtly, deftly, wisely. If we didn't know how to use it, we would be destroyed. Some of us have begun to give it high status by labeling it a privilege, the epistemological privilege of the oppressed.

This is vintage Katie Cannon: the vivid ninth-grade story of Kennedy's assassination, the analysis of its meaning in historical and cultural context, the use of the story as a lens for revealing broader societal patterns, philosophical insights, the easy return to the threads of the original story. "So for all these reasons, it is even more horrifying that Sara cried. I couldn't believe it!" (59–60)

Much of Katie's life story was shaped by her urgent desire to escape her roots. She was born and raised in Kannapolis, North Carolina — a segregated, rural town where the "Ku Klux Klan still rise at their whim and will," where, when Katie was a child, Blacks were not allowed to go to the library, eat at the restaurants, sit downstairs at the movie theater, or swim in the local pools and ponds. Katie hated the provincialism, the poverty, the racism, the claustrophobia, the ugly Jim Crow. Very early she began desperately plotting her "great escape." In Kannapolis, the home of Cannon Mills, Black women had three choices. They could work as domestics, do hard labor in the mills, or a tiny, elite group could do the dignified life-giving work of teaching. Katie saw the barriers, witnessed the violence and oppression, and felt the triple-barreled threat of her poverty, her Blackness, and her femaleness. In every fiber of her body, she knew that in order to realize her potential, in order to shape her identity, it would be necessary for her to leave. Flight was her great preoccupation. "My heart was breaking wide open...I was desperate to find a place to be *ME!*"

Her search took her all over the world: to New York, to Santa Fe, New Mexico (where her visit to Ghost Ranch "opened up the horizon and pushed it toward the sun"), to West Africa, to Israel and Jordan. But even when — at seventeen — she went off to Barber Scotia College, a tiny Black school seven miles up the road, she packed her trunk and exaggerated the distance by returning home only when they closed the school for Christmas vacation. Barber Scotia could have been on the other side of the country. Each journey away from her roots helped Katie discover new dimensions of her identity, helped her create and shape her complicated and unique perspective on the world. But after some time, the travel also forced her to reckon with the emptiness and futility of her single-minded pursuit. Identity and perspective are not formed merely through escape.

By the time Katie Cannon agreed to take the journey through *Rivers,* she was "ready to return home." She was ready to admit that identity and wholeness come with reconnection as well as retreat. She was ready to celebrate the richness of her impoverished past. At forty-one, she was ready to face what she enthusiastically refers to as "my middle-aged crisis." She now thinks of mid-life as a time of reckoning with loss, reconnecting with ancestors, "scraping the whites off of her eyeballs," honoring the goodness in her imperfect family, getting in touch with feelings, slowing down. It is also a time of making "the translation" from her childhood home (poor, Black, rural, chaotic) to her adult nest (abundant, predominantly White, urban, serene). "I come from a place," explains Katie, "where when people talk about *field work* they literally mean field work — work in the fields — not ethnographic research. I come from a place where there isn't but one kind of doctor, the person who takes care of you when you are sick...."

The work of "translation" is difficult, sometimes unbearably painful. For Katie, it has meant moving from a life dominated by thinking, logic, analysis, and rationality to a place where she "takes the time to feel," where she can "catch the dreams and interpret them." The essays in *Katie's Canon* reveal the fruits of this treacherous translation, the bringing together of the disparate worlds of childhood and adulthood; and they express the convergence of thought and feeling, analysis and emotion. As a matter of fact, the pieces in this volume represent a kind of courageous stocktaking, a critique and celebration of the power of duality, but also a recognition of the discomforts, anguish, and ambiguity that the two-ness inspires. Cannon's work reveals her brave confrontation with the dualities that society seems to construct — the dualities of Whiteness and Blackness, of feminism and African-Americanism, of southern and northern, of thinker and preacher, of beautiful and ugly, of literate and illiterate, of cosmopolitan and provincial. But Katie does something very interesting with these opposing forces: first she magnifies the differences; then she composes their convergence. As a matter of fact, her creativity grows out of embracing, naming, and exaggerating all of these dualisms. In them lies her wellspring of strength as well as her greatest vulnerabilities. By marking and intensifying the dualities (in her life, her teaching, and her writings), Katie Cannon is better able to transcend the boundaries between them.

W. E. B. Du Bois, whose work is quoted in this volume, spoke about the power and vulnerability of this double vision, dual perspectives that are captured and echoed in *Katie's Canon*. In his essay "Of Beauty and Death," from his collection *Darkwater: Voices from within the Veil* (1920), Du Bois tells of an attempt by a Black man to buy an orchestra ticket to see a Charlie Chaplin movie. The salesperson tells him that only the cheapest seats in the smoking gallery are available. Suspicious, the man lingers by. A White man rushes up. He is sold three tickets to the orchestra. "Suddenly your heart chills. You turn yourself away toward the golden twinkle of the purple night and hesitate again. What's the use?" Then rage comes. He confronts the seller, who contemptuously throws the demanded ticket at him. "Then you slink to your seat and crouch in the darkness before the film, with every tissue burning... God! What a night of pleasure."

Du Bois goes on to speak about the beautiful-ugly center of human experience, the life and death, the finity and infinity. "There is something in the nature of Beauty," he writes, "that demands an end. Ugliness may be indefinite. It may trail off into gray endlessness. But Beauty must be complete... whether it be a field of poppies or a great life — it must end, and the End is part and triumph of the Beauty. I know there are those who envisage a beauty eternal. But I cannot. I can dream of great and never ending processions of beautiful things and visions and acts. But each must be complete or it cannot for me exist."

"On the other hand," Du Bois claims, "Ugliness to me is eternal, not in the essence but in its incompleteness; but its eternity does not daunt me, for its eternal unfulfillment is a cause of joy. There is in it nothing new or unexpected; it is the old evil stretching out and ever seeking the end it cannot find; it may coil and writhe and recur in endless battle to days without end, but it is the same human ill and bitter hurt. But Beauty is fulfillment. It satisfies. It is always new and strange. It is the reassurable thing. Its end is Death — the sweet silence of perfection, the calm and balance of utter music. Therein is the triumph of Beauty."

In *Katie's Canon*, we hear the music and the chaos. We sense the fulfillment and the unfulfillment, the triumph and the defeat. "I magnify the dualities," she reminds us. Cannon's essays complicate. They rage. They provoke. They make us consider the "privileges" and impotence of our oppression and they challenge us to fight all forms of racism, sexism, classism, and homophobia in an effort to create a more just society. This work — Katie warns — is difficult, daily labor. It is unglamorous, incremental, unsentimental, often invisible. It demands vigilance and courage, and it must be lubricated by humor. Katie Cannon's work serves as challenge, admonition, and witness.

SARA LAWRENCE-LIGHTFOOT

Professor of Education
Harvard University

Preface

Recalling the title of this book will be as easy as remembering my name. Dr. Bernice Johnson Reagon, a cultural anthropologist at the Smithsonian Institution and the founder and leader of the African American women's vocal ensemble Sweet Honey in the Rock named this book, *Katie's Canon* during the Black Woman Writer and Diaspora Conference sponsored by Michigan State University in the fall of 1985. Following my presentation on "Black Women's Literature as Sacred Texts," Dr. Johnson Reagon commented that I live out the essence of my name by always opening up the canon. I attempted to dodge the responsibility of this authoritative task by explaining that I am a "cannon" *boom! boom!* Dr. Johnson Reagon remarked, "We are an oral people. A cannon is a canon." Indeed. Dr. Cheryl J. Sanders's essay "Womanist Ethics: Contemporary Trends and Themes"[1] bears witness to this ten-year old prophecy in the following way:

> Womanist ethics is a relatively recent development in religious studies, having its origins in 1985 when Katie G. Cannon appropriated Alice Walker's concept and definition in relation to black women's tradition of biblical interpretation in "The Emergence of Black Feminist Consciousness," a chapter written for the anthology *Feminist Interpretation of the Bible.*[2]

Katie's Canon: Womanism and the Soul of the Black Community is a selection from essays I wrote for diverse occasions over a period of ten years. Some of this writing took place at Harvard Divinity School in 1983 when I was a Women's Research Associate in Christian Social Ethics. A Mary Ingraham Bunting Fellowship allowed me to participate in the Bunting Institute of Radcliffe College in Cambridge, Massachusetts, in 1987–88 and to write the second part of this text. While a Rockefeller Scholar in Residence at the Center for Black Literature and Culture at the University of Pennsylvania in 1991–92, I was able to rethink some of my pedagogical concerns and to broaden the context of my ideas. In bringing this work together in one volume, I lay bare womanist norms for emancipatory praxis. In each essay I am conducting a three-pronged systemic analysis of race, sex, and class from the perspective of African American women in the academy of religion.

I want to thank a number of those who have helped with this project. Appreciation is extended to Sara Lawrence-Lightfoot, Emilie M. Townes, Benjamin A. Currence, Kerry L. Haynie, Elisabeth Schüssler Fiorenza, Mercy Amba Oduyoye, Peter Paris, John H. Cartwright, Judith Plaskow, Beverly W. Harrison, James H. Cone, Deborah McDowell, Cheryl Townsend Gilkes, Carol Robb, Delores S. Williams, Jacquelyn Grant, Marcia Y. Riggs, Martha Acklesberg, Renita J. Weems, Janie V. Ward, M. Susan Harlow, Nellie Y. McKay, Houston A. Baker, Jr., Minnie J. Wright, and Karen E. Reliford, whose intellectual companionship as well as personal friendship were crucial in the creation of this manuscript.

I am grateful to my former colleagues at the Episcopal Divinity School for their encouragement, sabbatical leaves, and the much-needed financial support through Conant Grants and the Young Scholars Fellowship of the Association of Theological Schools. Many seminarians have assisted my research. Joanna Kadi, Meck Groot, Laura Ruth Jarrett, Julie Wilson, Webb Brown, Ngozi Obi, Matt Watson, Peta Blake, Ann Sipko, Sue Phillips, Sheri Hostetler, Joann Vasconcellos, Carlene Larsson, and Melissa Cooper contributed immeasurably to this text.

I am also thankful to the faculty, staff, and students in the Department of Religion at Temple University and the members of First African Presbyterian Church in Philadelphia. For their support I am most grateful.

Homage is due to the African American women who belong to the American Academy of Religion and the Society of Biblical Literature. The extraordinary scholarship of women who are active in the Womanist Approaches to Religion and Society Working Group has profoundly influenced my work.

I am indebted to Carolyn S. Hopley, who continues to provide support and encouragement in times of frustration. In the final stages, she moved me off the dime of procrastination by reading the entire manuscript and proofreading the galleys.

Frank Oveis, my editor, has waited patiently for this project since 1990. His gentle persistence and enthusiastic prodding were extremely helpful throughout the process that converted this compilation of class notes into a book.

The dedication will never fully reveal the contributions that Joan D. Blackmer, the Reverend Angelin J. Simmons, and Etta Moon have made in transforming this work from dream into reality.

Last but not least are my parents, Esau and Corine Lytle Cannon; my sisters, Sara C. Fleming, Doris C. Love, Sylvia M. Edwards; and my brothers, James E. Cannon, John W. Cannon, and Jerry L. Cannon, whose unconditional love has made all the difference.

Katie's
Canon

Womanist 1. From *womanish*. (Opp. of "girlish," i.e., frivolous, irresponsible, not serious.) A black feminist or feminist of color. From the black folk expression of mothers to female children, "You acting womanish," i.e., like a woman. Usually referring to outrageous, audacious, courageous or *willful* behavior. Wanting to know more and in greater depth than is considered "good" for one. Interested in grown-up doings. Acting grown up. Being grown up. Interchangeable with another black folk expression: "You trying to be grown." Responsible. In charge. *Serious.*

2. *Also:* A woman who loves other women, sexually and/or nonsexually. Appreciates and prefers women's culture, women's emotional flexibility (values tears as natural counterbalance of laughter), and women's strength. Sometimes loves individual men, sexually and/or nonsexually. Committed to survival and wholeness of entire people, male *and* female. Not a separatist, except periodically, for health. Traditionally universalist, as in: "Mama, why are we brown, pink, and yellow, and our cousins are white, beige, and black?" Ans.: "Well, you know the colored race is just like a flower garden, with every color flower represented." Traditionally capable, as in: "Mama, I'm walking to Canada and I'm taking you and a bunch of other slaves with me." Reply: "It wouldn't be the first time."

3. Loves music. Loves dance. Loves the moon. *Loves* the Spirit. Loves love and food and roundness. Loves struggle. *Loves* the Folk. Loves herself. *Regardless.*

4. Womanist is to feminist as purple to lavender.

Definition of a "Womanist" from *In Search of Our Mothers' Gardens: Womanist Prose*, copyright © 1983 by Alice Walker, reprinted by permission of Harcourt Brace & Company.

Introduction

My grandmother, Rosa Cornelia White Lytle, was the gatekeeper in the land of "counterpain." She was always available with salves, hot towels, and liniments to cure physical aches and spiritual ills. As a charismatic healer, Grandma Rosie's practice consisted of diagnosis, treatment, and prevention in the maintenance of overall wholeness. Many days my soul struggled with whether to go to school or stay home and be healed from the injuries the world inflicted unknowingly.

In 1983, "Womanism" became the new gatekeeper in my land of counterpain. Early that spring, an African American woman poet, novelist, essayist and short story writer, Alice Walker, coined the term "womanist."[1] Walker's expertise lay in literature, not in etymology or theology. And yet her symbolic crafting of an all-encompassing definition was philosophically medicinal.

The creation of womanist as a confessional concept was a benchmark event for African American scholars in religion, arguably most significant for women in the American Academy of Religion and the Society of Biblical Literature. The chief function of womanism is not merely to replace one set of elitist, hegemonic texts that have traditionally ignored, dismissed, or flat-out misunderstood the existential realities of women of the African Diaspora with another set of Afrocentric texts that had gotten short shrift and pushed to the margins of the learned societies. Rather our objective is to use Walker's four-part definition as a critical, methodological framework for challenging inherited traditions for their collusion with androcentric patriarchy as well as a catalyst in overcoming oppressive situations through revolutionary acts of rebellion. My overall goal in this project is to recast the very terms and terrain of religious scholarship.

In developing the focus for the essays collected in this volume, I recalled the specific feedback I received time and time again after public lectures on womanism. Most of the time, an undesignated spokesperson in the audience makes a declaration that African American women scholars are non-political. I asked one gentleman who was getting very worked up about this what he meant by saying that womanists are apolitical. Not even sighing or missing a heartbeat, he responded, "Well, it seems to me that womanist work is not talking about White people." I said that is correct. We do not begin nor end our work with White people on our eyeballs. So he and others conclude that if Euro-Americans are not the focal point of departure then womanist work is without political significance.

While it is perfectly legitimate, indeed imperative, for each of us to assert and exercise our right to engage theoretical and critical activities in the academy, we must disentangle the power relations within American society wherein certain people whether by accident, design, providence, or the most complicated means of academic currency exchange high-handedly dictate the specific disciplinary aims, setting the parameters as well as the agenda, for each field of study.[2]

In a major sense, my desire to shift the intellectual paradigm grows out of one dynamic that emerges insistently after every womanist lecture. During the question and answer sessions the tension often mounts and continues to intensify until the conversation explodes into loud, chaotic babble. The bottom line concern is always the same: "How dare African American women exclude men from being the subject of womanist discourse, especially when men have always included women." The line of argument put forth is that rigorous, academically excellent scholarship is always universal. This type of so-called value neutrality of disinterested objectivity suppresses socioecclesial location.

It is important to note that too often when womanists are in dialogue with other communities of discourse there is an intentional attempt to obscure the power relations that constitutes pseudo-inclusivity. A significant number of colleagues protest any and all marginalization of their work and yet insist on subsuming African American women's scholarship under categories of White women and Black men. Professors of religion believe that they have the right to resist the expansion of the field by misinterpreting womanist scholarship as apolitical, inferior, and dangerously essentialist.

Womanism requires that we stress the urgency of the African American women's movement from death to life. In order to do this, we recount in a logical manner the historical consequences of what precedes us. We investigate contestable issues according to the official records, which seldom offer any indication why things have gone wrong nor why benefactors of oppression strive to maintain certain principles, values, and taboos as the center of social reality. In other words, womanist religious scholars insist that individuals look back at race, sex, and class constructions before it is too late and put forth critical analysis in such a way that the errors of the past will not be repeated.

Thinking about reputed inventors of normative social anatomy who have given little attention to the moral agency of Black, working, poor women from a liberation perspective has challenged me as a reader and writer of ethics. Whatever the reasons may have been for this failure, it must be rectified if we are to create a larger ethical scene against which the particularities of our various context might unfold.

Each essay in this book is a challenge to systems of domination. Each contains an imperative for women and men of African ancestry to map out survival strategies in such a way that moral wisdom is communicated. Each is a call for action wherein the individual social-self as well as the larger collective community can break out of brutal cycles of misery and violence.

The twentieth century will be ushered out by a prophecy similar to the one by which it was introduced. In the preface to his famous book of 1903, *The Souls of Black Folks,* W. E. B. Du Bois wrote: "The problem of the Twentieth Century is the problem of the colour line."[3] The essays in this book support the triumphs and struggles that have brought us to the edge of this new millennium. Still, my hope is that readers will join in generous cooperation and thoughtful collaboration in what appears to me as necessary work for a promising future. The problem of the twentieth-first century is the problem of the color line, the gender line, and the class line.

Chapter 1

Surviving the Blight

And when we (to use Alice Walker's lovely phrase) go in search
of our mothers' gardens, it's not really to learn who trampled on
them or how or even why — we usually know that already. Rather,
it's to learn what our mothers planted there, what they thought as
they sowed, and how they survived the blighting of so many fruits.
— Sherley Anne Williams[1]

I am most aware of the rich lore I inherited from my mother's garden in
Kannapolis, North Carolina. I recall particularly the stories shared during devastating thunderstorms. Whenever there were gusty winds and
heavy rain accompanied by lightning and thunder, the Cannon house-
hold became — and still becomes — a folklore sanctuary. We turn off
all the lights, unplug electrical appliances, and leave the supper dishes
sitting in the kitchen sink. When the whole family is seated strategically
around the kerosene lantern, my mother, Corine Lytle Cannon, moves
into her role as creative storyteller.[2]

My mother's style is to reminisce around a stock of historical images,
themes, and cultural expressions that tell the story of the origin of Black
people in America. Much of what she recounts is based on testimony
shared across generations that her father, Emmanuel Clayton Lytle, born
August 21, 1865, was the only free child in his family. My grandfather's
parents, siblings, and all others who preceded him were born into slavery. One of our favorite family legends centers around his mother, my
maternal great-grandmother, Mary Nance Lytle, born in 1832. When
freedom finally came, Grandma Mary walked hundreds of miles, from
plantation to plantation, looking for the children who had been taken
from her and sold as slaves. With only instinct to guide her, Grandma

This chapter was first published in Letty Russell, et al., eds., *Inheriting Our Mother's
Gardens* (Westminster Press, 1988), 75–90.

Mary persisted until she found all her children and brought the family back together.

As direct descendants of African American slaves, my family understands such tales as the indispensable source of Black people's historical confidence and spiritual persistence despite all oppression. My mother's keen memory and her extraordinary artistic sense enable her to pass on eyewitness accounts from freed relatives to succeeding generations. These narratives are the soil where my inheritance from my mother's garden grew.

Historical Context

As a student of slave narratives, seeking the interior garden of Afro-American culture, I discovered unmistakable evidence that racial slavery in the United States was the cruelest of institutions. The unmitigated severity of slavery was based on the assumed principle of human chattelhood. As early as 1660, it was decreed that henceforth all Africans — and only Africans and their descendants — entering the colonies would be subjected to an entire institutional framework that required them to be treated as objects, as possessions, rather than as human beings. The principle of chattelhood enabled the inner dynamics of racial slavery to expand until it penetrated the basic institutional and ideological underpinnings of the entire normative order of society.

Acquisition of Slaves

The "middle passage," the transoceanic travel of captive and enslaved Africans, has been described as the most traumatizing mass human migration in modern history. Over a period of nearly four centuries, somewhere between nine million and fifty million people from central and western areas of Africa were seized, loaded on ships, and transported to the Americas. Each year slavers systematically hunted tens of thousands of African women, men, and children, chained them in coffles, and packed them in barracoons. People of different tribes, languages, and cultures were driven along in caravans, placed in the dungeons of slave castles or corral-like stock pens, and branded with the slave company's mark. Then they were shackled and crammed into the poorly ventilated holds of small ships, with their faces pressed against the backs of those lying in front of them. The treatment was so harsh that one out of every eight Africans died en route. So much wretchedness was never condensed in so little room as in the slave ships.

Status of Slaves

The status of chattel — mere property — was permanent, hereditary, and strictly racial. African and African American women, men, and children were reduced to the condition of livestock, and their value was calculated in real estate terms. Of all Western slaveholding areas, it was in the United States that slaves were defined most completely as sources of capital accumulation and commodities. All Afro-Americans (Blacks) were presumed to be slaves unless they could establish that they had been legally freed. The legalization of chattel slavery meant that the overwhelming majority of Blacks lived permanently in subhuman status. No objective circumstance — education, skill, dress, or bearing — could modify this fundamentally racist arrangement. This mode of racial domination meant that as chattel slaves none of my ancestors were human beings legally, culturally, socially, or politically. They had no socially recognized personhood. Their status in U.S. society was literally as things. The institution of slavery and its corollaries, White supremacy and racial bigotry, excluded Black people from every normal human consideration.

Afro-Americans faced many assaults, both cultural and physical. Like domestic animals, they were literally called "stock." Their children were anticipated as "increase." My Black foremothers were referred to as "brood sows and breeders." My Black forefathers, when sold, were described, as were horses, as either "sound or unsound." At slave auctions, Black people were stripped naked, exposed to public view, and dehumanized with pokes, probes, and crude physical examinations. Often traders made slaves run, leap, and perform acts of agility to demonstrate their "value" as chattel.

Contemporary assessments of racial slavery cannot afford to ignore this history of the virtually unlimited power of White slaveholders. The submission required of slaves was unbounded. Armed with absolute dominion over the slave, the master's power extended to every dimension, including life and death. Slaveholders had the power to kill slaves with impunity. If a slave was injured or killed by someone else, the master could claim compensation comparable to damages due when an animal was harmed. A slave suffering from such a wrong was not considered the injured party. The slaveholder was considered to be the sufferer, damaged because of the loss of the slave's labor. The death of a slave required neither official investigation nor report, any more than did the death of cattle. Non-Blacks on the American scene portrayed Black slaves to be dumb, stupid, or contented, capable of doglike devotion, wanting in basic human qualities. They used such caricatures to convince themselves that the human beings whom they violated, degraded, and humiliated or whose well-being they did not protect were unworthy of anything better.

Conditions of Slavery

Classified as pieces of movable property, devoid of the minimum human rights society conferred on others, my great-grandparents could neither own property nor make contracts. As slaves, they were not permitted to buy or sell anything at all except as their masters' agents. They could not give or receive gifts. They could not travel without a pass. Afro-Americans had no security and no protection against insults and deliberate injuries inflicted on them. There was no one to hear their complaints of ill-treatment, no power of appeal, no redress whatever. In essence, Black women, men, and children were denied all the conventionalized prerogatives of the human condition defined by the American culture.

Forced into the precise and irrevocable category of perpetual servitude *durante vita,* for all generations, Black people could not be legally married. Without the legal status of marriage, the union of a female slave and a male slave was considered as "cohabitation," which was tolerated but might be terminated at will by slaveholders. White people differentiated between the basic rights and patterns of the family life they claimed for themselves as a "democratic" nation and those they deemed just treatment for their human merchandise. One former slave recalled:

> My pa b'longin' to one man and my mammy b'longin' to another, four or five miles apart, caused some confusion, mix-up, and heartaches. My pa have to git a pass to come to see my mammy. He come sometimes without de pass. Patrollers catch him way up de chimney hidin' one night; they stripped him right befo' mammy and give him thirty-nine lashes, wid her cryin' and a hollerin' louder than he did.[3]

Slaves were constantly being robbed of familiar social ties in order that slaveholders could maximize their profits. All of the slave's relationships existed under the shadowy but imminent threat of permanent separation. Black people lived in constant fear and regularly had to endure the reality of having their husbands, wives, and children sold away from them under conditions that made it unlikely that they would ever see one another again. Relationships between both blood kin and friends were broken up by the interstate migration of slave labor. Slaveholders were at liberty to give, sell, or bequeath African Americans to other persons.

> A slave owner who broke up a family was not heartless by his lights. The kindliest of masters saw nothing wrong in giving a slave child to his son or daughter when they married. An economically pressed planter might regret that husbands and wives would be

separated if he moved to the Southwest, but what could he do? Sometimes debts mounted and slaves were seized by the sheriff or owners died and estates were divided.[4]

Countless slave families were forcibly disrupted.

Exploitation of Slave Workers

Be it in the Piedmont section, tidewater Virginia, the rice districts of South Carolina, or the lower Mississippi Valley, stories abound concerning my ancestors' lot, memories of stripes and torture. Their labor was coerced without wages, extorted by brute force. Slaveholders inflicted on slaves any severity they deemed necessary to make slaves perform required tasks and meted out any sort or degree of punishment for failure to work as expected or for otherwise incurring their displeasure.

Answerable with their bodies for all offenses, slaves were beaten with horse whips, cow straps, and a variety of blunt weapons. They suffered from scalding, burning, rape, and castration, sometimes dying from such inflictions. The great cruelty exhibited toward slaves resulted in instances of gouged-out eyes, slit tongues, and dismembered limbs. Sometimes slaves were physically marked by brands or tattoos or by wooden yokes or iron collars with long extended spokes. The callous and brutal system of slavery required a considerable number of slaves to wear chains, not only in the field during working hours but also at night in their living quarters. Eli Coleman, born a slave in 1846, recalled:

> Massa whooped a slave if he got stubborn or lazy. He whooped one so hard that the slave said he'd kill him. So Massa done put a chain round his legs, so he jes' hardly walk, and he has to work in the fields that way. At night he put 'nother chain round his neck and fastened it to a tree.[5]

The stark fact is that even while slaves lived under differing degrees of harshness, all slaves served under continuous duress.

> A handsome mulatto woman, about 18 or 20 years or age, whose independent spirit could not brook the degradation of slavery, was in the habit of running away; for this offence she had been repeatedly sent by her master and mistress to be whipped by the keeper of the Charleston workhouse. This had been done with such inhuman severity, as to lacerate her back in a most shocking manner; a finger could not be laid between the cuts. But the love of liberty was too strong to be annihilated by torture; and as a last resort, she was whipped at several different times, and kept a close prisoner. A heavy iron collar, with three prongs projecting from it, was

placed around her neck, and a strong and sound front tooth was extracted, to serve as a mark to describe her, in case of escape.[6]

The atrocious mutilation, too often practiced, was deeply rooted in and closely bound up with the whole existing system of chattelhood. The forms of permitted coercion effected a more complete dehumanization of slaves than had other institutional forms of slavery in earlier societies. Never before U.S. chattel slavery was a people so systematically deprived of their human rights and submerged in abject misery. The intent was to crush the spirit and will in order to transform an entire race of people, their lives and their labor, into basic commodities of production and reproduction. White supremacists in the antebellum South believed that such systematic terrorism was absolutely necessary for the continuance of their highly prized way of life and of the economic organization, social relations, and political conditions necessary to it.

Even though the customary methods of enslavement were harsh and even ferocious, Black people worked in every branch of colonial trade and commerce. In addition to the gang labor on cotton, rice, tobacco, and sugar cane plantations, Black women and men worked as cooks, waiters, nurses, carpenters, masons, valets, gardeners, weavers, shoemakers, lumberjacks, and stevedores. Enslaved workers were also forced to work in mines, extracting coal, lead, iron, and gold. They built canals and pulled barges. Slaves dug tunnels, laid rails, and staffed the railroad system. Relegated to the quarries, slaves drilled and tapped explosives, cut and polished stones, and freighted them away. Working under the lash and guarded by overseers, bondswomen regularly performed virtually the same tasks as men.

The rigor of bondage meant that chattel slaves worked always at the discretion of their owners. They could not sell their own labor. My forebears had no say as to where, for whom, or how they would work. Slaveholders dictated the nature of the work, the times for labor and rest, and the amount of work to be performed. The fruit of Black labor could not convert to financial and material gains for Black people and their families. Black people were exploited both for White people's profit and for their pleasure.

Hovering over all my cultural inheritance is the devastating reality that chattel tenure excluded any sort of social recognition of Black people as thinking, religious, and moral beings. My ancestors were forbidden by stringent laws to acquire an education or obtain the means to buy their own freedom. The dominant legal and social attitude was that slaves were to be kept ignorant and living a marginal existence, fed or famished, clothed or left naked, sheltered or unsheltered as served the slaveholder. In North Carolina it was a crime to distribute any pamphlet or book, including the Bible, among slaves. Only under rigidly specified conditions could Black people take part in services of worship. Preaching the gospel, assembling together, and learning to read and write were understood simply as obstacles to the maximization of slave identity. Black people were the only people in the United States ever explicitly forbidden by law to become literate.

Cultural Inheritance

Despite the devastations of slavery, with its unremitting exercise of raw planter power and unconstrained coercion, my ancestors had the hours from nightfall to daybreak to foster, sustain, and transmit cultural mechanisms that enabled them to cope with such bondage. In spite of every form of institutional constraint, Afro-American slaves were able to create another world, a counterculture within the White-defined world, complete with their own folklore, spirituals, and religious practices. These tales, songs, and prayers are the most distinctive cultural windows through which I was taught to see the nature and range of Black people's response to the dehumanizing pressures of slavery and plantation life. Even with cultural self-expression outlawed, my ancestors never surrendered their humanity or lost sight of a vision of freedom and justice they believed to be their due. There was a critical difference between what Whites tried to teach and what slaves actually learned. Against all odds, Afro-American slaves created a culture saturated with their own values and heavily laden with their dreams.

Folklore

The folktales I have heard all my life were created by the slaves throughout the antebellum South as a strategy for coping with oppression and for turning their world upside down. Operating beneath a veil of pseudo-complacency, Black women and men tapped into a profound sense of cultural cohesion, creating an expressive system of coded messages to communicate what they considered good, worthy, and meaningful. Since their survival depended on keeping their true feelings undetected in the presence of Whites, Afro-Americans employed the wit, intelligence, and ingenuity of Br'er Fox, Br'er Rabbit, the Squinch Owl, and others to overwhelm and defeat the powerful foes, Ole Massa and his wife. An ancient Black verse describes the pro-active phenomenon of folktales in this way:

> Got one mind for white folks to see,
> Nother for what I know is me;
> He don't know, he don't know my mind.[7]

Many of the slave stories have a defensive verbal dimension so esoteric that White people miss their meanings altogether. Langston Hughes and Arna Bontemps elaborate this point in the following manner:

> While masters of slaves went to some length to get rid of tribal languages and some tribal customs, like certain practices of sorcery, they accepted the animal stories as a harmless way to ease time or entertain the master's children. That the folk tales of these Negro slaves were actually projections of personal experiences and hopes and defeats in terms of symbols appears to have gone unnoticed.[8]

Scores and scores of Blacks projected their everyday experiences and their own sensibilities onto legendary figures like High John de Conqueror, John the Trickster, and Efram as a challenge to the slave system. As C. Eric Lincoln has written:

> Every black community in the South has its multitudes of legends illustrating blacks' superior strength, sexual prowess, and moral integrity. "Mr. Charlie" is never a match for the cunning of "Ol' John." And "Miss Ann," though she is "as good a ol' white woman" as can be found anywhere, remains in the mind of the black southerner a white woman, and therefore a legitimate target for the machinations of her black servant, "Annie Mae."[9]

Living in a dialectical relationship with White supremacy, folklore was the essential medium by which the themes of freedom, resistance, and self-determination were evoked, preserved, and passed by word of mouth from generation to generation. Older slaves used folktales to reveal to their fellow slaves what they knew. As tradition bearers, they distilled this compendium of folk wisdom into instructional materials to teach younger slaves how to survive. The reappropriation of their own experiences afforded the slaves opportunities to strip away the social absurdity of chattelhood so carefully camouflaged in the dominant culture. In other words, folklore was the mask the slaves wore in order to indict slavery and to question the society in which it flourished. By objectifying their lives in folktales, Afro-American slaves were able to assert the dignity of their own persons and the invincibility of their cause.

Spirituals

Like many raconteurs, my mother always includes music in her storytelling sessions. While waiting for the ongoing storm to subside, my mother invites the family to join her in singing Afro-American spirituals. Beating time with our hands or feet, we sing about Mary weeping, Martha mourning, Peter sinking, and Thomas doubting. This genre of Black sacred music is a vital part of my family's religious tradition.

The music we listen to and sing at home is in the tradition of my ancestors, musicians who fashioned their songs from biblical lore, traditional African tunes, Protestant hymns, and the crucible of their experiences under slavery. Using their own distinct phrases, improvisational structure, polyrhythms, and call-and-response patterns, Black women and men expressed their consciousness and identity as a religious people. Some of their songs were slow, drawn-out "sorrow tunes" that reflected the mood of suffering in the midst of unspeakable cruelty.

> Nobody knows de trubble I sees,
> Nobody knows but Jesus,
> Nobody knows de trubble I sees,
> Glory hallelu!

Other spirituals were liturgical shouts and jubilees, songs with reference to a future happy time. These required upbeat tempos accompanied by rhythmic clapping and holy dancing.

> Oh, my soul got happy
> When I come out the wilderness,
> Come out the wilderness,
> Come out the wilderness,
> Oh, my soul got happy
> When I come out the wilderness,
> I'm leanin' on the Lawd.

A number of spirituals were veiled protest songs used to announce secret meetings, planned escapes, and the route and risk of the freedom trail.

> Steal away, steal away,
> Steal away to Jesus!
> Steal away, steal away home,
> I ain't got long to stay here!

In essence, spirituals were the indispensable device that slaves, forbidden by slaveholders to worship or, in most cases, even to pray, used to transmit a worldview fundamentally different from and opposed to that of slaveholders. For instance, slaveholders spoke of slavery being "God-ordained," while slaves sang

> O Freedom! O Freedom!
> O Freedom, I love thee!
> And before I be a slave,
> I'll be buried in my grave,
> And go home to my Lord and be free.

The spirituals express my ancestors' unflinching faith that they, too, were people of God.

As spiritual singers, slaves were not bothered by the chronological distance between the biblical era and their present. Operating on a sense of sacred time, they extended time backward so as to experience an immediate intimacy with biblical persons as faith relatives. In other words, the characters, scenes, and events from the Bible came dramatically alive in the midst of their estrangement. The trials and triumphs of Noah riding out the flood, Moses telling Pharaoh to let God's people go, Jacob wrestling all night with an angel, Daniel being delivered from the lion's den, Shadrach, Meshach, and Abednego walking in the midst of flames, Joshua fighting the battle of Jericho, and Jesus praying in the Garden of Gethsemane are some of the Bible stories my foreparents committed to music as they interpreted their own experience against a wider narrative of hope and courage.

Prayer

When the rainfall's intensity and the wind's velocity drop and the lightning and the thunder recede, I know that the end of the storytelling is near. Believing that a direct personal relationship with God exists, my mother always concludes her stories with a long prayer of intercession, praise, and thanksgiving. Kneeling beside the couch, she prays for the needs of both the immediate and the extended family. She celebrates God's goodness, majesty, and mercy. She frequently enunciates thanks for the gifts of the earth and for all the blessings received. After a period of silence, my mother then provides time for every family member to bear witness to the immediate power of Jesus as "heart fixer and mind regulator."

This sacred corporate event is the direct and natural successor to the oral folklore and the religious music inherited from Afro-American slaves. Hence I grew up understanding the Black prayer tradition to be the authentic living bridge between Black people's stories, Black people's music, and Black people's source of faith.

In the past, my ancestors met in secluded places — woods, gullies, ravines, and thickets (aptly called "hush harbors") — to pray without being detected. Adeline Hodges, born a slave in Alabama, attests to the importance of prayer:

> De slaves warn't 'lowed to go to church, but dey would whisper roun, and all meet in de woods and pray. De only time I 'members my pa was one time when I was a li'l chile, he set me on a log by him an' prayed.[10]

Sometimes they prayed while huddled behind wet quilts and rags that had been hung up in the form of a church or tabernacle, in order to prevent their words from carrying through the air. Other times they formed a circle on their knees and spoke their words into and over a vessel of water to drown out the sound. Ellen Butler, born a slave in Louisiana in 1859, witnesses to this dimension of slave religion:

> Massa never 'lowed us slaves to go to church but they have big holes in the fields they gits down in and prays. They done that way 'cause the white folks didn't want them to pray. They used to pray for freedom.[11]

The tradition of the slaves' "hush harbor" prayer meetings lives on in my parents' home. With the abiding strength of the family legends planted in our hearts, my mother invites each one of us to pray, quote Scripture, lead a song, or give a testimony. Speaking under the unction and guidance of the Holy Spirit, my father, Esau Cannon, testifies about his personal experience with God. My grandmother, Rosa Lytle, "lines out" in long-metered style her favorite psalms and spirituals. The rest of the family interjects Bible verses between the singing. The last thing we utter before retiring to bed is always Grandma Rosie's prayer:

> And when waste and age
> and shock and strife
> shall have sapped
> these walls of life,
> Then take this dust
> that's earthly worn
> and mold it
> into heavenly form.

Such is my inheritance.

Chapter 2

Slave Ideology and
Biblical Interpretation

Scholars of stature within mainline Christian denominations have produced immense literature on the Bible and slavery with very little unanimity. Some have written about the various types of antislavery arguments found in the Old and New Testaments. Others have engaged in rigorous historico-critical exegesis of selected Scriptures used to condone slavery. What is interesting in the analyses by liberationists is the direct correlation between apologetic selectivity and the exegetes' political-social commitments. Thus, my particular concern as a liberation ethicist is to unmask the hermeneutical distortions of White Christians, North and South, who lived quite comfortably with the institution of chattel slavery for the better part of 150 years. Slaveholders knew that, in order to keep racial slavery viable, in addition to legal, economic, and political mechanisms they needed religious legitimation within the White society.

Apostles of slavery kept their eyes on the economic benefits and power relations at all times. Beneath their rhetoric and logic, the question of using the Bible to justify the subordination of Black people was fraught with their desire to maintain their dominance, to guarantee their continued social control. If the powerbrokers of the antebellum society were to continue benefitting from the privileges and opportunities the political economy provided, then the slaveholding aristocrats must, as a basic precondition, maintain their domination over the ideological sectors of society: religion, culture, education, and media.[1] The control of material, physical production required the control of the means of mental, symbolic production as well.

The practice of slaveholding was, therefore, largely unquestioned. The majority of White Christians engaged in a passive acceptance of the givenness of the main feature of slavocracy. Any questioning of the system or identification of contradictions to social practices within

This chapter was first published in *Semeia* 47 (1989): 9–22.

Christianity was undermined by the substratum of values and perceptions justified theologically by biblical hermeneutics determined from above. The rank and file of White church membership accepted the prevailing racist ideology, identifying with the slaveholders and copying their rationales, rituals, and values. They regarded slave ideology and Christian life as inseparable; they were integral parts of the same system. The defense of one appeared to require the defense of the other.

Admittedly, there were a few antislavery women and men in the mainline churches prior to the aggressive abolitionist movement of the 1830s, but as a whole the White church evaded responsibility and surrendered its prerogatives to slavocracy. For most of the years that chattel slavery existed, the mainline Protestant churches never legislated against slavery, seldom disciplined slaveholders, and at most gently apologized for the "peculiar institution."

Drawing principally upon socio-ethical sources of the late eighteenth and early nineteenth centuries, I investigate three intellectual, hierarchical constructs that lie at the center of the Christian antebellum society. (1) At what point and under what conditions did Americans of African descent lose their status as members of the moral universe? (2) What are the ethical grounds that make the formula for "heathen conversion" intrinsically wrong? and (3) What are the hermeneutical distortions that shaped the slavocracy's polemical patterns of biblical propaganda?

The Mythology of Black Inferiority

The first ideological myth legitimizing the hermeneutical assumption of Christian slave apologists was the charge that Black people were not members of the human race. Most church governing boards, denominational missionary societies, local churches, and clergy held the position that human beings by nature were free and endowed with natural rights. Their basic concept of human relationships was equality of all people in the sight of God. No one was superior to another, none inferior. Black people had not forfeited their freedom nor relinquished their rights. This espoused oneness of humanity clashed directly with the perception that Black people must necessarily be possessed of low nature.[2]

To justify their enslavement, Black people had to be completely stripped of every privilege of humanity.[3] Their dignity and value as human beings born with natural rights had to be denied. Black Americans were divested so far as possible of all intellectual, cultural, and moral attributes. They had no socially recognized personhood. The institution of chattel slavery and its corollary, White supremacy and racial bigotry, excluded Black people from every normal human consideration.

The humanity of Black people had to be denied, or the evil of the slave system would be evident.

In other words, hereditary slavery was irreconcilable with doctrines of inalienable rights.[4] So as not to contradict their avowed principles, legislatures enacted laws designating Black people as property and as less than human.[5] Black people were assigned a fixed place as an inferior species of humanity. The intellectual legacy of slavocracy was the development of certain White preconceptions about the irredeemable nature of Black women and Black men as "beings of an inferior order," a sub-par species between animal and human. One of the many characterizations proposed was that Black people were irremediably different from Whites, as much as swine from dogs, "they are Baboons on two legs gifted with speech."[6]

Central to the whole hermeneutical approach was a rationalized biblical doctrine positing the innate and permanent inferiority of Blacks in the metonymical curse of Ham.[7] The Ham story in Genesis 9:25–27 was not only used to legitimize slavery in general, but it was also used by proslavery, pro-White supremacists to justify the enslavement of Blacks in particular. Ham became widely identified as the progenitor of the Black race, and the story of the curse that Noah pronounced against Canaan, the son of his son Ham, was symbolically linked to the institution of racial slavery. In a book entitled *Bible Defense of Slavery* Josiah Priest took the position that the enslaving of Black people by the White race was a judicial act of God.

> The servitude of the race to Ham, to the latest era of mankind, is necessary to the veracity of God Himself, as by it is fulfilled one of the oldest of the decrees of the Scriptures, namely that of Noah, which placed the race as servants under other races.[8]

Christians caught in the obsessive duality of understanding Black people as property rather than as persons concurred with both faulty exegesis and social pressure that depicted people with black skin as demonic, unholy, infectious progenitors of sin, full of animality and matriarchal proclivities.

During the early part of the eighteenth century, state laws adopted the principle of *partus sequitur ventrem* — the child follows the condition of the mother regardless of the race of the father. Absolving all paternal responsibilities, this principle institutionalized and sanctioned sexual prerogatives of "stock breeding" with Black men and the rape of Black women by White men. What this means is that the Black woman's life was estimated in terms of money, property and capital assets. She was a commodity to be bought and sold, traded for money, land, or other objects. Her monetary value was precisely calculated by her capacity to produce goods and services, combined with her capacity to reproduce "a herd of subhuman labor units."[9] Hence, the Black woman as the carrier of the hereditary legal status extended the status of slave to her children and her children's children, supposedly to the end of time. An entire race was condemned by the laws of a purportedly Christian people to perpetual, hereditary, unrequited servitude.[10]

The White antebellum church did not see the gross injustice of slavery. Outspoken supporters of slavery generally admitted that enslaved Blacks were mere property, a type of domesticated animal to serve as the White man's tool like any other beast of burden.[11] And as slaveholders, White Christian citizens must have the security that neither their property nor their privilege to own people as property would be taken from them. The church made every effort by admonition and legislation to see that the authority of slaveholders was not compromised. For them, the great truth written in law and God's decree was that subordination was the normal condition of African people and their descendants.[12]

Ideas and practices that favored equal rights of all people were classified as invalid and sinful because they conflicted with the divinely ordained structure that posited inequality between Whites and Blacks. The doctrine of biblical infallibility reinforced and was reinforced by the need for social legitimization of slavery. Thus, racial slavery was accepted as the necessary fulfillment of the curse of Ham. This had the effect of placing the truthfulness of God's self-revelation on the same level as Black slavery and White supremacy.[13] The institutional framework that required Black men, women, and children to be treated as chattel, as possessions rather than as human beings, was understood as being consistent with the spirit, genius, and precepts of the Christian faith.

The Mythologizing of Enslavement

The second ideological process that legitimated Christian slave apology was a reconstruction of history and divine action in it. It was claimed that God sent slavers to the wilds of Africa, a so-called depraved, savage, heathen world, in order to free Africans of ignorance, superstition, and corruption.[14] It is of more than passing significance that the proslavery writing portrayed Africa as the scene of unmitigated cannibalism, fetish worship, and licentiousness. Using gross caricatures, slave apologists mounted an ideological offensive in justification of the ravishing of the entire continent of Africa.[15] They argued that Africans by nature were framed and designed for subjection and obedience. Their preoccupation was that people designated by nature as "bestial savages" and "heathens" were destined by providence for slavery.[16]

Embracing false dogma of inherent African inferiority, beneficiaries of White supremacy described African character as the most depraved humanity imaginable. Africans were depicted as the epitome of heathenism, "wild, naked ... man-eating savages," and "the great ethnological clown." White Christians had to be enabled to consider it an unspeakable privilege for Africans to be brought to the Americas as slaves.[17] Repeatedly, they claimed that slavery saved poor, degraded, and wretched African peoples from spiritual darkness.

North American Christians credited themselves with weaning Africans of savage barbarity.[18] Their joy in converting Africans was that they were giving to "heathens" elements of Christian civilization. Being enslaved in a Christian country was considered advantageous to Africans' physical, intellectual, and moral development. Slavery exposed Africans to Christianity, which made them better servants of God and better servants of men.

The popularity of "heathen conversion" was disclosed in the public reception of George Fitzhugh's *Cannibals All! or, Slaves without Masters,* who asserted Africans, like wild horses, had to be "caught, tamed and civilized."[19] Resting upon irrational antipathies, White Christians — prominent and common-bred alike — clearly distinguished their personhood from that of Africans. Many were convinced that African peoples were somehow irreparably inferior to and less worthy than Europeans. Fixated on the fetish of heathenism, they believed that the color of white skin proved sufficient justification to rob Africans by force and fraud of their liberty. The proper social hierarchy upon which the slave system rested — the putative inferiority of Africans and the alleged superiority of Europeans — had to remain safely intact.[20] Historian Winthrop Jordan declares:

> Heathenism was treated not so much as a specifically religious defect, but as one manifestation of a general refusal to measure up to proper standards, as a failure to be English or even civilized.... Being Christian was not merely a matter of subscribing to certain doctrines; it was a quality inherent in oneself and one's society. It was interconnected with all other attributes of normal and proper men.[21]

Entirely under the power of Whites, against whom they dared not complain and whom they dared not resist, enslaved Africans were denied the right to possess property, and deprived of the means of instruction and of every personal, social, civil, political, and religious mode of agency. If they asserted their personhood in defiance of oppressive authority, slaveholders punished them severely. Never before U.S. chattel slavery was a people so systematically deprived of their human rights and submerged in abject misery.[22]

The prevailing sentiment of American Christians — Presbyterians, Congregationalists, Roman Catholics, Quakers, Lutherans, Baptists, Methodists, and Anglicans — was that African peoples deserved imperial domination and needed social control.[23] Many churches preached a gospel that declared that Black people were indebted to White Christians and bound to spend their lives in the service of Whites; any provisions for food, clothes, shelter, medicine, or any other means of preservation were perceived not as legal requirement but as an act of Christian charity. This "Christian feature" of Anglo-American enslavement was interpreted as an incalculable blessing to African peoples. Africans and their descendants were much better off bound in slavery with their souls free than vice versa.

These and similar judgments bolstered the belief that Anglo-Saxons, Spaniards, Danes, Portuguese, and Dutch had a divine right to defend themselves against the intolerable suffering and absolute despotism that they imposed so heavily on others. As long as the image of Africans as "heathens" was irrevocable, then the church's attempt to Christianize via enslavement could continue indefinitely, the exploitation of Africa's natural resources could proceed without hindrance, and White Christians could persist in enjoying a position of moral superiority. Ruthlessly exploiting African people was justifiable Christian action.

Remythologizing Divine Will

The third ideological myth needed to legitimize the hermeneutical circle of Christian slave apologists was the understanding that the law of God and the law of the land gave them an extraordinary right to deprive Black people of liberty and to offer Blacks for sale in the market like any other articles of merchandise. For almost two centuries, slave apologists maintained that slavery was constantly spoken of in the Bible without any direct prohibition of it, no special law against it. And therefore, on the basis of the absence of condemnation, slavery could not be classified as sin. The presumptive evidence for many White Christians was that the absence of slaveholding from the catalogue of sins and disciplinary offenses in the Bible meant that slavery was not in violation of God's law.

Biblical scholars, along with distinguished scientists, lawyers, and politicians, produced a large quantity of exegetical data denying the arbitrariness of divinely ordained slavery.[24] The foundation of the scriptural case for slavery focused on an argument that neither Jesus of Nazareth, the apostles, nor the early church objected to the ownership of slaves. The fact that slavery was one of the cornerstones of the economic system of the Greco-Roman world was stressed and the conclusion reached that for the early church the only slavery that mattered was spiritual slavery to sin, to which all were bound. Physical slavery was spiritually meaningless under the all-embracing spiritualized hope of salvation. This line of reasoning was of central importance in reconciling the masses of White Christians to the existing social order. Instead of recognizing that slavery was ameliorated by early Christianity, slave apologists used their interpretative principle to characterize slavery as a sacred institution.[25]

To elicit White Christians' consent and approval of racial chattel slavery, which theologically contradicted a liberation reading of the Christian gospel, some of the leading antebellum churchmen — Robert Lewis Dabney, a Presbyterian theologian, Augustine Verot, the Catholic bishop of Georgia and East Florida, and John Leadley Dagg, Baptist layman who served as president of Mercer University — presented slavery as conforming to the divine principles revealed in the Bible. White clergy were trained to use the Bible to give credence to the legitimacy of racial chattelhood.[26] In other words, they adopted an implacable line of reasoning that made slavery an accepted fact of everyday life, not only in the entire Near East but also within normative biblical ethical teaching. Needless to say, the New Testament instruction that slaves should be obedient to their masters was interpreted as unqualified support for the modern institution of chattel slavery. The slave system was simply a part of the cosmos.[27]

Slave apologists such as George Fitzhugh, Thomas R. Dew, and William A. Smith used a hermeneutical principle that functioned to conceal and misrepresent the real conflicts of slave ideology and Christian life. Smith, the president of Randolph Macon College in Virginia, was quite candid:

> Slavery, *per se,* is right.... The great abstract principle of slavery is right, because it is a fundamental principle of the social state: and domestic slavery, as an *institution,* is fully justified by the condition and circumstances (essential and relative) of the African race in this country, and therefore equally right.[28]

Fitzhugh, a well-known essayist, and Dew, a prominent lawyer, concluded that since slavery was part of a natural order and hence in accord with the will of God, it could not be morally wrong.

Christian commentators, working largely to the advantage of wealthy aristocrats, used biblical and philosophical arguments to present slaveholders' interests and claims in the best possible light.[29] For example, scholars such as How, Ross, and Priest constructed "biblical facts" that permitted them to claim that the eradication of chattel slavery was inapplicable to Christian living. By using selective appeals to customary practices, they disseminated moral teachings to reinforce what counted as good Christian conduct. Clergy were condemned for preaching against slavery because abolition sermons were considered to be a part of a traitorous and diabolical scheme that would eventually lead to the denial of biblical authority, the unfolding of rationalism, deistic philanthropism, pantheism, atheism, socialism, or Jacobinism. Members of churches were warned against subscribing to antislavery books, pamphlets, and newspapers. The church condoned mob violence against anyone with abolitionist tendencies, which in turn, reassured that the existing social order would go unchallenged.

Having no desire to divorce themselves from the institution of slavery, church governing boards and agencies issued denominational pronouncements on behalf of the official platitudes of slave ideology. Denominational assemblies reinforced publicly their compliance with the assumed principle of human chattelhood. Black people were classified as moveable property, devoid of the minimum human rights that society conferred to others.

The vast majority of White clergy and laity alike appropriated this ideology to convince themselves that the human beings whom they violated or whose well-being they did not protect were unworthy of anything better. White Christians seemed to have been imbued with the permissive view that the enslavement of Black people was not too great a price to pay for a stable, viable labor system.[30] In a political economy built on labor-intensive agriculture, slave labor seemed wholly "natural." The security and prosperity of slavocracy evidently enabled White Christians, slaveholders and non-slaveholders alike, to feel secure with the fruits of the system.

Through a close analysis of slave ideology and biblical interpretation we can discern the many ways that chattel slavery maintained itself even after it was no longer the most economically profitable method of utilizing natural and technological resources. The majority of White Christians had learned well not to accept the equal coexistence of Whites and Blacks in the same society.[31] They believed that giving Black people civil parity with the White population would threaten the ease and luxury of White happiness, and perhaps dissolve the Union. For the sake of the public welfare, people with ancestors born in Europe, and not in Africa, needed to be relieved of degrading menial labor so that they could be free to pursue the highest cultural attainment. Slavery, sanctioned not just by civil law but by natural law as well, was considered the best foundation for a strong economy and for a superior society.

Concluding Ethical Reflections

I have sketched three mythologizing processes that served as the foundational underpinnings for slave ideology in relation to White Christian life. I believe that it is important for us to trace the origin and expansion of these myths because the same general schemes of oppression and patterns of enslavement remain prevalent today and because the biblical hermeneutics of oppressive praxis is far from being dead among contemporary exegetes. As life-affirming moral agents we have a responsibility to study the ideological hegemony of the past so that we do not remain doomed to the recurring cyclical patterns of hermeneutical distortions in the present — i.e., violence against women, condemnation of homosexuality, spiritualizing Scripture to justify capitalism.

My analysis shows that slave apologists worked within an interpretative framework that represented the whole transcript of racial chattel slavery as ordained by God. They systematically blocked and refuted any discourse that presented contrary viewpoints. Using theo-ethical language, concepts, and categories White superordinates pressed their claims of the supposedly inherent inferiority of Black people by appealing to the normative ethical system expressed by the dominant slaveholders. The political and economic context incorporated a structure of discourse wherein the Bible was authoritatively interpreted to support the existing patterns of exploitation of Black people.

Antebellum Christians, abiding by the developing racial and cultural conceptions, resisted any threat to slavocracy or any challenge to the peace and permanency of the order of their own denomination. They conformed their ethics to the boundaries of slave management. It became their Christian duty to rule over African people who had been stricken from the human race and reclassified as a subhuman species.

Not surprisingly, denominations sprang officially to the defense of slave trading, slaveholding, and the Christianization of Africans with ingenious economic arguments. Wealthy slaveholders transmuted a portion of their disproportionate economic profit into modes of social control by public gestures that passed as generous voluntary acts of charity. They used revenue from slave labor to pay pastors, maintain church properties, support seminaries, and sustain overseas missionaries. Seduced by privilege and profit, White Christians of all economic strata were made, in effect, coconspirators in the victimization of Black people. In other words, slave apologists were successful in convincing at least five generations of White citizens that slavery, an essential and constitutionally protected institution, was consistent with the impulse of Christian charity.

Chapter 3

The Emergence of Black Feminist Consciousness

The feminist consciousness of Afro-American women cannot be understood and explained adequately apart from the historical context in which Black women have found themselves as moral agents. By tracking down the central and formative facts in the Black woman's social world, one can identify the determinant and determining structures of oppression that have shaped the context in which Black women discriminately and critically interpret Scripture, in order to apprehend the divine Word from the perspective of their own situation. Throughout the history of the United States, the interrelationship of White supremacy and male superiority has characterized the Black woman's reality as a situation of struggle — a struggle to survive in two contradictory worlds simultaneously, one White, privileged, and oppressive, the other Black, exploited, and oppressed. Thus, an untangling of the Black religious heritage sheds light on the feminist consciousness that guides Black women in their ongoing struggle for survival.

The Struggle for Human Dignity

The Black church is the crucible in which the systematic faith affirmations and the principles of biblical interpretation have been revealed. It came into existence as an invisible institution in the slave community during the seventeenth century. Hidden from the eyes of slave masters, Black women, along with Black men, developed an extensive religious life of their own. C. Eric Lincoln puts it this way:

> The blacks brought their religion with them. After a time they
> accepted the white man's religion, but they have not always ex-

This chapter was first published in Letty M. Russell, ed., *Feminist Interpretation of the Bible* (Westminster Press, 1985), 30–40.

pressed it in the white man's way.... The black religious experience is something more than a black patina on a white happening. It is a unique response to a historical occurrence that can never be replicated for any people in America.[1]

The biblical interpretation of the antebellum Black church served as a double-edged sword. Confidence in the sovereignty of God, in an omnipotent, omnipresent, and omniscient God, helped slaves accommodate to the system of chattel slavery. With justice denied, hopes thwarted, and dreams shattered, Black Christians cited passages from the Bible that gave them emotional poise and balance in the midst of their oppression. In the prayer meetings and song services, in the sermons and spirituals, the biblical texts provided refuge in a hostile White world. Howard Thurman argued that this stance enabled enslaved Black women and Black men to make their worthless lives worth living.[2] "Being socially proscribed, economically impotent, and politically brow-beaten," Benjamin Mays wrote, "they sang, prayed, and shouted their troubles away."[3]

The biblical interpretation of the Black church also made slaves discontent with their servile condition. Under slavery the Black woman had the status of property: her master had total power over her, and she and her children were denied the most elementary social bonds — family and kinship. The Black woman was defined as "brood sow" and "work ox." Concession was given to her gender only when it was expedient for the slaveowner. Much of the theology of this period encouraged slave women to eliminate the sources of their oppression. The Black religious experience equipped slaves with a biblical understanding that called them to engage in acts of rebellion for freedom. The faith assertions of the Black church encouraged slaves to reject any teachings that attempted to reconcile slavery with the gospel of Jesus Christ. As George Rawick points out:

> It was out of the religion of the slaves, the religion of the oppressed, the damned of this earth, that came the daily resistance to slavery, the significant slave strikes, and the Underground Railroad, all of which constantly wore away at the ability of the slave masters to establish their own preeminent society.[4]

The slave woman's religious consciousness provided her with irrepressible talent in humanizing her environment. Having only from midnight to daybreak to provide love and affection for her own offspring, the Black woman returned at night with leftovers, throwaways, discarded shells of the White slaveowner's rubbish to the small, crude, squalid dwelling where she made a home for her family. Often she took into her quarters Black children whose parents had been sold away from them or they from their parents with the full knowledge that she could expect to have her own offspring with her for a few years, at the most.

Being both slave and female, the Black woman survived wanton misuse and abuse. She was answerable with her body to the sexual casualness of "stock breeding" with Black men and to the sexual whims and advances of White men. Virtually all the slave narratives contain accounts of the high incidence of rape and sexual coercion. La Frances Rodgers-Rose, in *The Black Woman,* describes the sexual exploitation of the Black slave woman in this manner:

> The Black woman had to withstand the sexual abuse of the white master, his sons and the overseer. A young woman was not safe. Before reaching maturity, many a Black woman had suffered the sexual advances of the white male. If she refused to succumb to his advances, she was beaten and in some cases tortured to death.[5]

White men, by virtue of their economic position, had unlimited access to Black women's bodies. At the crux of the ideology that Black women were an inferior species was the belief that Black women, unlike White women, craved sex inordinately. "The rape of the black woman by white men or the use of their bodies for pleasure could be rationalized as the natural craving of the black women for sex, rather than the licentiousness of the white men."[6] The mixed blood of thousands upon thousands of African peoples' descendants is incontrovertible proof of sexual contact between White slave masters and Black slave women.

Reduced to subservient marginality, the Black slave woman was constantly being stripped of familiar social ties in order for her owner to maximize his profit. All of the Black woman's relationships existed under the shadowy threat of a permanent separation. As an outsider in society, the Black woman lived with constant fear, and most of the time she had to endure the reality of having her husband and her children sold away from her with the likelihood that she would never see them again. Countless slave families were forcibly disrupted. "This flow of enslaved Afro-Americans must count as one of the greatest *forced* migrations in world history."[7]

> In nothing was slavery so savage and so relentless as in its attempted destruction of the family instincts of the negro [sic] race in America. Individuals, not families; shelters, not homes; herding, not marriages, were the cardinal sins in that system of horrors. Who can ever express in song or story the pathetic history of this race of unfortunate people when freedom came, groping about for their scattered offspring with only instinct to guide them, trying to knit together the broken ties of family kinship?[8]

The Black woman's consciousness in the first two centuries of the American colonies' existence focused on identifying resources that would help her sustain the inescapable theological attacks — either Black people were human beings and could not be property, or they were property and something less than human. "Black and white were constantly presented as antipodes, negative and positive poles on a continuum of goodness. In the minds of whites, Negroes stood as the antithesis of the character and properties of white people."[9] All of life was graded according to an elaborate hierarchy, inherited from the Middle Ages, known as the "great chain of being." Blacks were assigned a fixed place as an inferior species of humanity. The common property of White culture included certain preconceptions about the irredeemable nature of Black women and Black men as "beings of an inferior order,"[10] a species between animal and human. Unwavering faith in God provided Black Christians with patience and perseverance in the ongoing struggle for survival.

The Struggle against White Hypocrisy

The institution of chattel slavery in America was destroyed by the most momentous event of the nineteenth century, the Civil War, from 1861 to 1865. Emancipation removed the legal and political slave status from approximately four million Black people in the United States, which meant that, in principle, these Blacks owned their person and their labor for the first time. Unfortunately, for the vast majority of Afro-Americans, the traditional practices of racial and gender subordination subjected them to incredible suffering. The general patterns of de facto social segregation and disenfranchisement of Blacks, which were integral to the raison d'être of the peculiar institution, continued as the norm. White southerners accepted the abolition of slavery as one of the consequences of their military defeat and surrender at Appomattox in 1865, but they were totally unwilling to grant Black women and men respect as equal human beings with rights of life, liberty, and property. The "rightness of whiteness" counted more than the basic political and civil rights of any Black person. Southern apologists received widespread acceptance from many Northerners who had opposed slavery on the ground of an indivisible United States while avidly supporting racial subordination. Many academic historians, sociologists, anthropologists, theologians, and biblical scholars dredged up every conceivable argument to justify the natural inferiority of Blacks and their natural subordination to Whites. Institutional slavery ended, but the virulent and intractable hatred that supported it did not.

During the Reconstruction Era, the Black church continued to assume its responsibility for shaping the expository and critical biblical reflections that would help the adherents of the faith understand the interplay of historical events and societal structures. The biblical teachings of the church continued to develop out of the socioeconomic and political context in which Black people found themselves. In every sphere where Black people were circumscribed and their legal rights denied, the Black church called its members to a commitment of perfecting social change and exacting social righteousness here on earth. The Scripture lessons that were most important after emancipation were those texts that focused on Christians working to help the social order come into harmony with the divine plan.

When the Freedmen's Bureau was effectively curtailed and finally dismantled, Blacks were left with dead-letter amendments and nullified rights acts, with collapsing federal laws and increasing White terrorist violence. Beyond the small gains and successes of a few Blacks, the optimism of ex-slaves about full citizenship was soon extinguished. Hence, the aftereffects of Reconstruction called the Black church forth as the community's sole institution of power. Whether urban or rural, the Black church was the only institution totally controlled by Black people. It was the only place outside the home where Blacks could express themselves freely and take independent action. The church community was the heart, center, and basic organization of Black life. And those who were the religious leaders searched the Scriptures to give distinctive shapes and patterns to the words and ideas that the Black community used to speak about God and God's relationship to an oppressed people.

The Black woman began her life of freedom with no vote, no protection, and no equity of any sort. Black women, young and old, were basically on their own. The patterns of exploitation of the Black woman as laborer and breeder were only shaken by the Civil War; by no means were they destroyed. Throughout the late nineteenth and early twentieth centuries, Black women were severely restricted to the most unskilled, poorly paid, menial work. Virtually no Black woman held a job beyond that of domestic servant or field hand. Keeping house, farming, and bearing and rearing children continued to dominate all aspects of the Black woman's life. The systematic exclusion of Black females from other areas of employment served as confirmation for the continuation of the servile status of Black women. As Jeanne Noble describes it, "While freedom brought new opportunities for black men, for most women it augmented old problems."[11] After emancipation, racism and male supremacy continued to intersect patriarchal and capitalist structures in definitive ways.

The religious consciousness of the Black freedwoman focused on "uplifting" the Black community. The Black female was taught that her education was meant not only to uplift her but also to prepare her for a life of service in the overall community. It was biblical faith grounded in the prophetic tradition that helped Black women devise strategies and tactics to make Black people less susceptible to the indignities and proscriptions of an oppressive White social order.

The unique alliance between northern missionary and philanthropic societies afforded an increasing number of Black women opportunities of education. The Black woman as educator attended Sunday services at local churches, where she often spoke in order to cultivate interest in the Black community's overall welfare. Churchwomen were crusaders in the development of various social service improvement leagues and aid societies. They sponsored fund-raising fairs, concerts, and all forms of social entertainment in order to correct some of the inequities in the overcrowded and understaffed educational facilities in the Black community. These dedicated women substantially reduced illiteracy among Black people.

The biblical teachings of the Black church served as a bulwark against laws, systems, and structures that rendered Black people nonentities. Fearful of the emerging competitive race relations with Blacks, White America instituted a whole set of policies and customs in order to maintain White supremacy. White people wanted to regulate and eventually stamp out all notions of social equality between the races. Terror of Black encroachment in areas where Whites claimed power and privileges even caused southern state legislatures to enact Black Codes, similar to slave codes, designed to limit drastically the rights of ex-slaves.

> Although their provisions varied among states, the Black Codes essentially prevented the freedmen from voting or holding office, made them ineligible for military service, and disbarred them from serving on juries or testifying in court against whites. Moreover, blacks were forbidden to travel from place to place without passes, were not allowed to assemble without a formal permit from authorities, and could be fined and bound out to labor contractors if they were unwilling to work.[12]

"Jim Crowism" became a calculated invidious policy to exclude the mass of Black folk from interracial contacts in public places and on public transportation facilities. With *de jure* segregation, civil rights for Black people fell outside the realm of legal contract. Not only were Blacks granted no protection under the law, but direct steps were taken to control even the most personal spatial and social aspects of Black life. Segregation took a less blatantly visible form in the North, but it was only slightly less rigid.

The Black woman's consciousness during this period caused her to evaluate this extreme social impoverishment — caused by a panoply of state laws requiring a rigid system of segregation — as an abominable evil. She believed that Jim Crowism was contrary to nature and against the will of God. The Black church with its own ideas of morality condemned the hypocrisy of White Christians. How could Christians who were White refuse flatly and openly to treat as fellow human beings Christians who had African ancestry? Was not the essence of the gospel mandate a call to eradicate affliction, despair, and systems of injustice? The Black church's identification with the children of Israel was a significant theme in the consciousness of the Black woman.

During the migratory period (1910–25), the Black church was the citadel of hope. A series of floods and boll weevil infestations, diminishing returns on impoverished soil, wartime curtailment of European immigrants for industrial labor markets, and rampaging racial brutality accelerated Black emigration from South to North and from rural to urban areas. Tens of thousands of Black women and men left home, seeking social democracy and economic opportunities. Black churches were used for almost every sort of activity: as boarding quarters for migrant people who had nowhere else to go, as centers for civic activities, as concert halls for artists and choirs, and as lecture rooms for public-spirited individuals. During this colossal movement of Black people, the church continued to serve as the focal point for the structure of Black life.

This accelerated movement of Blacks out of the South impinged upon the Black woman's reality in very definite ways. Black women migrated North in greater numbers than Black men.[13] Economic necessity dictated that most Black women who migrated to the urban centers find work immediately in order to survive themselves and to provide for their families. Black women once again found only drudge work available to them. Small numbers of Black women were allowed inside the industrial manufacturing system but were confined to the most tedious, strenuous, and degrading occupations.

> White women had no intentions of working alongside black women; even if some of them did speak of sexual equality, most did not favor racial equality.... Fear of competing with blacks as well as the possible loss of job status associated with working with blacks caused white workers to oppose any efforts to have blacks as fellow workers.[14]

The interaction of race and sex in the labor market exacted a heavy toll on the Black woman, making all aspects of migration a problem of paramount religious significance. Her experience as wife and mother, responsible for transmitting the culture, customs, and values of the Black community to her children, served as a decisive factor in determining how the Bible was read and understood. At the same time that the Black woman was trying to organize family life according to her traditional roles, the male-dominated industrial society required that she serve as catalyst in the transition process. Her own unfamiliarities and adaptation difficulties had to be repressed because she was responsible for making a home in crowded substandard housing, finding inner-city schools that provided literacy for her children, and earning enough income to cover the most elementary needs.

The Struggle for Justice

Black religion and the Black church served as a sustaining force, assuring boundless justice. During these stormy times, the Black church tradition renewed hope and spiritual strength, touching these women's lives in all their ramifications, enabling migrant women to carry on in spite of obstacles and opposition. It was the interpretive principle of the Black church that guided Black women in facing life squarely, in acknowledging its raw coarseness. The White elitist attributes of passive gentleness and enervative delicacy, considered particularly appropriate to womanhood, proved nonfunctional in the pragmatic survival of migrant Black women. Cultivating conventional amenities was not a luxury afforded them. Instead, Black women were aware that their very lives depended upon their being able to decipher the various sounds in the larger world, to hold in check the nightmare figures of terror, to fight for basic freedoms against the sadistic law enforcement agencies in their communities, to resist the temptation to capitulate to the demands of the status quo, to find meaning in the most despotic circumstances, and to create something where nothing existed before. Most of the time this was accompanied by the unceasing mumbling of prayers. "But nothin' never hurt me 'cause de Lawd knowed how it was."[15]

World Wars I and II brought the most visible changes in Black life. Under coercive pressure from the Black community, the federal government was forced to take definite steps to halt discrimination in war industries. With White labor reserves depleted, large numbers of Black women and men were hired. In segregated plants and factories, Black women attained semiskilled, skilled, and supervisory positions. A few were even granted limited rights in auxiliary unions. Most Black women, however, were assigned the most arduous tasks, worked in the least skilled jobs, and received lower wages than their White counterparts.

The biblical teachings of the Black church continued to initiate and envision the fundamental truth claims operative in the community. The ministers' expositions of the biblical faith corresponded to the efficacious ways that the Black community dealt with contingencies in the real-lived context. The Scriptures made a significant difference in the notions Blacks used to see and to act in situations that confronted them.

For instance, during this period segregation was still legally maintained in almost every area of social contact, the horrors of lynching became an accepted reality, and blackface minstrel-burlesque shows were used to reinforce the stereotype of Black people as inferior. Black churchwomen became crusaders for justice. They recorded and talked about the grimness of struggle among the least visible people in the society. Given their hostile environment, deteriorating conditions, and the enduring humiliation of the social ostracism of the war years, these women exposed the most serious and unyielding problem of the twentieth century — the single most determining factor of Black existence in America — the question of color.

In the years following the world wars, White mob violence, bloody race riots, and "hate strikes" broke out in northern and southern cities alike. Innocent Blacks were beaten, dragged by vehicles, and forced out of their homes. Substantial amounts of Black-owned property were destroyed. Throughout the country, extralegal barriers resurged to prevent social equality. Lynching, burning, castrating, beating, cross-burning, tarring and feathering, masked night rides, verbal threats, hate rallies, public humiliations, and random discharging of shotguns at windows were all used by White vigilante groups "to shore up the color line."

Blacks served in World War II as soldiers and civilians. Thousands worked in noncombatant labor battalions. All returned home calling for the "double V" — victory abroad and victory at home. Black veterans objected to the second-class treatment traditionally accorded to them. In their cry against the ideological supremacy of racist practices and values, they appealed to the religious heritage of Blacks that began in the invisible church during slavery.

Black Womanist Consciousness

From the period of urbanization of World War II to the present, Black women find that their situation is still a situation of struggle, a struggle to survive collectively and individually against the continuing harsh historical realities and pervasive adversities in today's world. The Korean and Vietnam wars, federal government programs, civil rights movements, and voter education programs have all had a positive impact on the Black woman's situation, but they have not been able to offset the negative effects of inherent inequities that are inextricably tied to the history and ideological hegemony of racism, sexism, and class privilege.

The Black woman and her family continue to be enslaved to hunger, disease, and the highest rate of unemployment since the Depression of the 1930s. Advances in education, housing, health care, and other necessities that came about during the mid- and late 1960s are deteriorating faster now than ever before. Both in informal day-to-day life and in the formal organizations and institutions in society. Black women are still the victims of the aggravated inequities of the tridimensional phenomenon of race/class/gender oppression. This is the backdrop of the historical context for the emergence of the Black feminist consciousness.

In essence, the Bible is the highest source of authority for most Black women. In its pages, Black women have learned how to refute the stereotypes that depict Black people as minstrels or vindictive militants, mere ciphers who react only to omnipresent racial oppression. Knowing the Jesus stories of the New Testament helps Black women be aware of the bad housing, overworked mothers, underworked fathers, functional illiteracy, and malnutrition that continue to prevail in the Black community. However, as God-fearing women they maintain that Black life is more than defensive reactions to oppressive circumstances of anguish and desperation. Black life is the rich, colorful creativity that emerged and reemerges in the Black quest for human dignity. Jesus provides the necessary soul for liberation.

Understanding the prophetic tradition of the Bible empowers Black women to fashion a set of values on their own terms, as well as mastering, radicalizing, and sometimes destroying the pervasive negative orientations imposed by the larger society. Also, they articulate possibilities for decisions and action that address forthrightly the circumstances that inescapably color and shape Black life. Black women serve as contemporary prophets, calling other women forth so that they can break away from the oppressive ideologies and belief systems that presume to define their reality.

Black feminist consciousness may be more accurately identified as Black womanist consciousness, to use Alice Walker's concept and definition.[16] As an interpretive principle, the Black womanist tradition provides the incentive to chip away at oppressive structures, bit by bit. It identifies those texts that help Black womanists to celebrate and rename the innumerable incidents of unpredictability in empowering ways. The Black womanist identifies with those biblical characters who hold on to life in the face of formidable oppression. Often compelled to act or to refrain from acting in accordance with the powers and principalities of the external world, Black womanists search the Scriptures to learn how to dispel the threat of death in order to seize the present life.

Chapter 4

Moral Wisdom in the Black Women's Literary Tradition

Origins

I first began pondering the relationship between faith and ethics as a schoolgirl while listening to my grandmother teach the central affirmations of Christianity within the context of a racially segregated society. My community of faith taught me the principles of God's universal parenthood, which engendered a social, intellectual, and cultural ethos embracing the equal humanity of all people. Yet my city, state, and nation declared it a punishable offense against the laws and mores for Blacks and Whites "to travel, eat, defecate, wait, be buried, make love, play, relax and even speak together, except in the stereotyped context of master and servant interaction."[1]

My religious quest tried to relate the Christian doctrines preached in the Black church to the suffering, oppression and exploitation of Black people in the society. How could Christians who were White flatly and openly refuse to treat as fellow human beings Christians who had African ancestry? Inasmuch as the Black church expressed the inner ethical life of the people, was there any way to reconcile the inherent contradictions in Christianity as practiced by Whites with the radical indictments of and challenges for social amelioration and economic development in the Black religious heritage? How long would the White church continue to be the ominous symbol of White dominance, sanctioning and assimilating the propagation of racism in the mundane interests of the ruling group?

In the 1960s my quest for the integration of faith and ethics was influenced by scholars in various fields who surfaced the legitimate con-

This chapter was first published in the *Annual of the Society of Christian Ethics,* ed. Larry L. Rasmussen, with assistance from David Hollenbach, Robin Lovin, Peter Paris, and Jane Cary Peck (Vancouver, B.C.: Society of Christian Ethics, Vancouver School of Theology, 1984), 171–92.

tributions of Afro-Americans that had been historically distorted and denied. Avidly I read the analysis exposing the assumptions and dogmas that made Blacks a negligible factor in the thought of the world. For more than three and a half centuries a "conspiracy of silence" rendered invisible the outstanding contributions of Blacks to the culture of humankind. From cradle to grave the people in the United States were taught the alleged inferiority of Blacks in every place in society.

When I turned specifically to readings in theological ethics, I discovered that the assumptions of the dominant ethical systems implied that the doing of Christian ethics in the Black community was either immoral or amoral. The cherished ethical ideas predicated upon the existence of freedom and a wide range of choices proved null and void in situations of oppression. The real-lived texture of Black life requires moral agency that may run contrary to the ethical boundaries of mainline Protestantism. Blacks may use action guides that have never been considered within the scope of traditional codes of faithful living. Racism, gender discrimination, and economic exploitation, as inherited, age-long complexes, require the Black community to create and cultivate values and virtues in their own terms so that they prevail against the odds with moral integrity.

For example, dominant ethics makes a virtue of qualities that lead to economic success — self-reliance, frugality, and industry. These qualities are based on an assumption that success is possible for anyone who tries. Developing confidence in one's own abilities, resources, and judgments amid a careful use of money and goods in order to exhibit assiduity in the pursuit of upward mobility have proven to be positive values for Whites. But when the oligarchic economic powers and the consequent political power they generate own and control capital and distribute credit as part of a legitimating system to justify the supposed inherent inferiority of Blacks, these same values prove to be ineffectual. Racism does not allow most Black women and Black men to labor habitually in beneficial work with the hope of saving expenses by avoiding waste so that they can develop a standard of living that is congruent with the American ideal.

Work may be a "moral essential," but Black women are still the last hired to do the work that White men, White women, and men of color refuse to do, and at a wage that men and White women refuse to accept. Black women, placed in jobs that have proven to be detrimental to their health, are doing the most menial, tedious, and by far the most underpaid work, if they manage to get a job at all.

Dominant ethics also assumes that a moral agent is to a considerable degree free and self-directing. Each person possesses self-determining power. For instance, one is free to choose whether he or she wants to suffer and make sacrifices as a principle of action or as a voluntary vocational pledge of crossbearing. In dominant ethics a person is free to make suffering a desirable moral norm. This is not so for Blacks. For the masses of Black people, suffering is the normal state of affairs. Mental anguish, physical abuse, and emotional agony are all part of the lived truth of Black people's straitened circumstances. Due to the extraneous forces and the entrenched bulwark of White supremacy and male superiority that pervade this society, Blacks and Whites, women and men are forced to live with very different ranges of freedom. As long as the White-male experience continues as the ethical norm, Black women, Black men, and others will suffer unequivocal oppression. The range of freedom has been restricted by those who cannot hear and will not hear voices expressing pleasure and pain, joy and rage as others experience them.

In the Black community, the aggregate of the qualities that determine desirable ethical values, uprightness of character, and soundness of moral conduct must always take into account the circumstances, the paradoxes, and the dilemmas that constrict Blacks to the lowest rungs of the social, political, and economic hierarchy. Black existence is deliberately and openly controlled: "how we travel and where, what work we do, what income we receive, where we eat, where we sleep, with whom we talk, where we recreate, where we study, what we write, what we publish."[2] The vast majority of Blacks suffer every conceivable form of denigration. Their lives are named, defined, and circumscribed by Whites.

The moral wisdom that exists in the Black community is extremely useful in defying oppressive rules or standards of "law and order" that unjustly degrade Blacks in the society. It helps Blacks purge themselves of self-hate, thus asserting their own validity. But the salient point here is that the ethical values that the Black community has fashioned for itself are not identical with the body of obligations and duties that Anglo-Protestant American society requires of its members. Nor can the ethical assumptions be the same, as long as powerful Whites who control the wealth, the systems, and the institutions in this society continue to perpetuate brutality and criminality against Blacks.

Method

The method used in this study departs from most work in Christian and secular ethics. The body of data is drawn from less conventional sources and probes more intimate and private aspects of Black life. The Black women's literary tradition has not previously been used to interpret and explain the community's socio-cultural patterns from which ethical values can be gleaned. I have found that this literary tradition is the nexus between the real-lived texture of Black life and the oral-aural cultural values implicitly passed on and received from one generation to the next.

Black women are the most vulnerable and the most exploited members of the American society. The structure of the capitalist political economy in which Black people are commodities, combined with patriarchal contempt for women, has caused the Black woman to experience oppression that knows no ethical or physical bounds.

> As a black, she has had to endure all the horrors of slavery and living in a racist society; as a worker, she has been the object of continual exploitation, occupying the lowest place on the wage scale and restricted to the most demeaning and uncreative jobs; as a woman she has seen her physical image defamed and been the object of the white master's uncontrollable lust and subjected to all the ideals of white womanhood as a model to which she should aspire; as a mother, she has seen her children torn from her breast and sold into slavery, she has seen them left at home without attention while she attended to the needs of the offspring of the ruling class.[3]

The focus of this essay is to show how Black women live out a moral wisdom in their real-lived context that does not appeal to the fixed rules or absolute principles of the White-oriented, male-structured society. Black women's analysis and appraisal of what is right or wrong and good or bad develop out of the various coping mechanisms related to the conditions of their own cultural circumstances. In the face of this, Black women have justly regarded survival against tyrannical systems of triple oppression as a true sphere of moral life.

Black women are taught what is to be endured and how to endure the harsh, cruel, inhumane exigencies of life. The moral wisdom does not rescue Black women from the bewildering pressures and perplexities of institutionalized social evils; rather, it exposes those ethical assumptions that are inimical to the ongoing survival of Black womanhood. The moral counsel of Black women captures the ethical qualities of what is real and what is of value to women in the Black world.

Black women writers function as continuing symbolic conveyors and transformers of the values acknowledged by the female members of the Black community. In the quest for appreciating Black women's experience, nothing surpasses the Black women's literary tradition. It cryptically records the specificity of the Afro-American life.

My goal is not to arrive at any prescriptive or normative ethic. Rather what I am pursuing is an investigation (1) that will help Black women, and others who care, to understand and to appreciate the richness of their own moral struggle through the life of the common people and the oral tradition; (2) to further understanding of some of the differences between ethics of life under oppression and established moral approaches that take for granted freedom and a wide range of choices. I am being suggestive of one possible ethical approach, not exhaustive.

I make no apologies for the fact that this study is a partisan one. However, it is not merely a glorification of the Black female community, but rather an attempt to add to the far too few positive records concerning the Black woman as moral agent. For too long the Black community's theological and ethical understandings have been written from a decidedly male bias. The particular usefulness of this method should enable us to use the lives and literature of Black women to recognize through them the contribution to the field of ethics that Black women have made. One test will be whether those who know this literary tradition find that I have done justice to its depth and richness. The second test is whether Black women recognize the moral wisdom they utilize. The third test is whether Black feminists who have given up on the community of faith will gain new insights concerning the reasonableness of theological ethics in deepening the Black woman's character, consciousness, and capacity in the ongoing struggle for survival. If these criteria are met, I will have reached my objective.

It is my thesis that the Black women's literary tradition is the best available literary repository for understanding the ethical values Black women have created and cultivated in their participation in this society. To prevail against the odds with integrity, Black women must assess their moral agency within the social conditions of the community. Locked out of the real dynamics of human freedom in America, they implicitly pass on moral formulas for survival that allow them to stand over against the perversions of ethics and morality imposed on them by Whites and males who support racial imperialism in a patriarchal social order.

Findings

The story of the Afro-American has been told quite coherently but has repeatedly left out the Black woman in significant ways. Seldom in history has a group of women been so directly responsible for exerting indispensable efforts to insure the well-being of both their own families and those of their oppressors. At the same time the Black woman is placed in such a sharply disadvantaged position that she must accept obligingly the recording of her own story by the very ones who systematically leave her out. But, the work of Black women writers can be trusted as seriously mirroring Black reality. Their writings are important chronicles of the Black woman's survival.

Despite their tragic omission by the literary establishment, Black women have been expressing ideas, feelings, and interpretations about the Black experience since the early days of the eighteenth century. Throughout the various periods of their history in the United States, Black women have used their creativity to carve out "living space." From the beginning, they had to contend with the ethical ambiguity of racism, sexism, and other sources of fragmentation in this land acclaimed to be of freedom, justice, and equality. The Black women's literary tradition delineates the many ways that ordinary Black women have fashioned value patterns and ethical procedures in their own terms, as well as mastering, transcending, radicalizing, and sometimes destroying pervasive, negative orientations imposed by the mores of the larger society.

Toni Morrison describes the moral agency of old Black women reared in the South in this way:

> Edging into life from the back door. Becoming. Everybody in the world was in a position to give them orders. White women said, "Do this." White children said, "Give me that." White men said, "Come here." Black men said, "Lay down." The only people they need not take orders from were black children and each other. But they took all of that and recreated it in their own image. They ran the houses of white people, and knew it. When white men beat their men, they cleaned up the blood and went home to receive abuse from the victim. They beat their children with one hand and stole for them with the other. The hands that felled trees also cut umbilical cords; the hands that wrung the necks of chickens and butchered hogs also nudged African violets into bloom; the arms that loaded sheaves, bales and sacks rocked babies to sleep. They patted biscuits into flaky ovals of innocence — and shrouded the dead. They plowed all day and came home to nestle like plums under the limbs of their men. The legs that straddled a mule's back were the same ones that straddled their men's hips. And the difference was all the difference there was.[4]

The bittersweet irony of the Afro-American experience forces Black women to examine critically the conventional, often pretentious, morality of middle-class American ideals.

The Black women's literary tradition provides a rich resource and a coherent commentary that brings into sharp focus the Black community's central values, which in turn frees Black folks from the often deadly grasp of parochial stereotypes. The observations, descriptions, and interpretations in Black literature are largely reflective of cultural experiences. They identify the frame of social contradiction in which Black people live, move, and have their being. The derogatory caricatures and stereotypes ascribed to Black people are explicitly rejected. Instead, writings by Blacks capture the magnitude of the Black personality. Spanning the antebellum period to today's complex technological society, Black women writers authenticate, in an economy of expression, how Black people creatively strain against the external limits in their lives, how they affirm their humanity by inverting assumptions and, how they balance the continual struggle and interplay of paradoxes.

The Black Women's Literary Tradition Parallels Black History

The Black women's literary tradition is a source in the study of ethics relative to the Black community because the development of the Black women's historical and literary legacy is tied to the origin of Black people in America. Most of the writing by Black women captures the values of the Black community within a specific location, time, and historical context. The literary tradition is not centered automatically upon the will and whims of what an individual writer thinks is right or obligatory, nor even upon whatever she personally believes to be true for her own localized consciousness. The majority of Black women who engage in literary compositions hold themselves accountable to the collective values that underlie Black history and culture. Dexter Fisher makes the point this way:

> To be totally centered on the self would be to forget one's history, the kinship of a shared community of experience, the crucial continuity between past and present that must be maintained in order to insure the future.[5]

As creators of literature these women are not formally historians, sociologists, or theologians, but the patterns and themes in their writings are reflective of historical facts, sociological realities, and religious convictions that lie behind the ethos and ethics of the Black community. As recorders of the Black experience, Black women writers convey the community's consciousness of values that enables them to find meaning in spite of social degradation, economic exploitation, and political oppression. They record what is valued or regarded as good in the Black community. Seldom, if ever, is their work art-for-art's-sake. "Whatever else may be said of it, Black American writing in the United States has been first and last, as Saunders Redding once observed, a 'literature of necessity.' "[6]

> The appeal of a basically utilitarian literature written to meet the exigencies of a specific historical occasion usually declines after the occasion has passed. That this is much less true of Black literature is due to constant factors in Afro-American history — the Black presence and white racism.[7]

The Black Women's Literary Tradition Uses the Oral Narrative Devices of the Black Community

The irresistible power in the Black women's literary tradition is its power to convey the values of the Black community's oral tradition in its grasp for meaning. The suppression of book learning and the mental anguish of intellectual deprivation obliged the Black tradition to be expressed mainly in oral form. What is critical for my purpose is that these women reveal in their novels, short stories, love lyrics, folktales, fables, drama, and nonfiction a psychic connection with the cultural tradition transmitted by the oral mode from one generation to the next. As serious writers who have mastered in varying degrees the technique of their craft, Black women find themselves causally dependent on the ethics of the Black masses. Black women writers draw heavily upon the Black oral culture.

The folk tales, song (especially the blues), sermons, the dozens, and the rap are all expressions of creativity that provide Black writers with the figurative language and connotations of dim hallways and dank smells, caged birds and flowers that won't sprout, curdled milk and rusty razors, of general stores and beauty parlors, nappy edges and sheened legs. The social and cultural forces within the Black oral tradition form the milieu out of which Black writers create.

Black women writers document the attitudes and morality of women, men, girls, and boys who chafe at and defy the restrictions imposed by the dominant White capitalist value system. They delineate in varying artistic terms the folk treasury of the Black community: ways to deal with poverty and the ramifications of power, sex as an act of love and terror, the depersonalization that accompanies violence, the acquisition of property, the drudgery of a workday, the inconsistencies of chameleon-like racism, teenage mothers, charlatan sorcerers, swinging churches, stoic endurance, and stifled creativity. Out of this storehouse of Black experience comes a vitally rich, ancient continuum of Black wisdom.

This capacity to catch the oral tradition also means an ability to portray the sense of community. Barbara Christian recognizes this unique characteristic common to Black women's literature as the "literary counterpart of their communities' oral tradition."

> The history of these communities, seldom related in textbooks, is incorporated into the tales that emphasize the marvelous, sometimes the outrageous, as a means of teaching a lesson. In concert with their African ancestors, these storytellers, both oral and literary, transform gossip, happenings, into composites of factual events, images, fantasies and fables.[8]

This important characteristic of Black women's writing is increasingly recognized by literary interpreters. Jeanne Noble says, "We would be scripted in history with little true human understanding without the black writer telling it like it is."[9] Mary Helen Washington says that this deeper-than-surface knowledge of and fondness for the verbal tradition is a truth that is shared by the majority of Black women writers:

> This remembrance of things past is not simply self-indulgent nostalgia. It is essential to her vision to establish connections with the values that nourish and strengthen her.[10]

Verta Mae Grosvenor captures the essence of the oral tradition at the very outset of her book *Vibration Cooking:*

> Dedicated to my mama and my grandmothers and my sisters in appreciation of the years that they have worked in miss ann's kitchen and then came home to TCB in spite of slavery and the moynihan report.[11]

Marcia Gillespie, in the May 1975 editorial of *Essence Magazine,* concludes that recording the oral tradition is a way of releasing the memories of mamas and grandmamas:

> ... the race memory of our women who, though burdened, neither broke nor faltered in their faith in a better world for us all.[12]

Black women's combination of the Western literate form with their unique sensibility to the oral narrative devices expresses with authority, power, and eloquence the insidious effects of racism, sexism, and class elitism on members of their communities. By not abandoning the deeply ingrained traditions of the Black community, these writers are able to utilize common sources that illustrate common values that exist within the collective vision of Black life in America.

The Black Women's Literary Tradition Capsulizes the Insularity of the Black Community

Black female writers, as participant-observers, capsulize on a myriad of levels the insularity of their home communities. Due to systemic, institutionalized manifestations of racism in America, the Black community tends to be situated as marginated islands within the larger society. The perpetual powers of White supremacy continue to drop down on the inhabitants of the Black community like a bell jar — surrounding the whole, while separating the Black community's customs, mores, opinions, and system of values from those in other communities. Black female authors emphasize life within the community, not the conflict with outside forces. In order to give faithful pictures of important and comprehensive segments of Black life, these writers tie their character's stories to the aesthetic, emotional, and intellectual values of the Black community.

For instance, Ann Petry's *The Street* (1946) depicts the inevitability of crime for Black mothers who provide for their families against all odds in hostile urban environments:

> A lifetime of pent-up resentments went into the blows. Even after he lay motionless, she kept striking him, not thinking about him, not even seeing him. First she was venting her rage against the dirty, crowded street. She saw the rows of dilapidated old houses; the small dark rooms; the long steep flight of stairs; the narrow dingy hallways; the little lost girls in Mrs. Hedges' apartment, the smashed homes where the women did drudgery because their men had deserted them. She saw all of these things and struck them.
>
> Then the limp figure on the sofa became in turn Jim and the slender girl she'd found him with; became the insult in the moist-eyed glances of white men on the subway; became the greasy, lecherous man at the Crosse School for Singers; became the gaunt Super pulling her down into the basement.
>
> Finally, and the blows were heavier, faster, now, she was striking at the white world which thrust black people into a walled enclosure from which there was no escape; and at the turn of events which had forced her to leave Bub alone while she was working so that he now faced reform school, now had a police record.
>
> She saw the face and the head of the man on the sofa through waves of anger in which he represented all these things and she was destroying them.[13]

Again, for instance, Gwendolyn Brooks's novel *Maud Martha* (1953) focuses on the coming of age for the Black woman-child who has a dark complexion and untamable hair and must learn how to ward off assaults to her human dignity.

> I am what he would call sweet. But I am certainly not what he would call pretty. Even with all this hair (which I have just assured him, in response to his question, is not "natural," is not good grade or anything like good grade) even with whatever I have that puts a dimple in his heart, even with these nice ears, I am still definitely not what he can call pretty if he remains true to what his idea of pretty has always been. Pretty would be a little cream-colored thing with curly hair. Or at the very lowest pretty would be a little curly-haired thing the color of cocoa with a lot of milk in it. Whereas, I am the color of cocoa straight, if you can be even that "kind" to me.[14]

And, still again, Margaret Walker's *Jubilee* (1966) captures the richness of Black folk culture: the songs, sayings, customs, foods, medicinal remedies, and language. This historical novel portrays the character of Vyry's movement from slavery to freedom.

> I wants you to bear witness and God knows I tells the truth, I couldn't tell you the name of the man what whipped me, and if I could it wouldn't make no difference. I honestly believes that if airy one of them peoples what treated me like dirt when I was a slave would come to my door in the morning hungry, I would feed 'em. God knows I ain't got no hate in my heart for nobody. If I is and doesn't know it, I prays to God to take it out. I ain't got no time to be hating. I believes in God and I believes in trying to love and help everybody, and I knows that humble is the way. I doesn't care what you calls me, that's my doctrine and I'm gwine preach it to my childrens, every living one I got or ever hopes to have.[15]

Black women writers find value consciousness in their home communities, which serve as the framework for their literary structure. They transform the passions and sympathies, the desires and hurts, the joys and defeats, the praises and pressures, the richness and diversity of real-lived community into the stuff for art through the medium of literature. As insiders, Black women writers venture into all strata of Black life.

Using the subject matter close to the heart of Black America, the Black women's literary tradition shows how the slavery and its consequences forced the Black woman into a position of cultural custodian. Black female protagonists are women with hard-boiled honesty and down-to-earth thinking, the ones who are forced to see through the shallowness, hypocrisy, and phoniness in their continual struggle for survival. Alice Childress paints the picture in this manner:

> The emancipated Negro woman of America did the only thing she could do. She earned a pittance by washing, ironing, cooking, cleaning, and picking cotton. She helped her man, and if she often stood in the front line, it was to shield him from the mob of men organized and dedicated to bring about his destruction.
>
> The Negro mother has had the bitter job of teaching her children the difference between the White and the Colored signs before they were old enough to attend school. She had to train her sons and daughters to say "Sir" and "Ma'am" to those who were their sworn enemies.
>
> She couldn't tell her husband "a white man whistled at me," not unless she wanted him to lay down his life before organized killers who strike only in anonymous numbers. Or worse, perhaps to see him helpless and ashamed before her.

Because he could offer no protection or security, the Negro woman has worked with and for her family. She built churches, schools, homes, temples and college educations out of soapsuds and muscles.[16]

Conclusion

The work of Black women writers can be trusted as seriously mirroring Black reality. Their writings are chronicles of Black survival. In their plots, actions, and depictions of characters, Black women writers flesh out the positive attributes of Black folks who are "hidden beneath the ordinariness of everyday life." They also plumb their own imaginations in order to crack the invidiousness of worn-out stereotypes. Their ideas, themes, and situations provide truthful interpretations of every possible shade and nuance of Black life.

Black women writers partially, and often deliberately, embrace the moral actions, religious values, and rules of conduct handed down by word of mouth in the folk culture. They then proceed in accordance with their tradition to transform the cultural limitations and unnatural restrictions in the community's move toward self-authenticity.

The special distinctiveness of most Black women writers is their knack of keeping their work intriguing and refreshing without diminishing its instructiveness. They know how to lift the imagination as they inform, how to touch emotions as they record, how to delineate specifics so that they are applicable to oppressed humanity everywhere. In essence, there is no better source for comprehending the "real-lived" texture of Black experience and the meaning of the moral life in the Black context than the Black women's literary tradition. Black women's literature offers the sharpest available view of the Black community's soul.

Chapter 5

Womanist Perspectival Discourse and Canon Formation

My fascination with words has no conscious beginning. I cannot recall the year, the month, the week, or the day when I first realized the magic that lay in the mix of alphabets, words, and stories. However, I do remember as a preschooler spending recess romping through the graveyard at the Mt. Calvary Lutheran Church. The words inscribed on the tombstones mesmerized me. I loved tracing the outline of the granite-carved letters, reading the epitaphs aloud, and spellbinding my classmates with creative stories about the deceased. Even as a small child I was participating in a ritual of honor for my ancestors whose lives and words belong not merely to the past but live on — in, with, and beyond their descendants.

As a womanist theological ethicist my research continues to look directly at ancestral cultural material as well as relatively fixed literary forms. Womanist ethics examines the expressive products of oral culture that deal with our perennial quest for liberation, as well as written literature that invites African Americans to recognize "the distinction between nature in its inevitability and culture in its changeability."[1] When understood in its essentials, my work as a womanist ethicist focuses on the four following areas.

1. *The creation of womanist pedagogical styles.* African American women in the academy design new modes of rigorous inquiry for teaching critical consciousness in our various disciplines. We invite women and men of contemporary faith communities to a more serious encounter with the contributions Black women and Black men have made and continue to make to theological and religious studies.

2. *The emergence of distinctive investigative methodologies.* Black women scholars engage in constructing cognitive maps of the "logic"

This chapter was first published in the *Journal of Feminist Studies in Religion* 9, nos. 1–2 (Spring/Fall 1993): 29–37. I would like to thank Angelin Jones Simmons for her help with this essay.

that sets the perimeters for the intelligibility and legitimacy of race, sex, and class oppression, so that we may discern the hierarchical, mechanistic patterns of exploitation that must be altered in order for justice to occur.

3. *Reconsideration of the established theories, doctrines, and debates of Eurocentric, male-normative ethics.* By juxtaposing traditional principles of character and the regulative standards of action with the judgment and criticism of ourselves in relation to others, we define, elaborate, exemplify, and justify the integration of being and doing.

4. *The adjudicative function of womanist scholars.* We formulate fresh ethical controversies relevant to our particular existential realities as they are recorded in the writings of African American women. I maintain that Black women writers stay intimately attuned to the social, cultural, and political environment in which Black life is lived and that their writings enlarge our theopolitical consciousness and our concept of ethics altogether. This aspect of womanist scholarship is built on the assumption that the African American women's literary tradition is a many-splendored art form and that our task as ethicists is not to read theoethical meaning into texts but to resonate with what is there. By respecting the autonomy of the novel and short story as literary art, I do not explain African American women's literature away by referencing it to Christian symbolic function nor do I dwell on thematic elements that are traditionally related to religious beliefs and moral conduct (i.e., immanence, transcendence, sin, salvation, grace, and forgivenness). Instead, what seems most reasonable for my purpose in this aspect of womanist research are the organizing intertextuality questions: What books are important in the writing of womanist ethics? Whose texts are we conscious of when we write? In this essay, therefore, I will identify some of the generative themes in the texts of African American women writers that womanist ethicists need to address.

My personal title for this essay is "Katie's Canon," wherein I identify the critical contestable issues at the center of Black life — issues inscribed on the bodies of Black people.[2] As a womanist liberation ethicist I have a solemn responsibility to investigate the African American women's literary tradition by asking hard questions and pressing insistently about the responsibility of this canon of books to the truthful, consistent, and coherent representation of Black existence in contemporary society. I am arguing that there is a certain distinguishable body of writings by African American women characterized by fidelity in communicating the baffling complexities and the irreducible contradictions of the Black experience in America. When seen through critical, theoethical lenses, Black women writers skillfully and successfully supply the patterns of conduct, feeling, and contestable issues that exist in the real-lived context that lies behind this literature.

The short story anthologies *Black-Eyed Susans, Midnight Birds, Invented Lives,* and *Memory of Kin* (edited with detailed commentary by Mary Helen Washington) belong to the realm of everyday experience while at the same time pushing beyond the boundaries of the known into the unknown. Washington's collections of representative literary texts erect a larger context of experience within which we may define and understand new contestable issues. These works of fiction, written primarily by African American women, inform and instruct us about moral agency within the framework of African American culture, but more importantly, they highlight aspects of Black women's ethical issues that would not be quite as perceptible otherwise.

In particular, one of the pressing concerns that these texts compel womanist scholars to bring to the table of ethical discourse is *colorism*.[3] The protagonists reveal something of the reader's own survival and travail of outsiderliness, being Black and female in a society that despises both. This interiorized color consciousness enables us to see the various shades of our complexion, hair texture, and physical features as others see us.

> In almost every novel or autobiography written by a black woman, there is at least one incident in which the dark-skinned girl wishes to be either white or light-skinned with "good" hair. Often the child experiences this desire with frightening intensity.[4]

Mary Helen Washington's essay "The Intimidation of Color"[5] clarifies the blatant injustice and the pain that African American women experience in the area of color complexion. Washington says that the subject of the distorted standards for African American women's physical beauty occurs with such frequency in the writing of Black women that it indicates how deeply we have been affected by the discrimination against the shade of our skin and the texture of our hair.

> Besides Shirley Temple movies, white-baby dolls, and other little black kids, what really convinced the black girl that she was truly undesirable was the reaction of adults to a "high-yellow" child. The classic example of this phenomenon is Maureen Peal, from Toni Morrison's *The Bluest Eye*.[6]

Washington's descriptive analysis of colorism penetrates to the soul of African American women's existence across the expanse of four centuries. She provides us with texts that detail the workings of colorism in the commonplaces of daily life.

> If the stories of these writers are to be believed, then the color/hair problem has cut deep into the psyche of the black woman. It is that particular aspect of oppression that has affected, for the most

part, *only women*. . . . Toni Morrison says in *The Bluest Eye* that the concept of physical beauty is one of the most destructive ideas in the history of human thought.[7]

Washington has collected short stories that gather into patterned episodes simplified, "sheroized," and impressive figures who deal with this issue in ways that are recognizable and accessible to the reader.

Some folk prefer to define the issue not as colorism but rather to identify this value system as *pigmentocracy:* an African American person's worth as a human being is determined on an ascending scale based on an admixture of Caucasian blood. The more white-skinned a person is, (supposedly) the greater that person's psychocultural superiority and capacity to dominate others. "The goal for the dark woman," Washington argues, "is not even beauty. The 'ideal' is completely out of the question. The goal is not true beauty, but to be passable, not to be offensive."[8]

Still others choose to classify this ethical dilemma under the category of *physiognomy:* determining the quality of the mind, character, and temperament based on the external physical features of white skin, blond hair, blue eyes, inverted lips, narrow nose, and nonprotruding jaw — all of which have to do with the value-ladenness of physicality. Abby Lincoln sums up this ontological problem in this way:

> We are the women whose hair is compulsively fried, whose skin is bleached, whose nose is "too big," whose mouth is "too loud," whose behind is "too broad," whose feet are "too flat" whose face is "too black," and whose suffering and patience is too long and enduring to be believed.[9]

Another contestable issue in African American women's texts that womanist scholars bring to the table of ethical discourse is found in the writings of Alice Walker. The phrase that best summarizes this issue is "moving beyond a single vision of vaginas." Especially as we read and teach ethics from texts written by Alice Walker, such as *Possessing the Secret of Joy, The Temple of My Familiar,* and *The Color Purple,* we are called to embrace a wholistic justice agenda, casting our lot with the liberation of the darkest women of color. The writings of Alice Walker identify the operative moral assumptions that oppress Black women. Her texts aid us in our quest and desire to transform patriarchal structures and relationships of inequality within the private and public spheres.

In her essay "One Child of One's Own," which she wrote after visiting Judy Chicago's art exhibit "The Dinner Party," Walker insists that some White feminists as well as some Black people deny Black women our womanhood.[10] We seem unable to escape society's vision that "all the women are white, all the Blacks are men."[11] Such individuals are not yet conscientized to experience even the tiniest bit of cognitive dissonance when they hear phrases like "women and Blacks" or "women and minorities."

I remember once in class when I quoted Alice Walker's statement that some White women act as if Black women don't have vaginas, a visiting White woman scholar got indignant: "That makes me angry, to hear you make a statement like that makes me very angry." I chuckled and continued the lecture by saying, "If the statement makes you angry, just imagine how I feel as a Black woman who lives in solidarity with other Black women who have this essential denial of our embodiment used as an operating principle in the making of social and public policies in this so-called Great Society of ours." The White woman came at me again, declaring even more boldly that Walker's statement made her angry; once again I shrugged my shoulders at her disconnected arrogance and asked, "And if the statement makes you angry how do you think the rest of us feel?"

Alice Walker continues her argument from a single vision of vaginas in the following way:

> It occurred to me that perhaps white women feminists, no less than white women generally, cannot imagine that black women have vaginas. Or if they can, where imagination leads them is too far to go.
>
> However, to think of black women is impossible if you cannot imagine them with vaginas.
>
> Perhaps it is the black woman's children, whom the white woman — having more to offer her own children, and certainly not having to offer them slavery or a slave heritage or poverty or hatred, generally speaking: segregated schools, slum neighborhoods, the worst of everything — resents. For they must always make her feel guilty. She fears knowing that black women want the best for their children just as she does. But she also knows black children are to have less in this world so that her children, white children, will have more. (In some countries, all.)
>
> Better then to deny that the black woman has a vagina. Is capable of motherhood. Is a woman.[12]

Alice Walker is in solidarity with our foremother Sojourner Truth, who asked in 1852, "Ain't I a woman?" Walker is also in alliance with Nikki Giovanni, who writes,

> ...get back fat black woman be a mother grandmother strong thing but not woman.[13]

The final embodiment issue womanist scholars bring to the table of ethical discourse is what Mae Henderson, an African American literary critic, identifies as "Black women's bodies as texts." Historically, Henderson writes, the Black woman's body *is* the text.[14] According to Toni Morrison, heteropatriarchs have worked out, have worked on, and have inscribed their death-dealing ideologies, theologies, and systems of value on the "canvas," that is, the flesh of Black people. Morrison even dedicates her novel *Beloved* to the "sixty million and more" who did not survive the Middle Passage, whose bodies are unaccounted for, somewhere in watery graves at the bottom of the Atlantic Ocean. If we want to read of the atrocities that have gone on for centuries, throughout civilization, both Henderson and Morrison urge us to read the texts of women's bodies, especially the bodies of women of African ancestry.

The heart of Morrison's *Beloved* is the mind of the slave. The mind that carries the memories of the body, the memories of eight children and six fathers, of men and women "moved around like checkers." What Baby Suggs "called the nastiness of life was the shock she received upon learning that nobody stopped playing checkers just because the pieces included her children."[15] During chattel slavery children were stolen and sold away at such a young age that the mother had not formed many memories. Imagine the trauma of giving birth to children and not being able to recognize your children's hands in a pile of hands? To have no idea of what their permanent teeth look like? To not know how their jaw bones changed over the years? It was at this point that Sethe, the main protagonist in *Beloved,* knew that she could not love, that she would not love.

Morrison continues, "The way in which we remember is by taking a slice of history and undeliberately trying not to remember." Our bodies are the texts that carry the memories and therefore rememory is no less than reincarnation. Sometimes the rememories are so ordinary that they cannot be remarked upon.

Sethe, like so many women of African ancestry, knew that she would endure slavery but was convinced that her children would not have to undergo such horror. Sethe kills her baby, Beloved, because she is forced to do something so that her daughter will not have to experience the beatings, the torture, the lynching — the brutalization. In *Deep River* Howard Thurman allows us to organize Sethe's ethical dilemma around the following questions: How does the human spirit accommodate such desolation? How long can we hold our breath against such agony? If only death of the body would come to deliver the soul from dying![16] Toni Morrison sums it up this way, "to kill children is preferable to letting them die."[17]

And, still again, Sethe's mother's milk was stolen. Sethe was milked like a cow by White boys with mossy teeth while "schoolteacher watched," all the time writing his text about Black people's size, density, details; human characteristics on the left-hand side of the ledger and so-called animal ones on the right. Henderson argues that schoolteacher beats, batters, and assaults Sethe by using the pen as a symbol and instrument of masculine authority.[18] "Schoolteacher" uses the writing of racist texts to re-mark African women's bodies with the signature of his paternity.

Over and over again, slaveholders wrote their texts on Black women's bodies. The scars and welts on Sethe's back from so many beatings looked and felt like a whole chokecherry tree to Amy, the runaway White girl who serves as the midwife.

> See, here's the trunk — it's red and split wide open, full of sap, and this here's the parting for the branches. You got a mighty lot of branches. Leaves, too, look like, and dern if these ain't blossoms. Tiny little cherry blossoms, just as white. Your back got a whole tree on it. In bloom.[19]

To Baby Suggs, Sethe's mother-in-law, the wounds on Sethe's body are so grotesque that Baby Suggs is speechless, without words, struck silent. Baby Suggs covers her mouth with her hand and gets busy with the ritual of healing, all the time thinking to herself that the open wounds, full of sap running down her daughter-in-law's back, were like a pattern of "roses of blood." Marcia Gillespie wrote in an issue of *Ms.* magazine that sometimes as women we witness so much death-dealing before our eyes that, in a form of self-protection our minds no longer allow our eyes to see and, I would add, our mouths to speak.[20]

When Paul D arrives he is the last to offer an alternative reading of what White men have stenciled and carved with whips on Sethe's body. By the time he shows up, the last survivor from the Kentucky plantation Sweet Home, Sethe's back is numb. The skin has been dead for years. Nevertheless, Paul D reads the text on Sethe's back as the decorative, intricate filigree work of an ironsmith.

One of the questions that we need to wrestle with is what does it mean *in* and *for* the womanist academy when African American women are rendered speechless when we read one another's bodies, and yet White women and Black men seem to have very little problem in reading from their viewpoint what has been written on our backs by White men?

In Toni Morrison's novels *Beloved* and *Jazz* this theme of embodiment as rememory and rememory as reincarnation is the basic motif. Flesh houses memories — the color of flesh, the reproductive character of flesh, and the manifold ways that the flesh of African women is the text on which androcentric patriarchy is written. In essence, Morrison maintains that we must wrestle with the question, What are the emotional resources for dealing with forgotten memories that lie dormant in our bodies and therefore in our souls? Having no language to carry the memory is the final devastation. And yet Morrison says that the need is deep: "If we had had more water we would have made more tears."[21]

So *in toto* womanist perspectival discourse identifies texts that comprise the canon. The four areas of womanist research make connections to the received "normative" tradition without succumbing to conservative values implicit in it. In other words, the literature of African American women frees womanist scholars from the matrix of dominant Western ethics so that we can get some sense of the sublimated ethical concerns and the "handing on" of moral insights that communicate emancipatory praxis. Canon formation is a way of establishing new and larger contexts of experience within which African American women can attend to the disparity between sources of oppression and sources for liberation. African American women's literature records the narrative events that are most recognizable in the lives of the Black community, which in turn enables womanist scholars to retrieve judiciously the complex series of ethical moves, thus helping the community as a whole to conserve what has survived from the past and release what may shape the present and the future.

Chapter 6

Resources for a Constructive Ethic

The Life and Work of Zora Neale Hurston

Of all the women in the Black women's literary tradition who have contributed to the concrete depiction of Black life, Zora Neale Hurston (1901–60) is "par exemplar." As an outstanding novelist, journalist, folklorist, anthropologist, and critic, Hurston possessed a sharp accuracy in reporting the positive sense of self that exists among poor, marginal Blacks, "the Negro farthest down."[1] The primary impetus for all her writings was to capture the density of simple values inherent in the provincialism of Blacks who worked on railroads, lived in sawmill camps, toiled in phosphate mines, earning their keep as common laborers. In her short story "John Redding Goes to Sea," Hurston describes the microcosmic world of her main characters:

> No one in their community has ever been farther than Jacksonville. Few, indeed had ever been there. Their own gardens, general store, and occasional trips to the country seat — seven miles away — sufficed for all their needs. Life was simple indeed with these folks.[2]

In a letter to Langston Hughes in 1929, Hurston summed up her deep dedication and abiding commitment to recording Black life:

> For I not only want to present the material with all the life and color of my people, I want to leave no loopholes for the scientific crowd to rend and tear us. I am leaving the story material almost untouched. I have only tampered with it where the story teller was not clear. I know it is going to read different, but that is the glory of the thing, don't you think?[3]

This chapter was first published in the *Journal of Feminist Studies in Religion* 1, no. 1 (1984): 37–51.

Zora Neale Hurston was the most prolific Black woman writer in America from 1920 to 1950, and her life and literature are paradigmatic of Black culture and Black women's lives.

Between the middle of the Harlem Renaissance and the end of the Korean War, Zora Neale Hurston wrote four novels, two books of folklore, an autobiography, and more than fifty short stories and essays. In 1934, Hurston was praised by the *New York Herald Tribune* for being in "the front rank" of all American writers. In 1935–36, she was the recipient of two Guggenheim Research Fellowships. During this time Hurston was offered a Rosenwald Fellowship to study for her doctorate in anthropology and folklore at Columbia University. However, within a month, the officers reneged on the offer because they found Hurston's degree plan unacceptable. Two important honors were bestowed on Hurston in 1943: Howard University presented her with the Alumni Award for distinguished postgraduate work in literature, and the *Saturday Review* presented her with the Anisfield-Wold Award for her autobiography, *Dust Tracks on a Road*. It was heralded as "the best book on race relations and as the best volume in the general field of fiction, poetry or biography which is of such character that it will aid in the sympathetic understanding and constructive treatment of race relations."

In both her life and her work Hurston embodied a sensitized candor in relation to the subtle, invisible ethos as well as the expressed moral values emanating from within the cultural institutions in the Black community. Unlike most of the other writers in her time, Hurston emphasized the unique cultural heritage and wholeness of Black life.

Zora Hurston always looked first and foremost to the Black experience as the source of her living texts. She used "folk language, folkways, and folk stories" as symbols to measure the intrinsic values of the Black oral/aural cultural tradition. In order to refute assumptions of genetic racism and to vindicate the Black community in the face of the oppressive slander of White supremacy, Hurston used a presentational method to document the culture, history, imagination, and fantasies of Black people.

Hurston depicted the inaudible stoutheartedness of Black folk. She maintained that Black life was more than defensive reactions to the oppressive circumstances of anguish and desperation perpetrated by a Western system of White male patriarchy. Hurston invested her energies in staying in touch with the rich, colorful creativity that emerged and reemerges in the Black quest for human dignity. The cultural traditions that Hurston wrote about tend to represent statements of belief about the world, its creation, and people's connectedness and estrangement within the insular community. The characters are women, men, and children who know how to grasp the affirmative side of life amid a system of brutalization. They learn early how to find personal fulfillment in the basic push-pull ambivalence of the do-it-yourself-or-do-without reality.

As a Black woman artist, subjected to the violence of Whites, of male superiority, and of poverty, Zora Neale Hurston offered an especially concrete frame of reference for understanding the Black woman as moral agent. Karla Holloway describes Hurston's moral agency as being both the mirror and the lamp, both the visual image and the mechanism that illuminates that image.[4] Hurston's own being is both the subject and the object of her work. Thus, Hurston's life and work serve as a prophetic paradigm for understanding the modes of behavior and courses of action that are passed from generation to generation by the most oppressed segments of the Black population.

Beginning in early childhood, Hurston embraced a set of values that allowed her to prevail against the odds with integrity. Through the Black community's oral tradition Hurston learned how to live on Black terms — how to resist, to oppose, and to endure the immediate struggles within terrifying circumstances. Hurston's parents schooled her in how to live with the tension of the irrational facticity of life. Even though Hurston was born and grew up in the first all-Black incorporated town in the United States (Eatonville, Florida, in 1865), where her father served three terms as mayor, Hurston's parents still made her aware of the evil systems and social institutions that existed outside of her supportive, nourishing environment. During her prepuberty years, Hurston's parents tried to teach her how to deal with the insults and humiliations of the larger society so that she would not make the wrong step or wrong response that could literally jeopardize her life.

Hurston's mother was Lucy Ann Potts, a former schoolteacher. She exhorted Zora to "jump at de sun" so that she would not "turn out to be a mealy-mouthed rag doll" with a squinched spirit by the time she was grown. "We might not land on the sun, but at least we would get off the ground."[5] In other words, Lucy Potts encouraged her daughter to strive continually for individuality and self-expression. She did not want Hurston to feel hampered and held down by the heinous pressures of racist/sexist reality.

At the same time, Hurston's father, a carpenter, a Baptist preacher, and the moderator of the South Florida Baptist Association, tried to induce a spirit of docile compliancy. He warned that it did not do for Blacks to have too much spirit because White folks would not tolerate it. In her autobiography, Hurston recorded her father's speech to her:

He predicted dire things for me. The white folks were not going to stand for it. I was going to be hung before I was grown. Somebody was going to blow me down for my sassy tongue. Mama was going to suck sorrow for not beating my temper out of me before it was too late. Posses with ropes and guns were going to drag me out sooner or later on account of that stiff neck I toted. I was going to tote a hungry belly by reason of my forward ways.[6]

Hurston's father wanted her to be aware of the burgeoning complexities imposed by discrimination. He attempted to inculcate in her the awareness of what happens when Whites and males support imperialism in a patriarchal social order.

Living on her memories, Zora Hurston's maternal grandmother — Grandma Potts — offered moral counsel in light of events and their possible consequences. She tried to warn Hurston of how her actions would affect the prospects of her survival: "Git down offa dat gatepost! You li'l sow you! Git down! Setting up dere looking dem white folks right in de face! They's gwine to lynch you, yet."[7]

Like the vast majority of Black children, Hurston by the age of nine had learned how life goes awry. With the death of her mother, Hurston moved swiftly from the tranquility of childhood to womanhood:

Mama died at sundown and changed a world. That is the world which had been built out of her body and heart. Even the physical aspects fell apart with suddenness that was startling....I was deprived of the loving pine, the lakes, the wild violets in the woods and the animals I used to know. No more holding down first base on the team with my brothers and their friends. Just a jagged hole where my home used to be.[8]

The counsel of her dying mother helped Hurston to leave behind the carefree days of childhood. The thirty-seven-year-old woman's deathbed speech, captured in the fictional character of Lucy in *Jonah's Gourd Vine,* is a series of proverbial sayings that were a sort of ethical treatise to help Hurston consider more deeply the worth and meaning of her life:

Stop cryin', Isie, you can't hear whut Ahm sayin', 'member tuh git all de education you kin. Dat's de onliest way you kin keep out from under people's feet. You always strain tuh be de bell cow, never be de tail uh nothin'. Do de best you kin, honey, 'cause neither yo' paw or dese older chilun is goin' tuh be bothered too much wid youh, but you goin' tuh git 'long. Mark mah words. You got spunk, but mah po' li'l sandy-haired child goin' suffer uh lot 'fo she git tuh de place she can 'fend fuh herself. And Isie, honey, stop cryin' and lissen tuh me. Don't you love nobody better'n you do yo'self. Do, you'll be killed 'thout being struck uh blow. Some uh dese things Ahm tellin' yuh, you won't understand 'em fuh years tuh come, but de time will come when you'll know.[9]

Her mother's instructions were concerned not so much with ascertaining fact or elaborating theories as with the means and ends of practical life. Hurston's mother pointed to the people, attitudes, and structures that were inimical to Hurston's ongoing survival. She spelled out those things that Hurston needed to do in order to protect the quality and continuity of her life. Hurston need not be a muzzled, mutilated individual but must continue to grow as a woman-child with a vibrant, creative spirit. This moral wisdom, handed down from mother to daughter as the crystallized result of experience, aimed to teach Hurston not only how to survive but also how to prevail with integrity against the cruel system of triple oppression.

During her middle years Hurston incarnated a personality of harmonious complex opposites. In the most comprehensive and thorough biography of Hurston so far written, Robert E. Hemenway describes the reconciling polarities of Hurston's personality as "fiercely flamboyant yet incredibly secretive, self-centered yet kind, a Republican conservative yet an early Black nationalist — a sophisticated writer who was never afraid to be herself."[10] Joyce O. Jenkins says that Hurston's personality was one carved out of a pragmatic philosophy of life, wherein she made up her own rules, refusing to be bound by what she ought to do and think.[11]

In 1925 Hurston arrived in New York City at a most opportune time. The Harlem Renaissance was flourishing. At the 1925 Urban League award dinner, Hurston met one of the contest judges, novelist Fannie Hurst. This initial meeting resulted in Hurston working for Hurst as live-in secretary, chauffeur, and confidante for several years. At the award dinner, Hurston also met Annie Nathan Meyer, a novelist and one of the founders of Barnard College. Meyer was so keenly impressed with Hurston that she arranged for her to enroll at Barnard on scholarship the following semester. While completing the requirements for the B.A. degree (1925–28), Hurston studied with Gladys Reichard, an anthropology professor at Barnard who was so excited by the quality of Hurston's work that she introduced her to Columbia's famed anthropology professor Franz Boas. The result was an opportunity for Hurston to work as an anthropological apprentice with Boas.

Two weeks before Hurston graduated from Barnard, she received a fellowship from Carter G. Woodson's Association for the Study of Negro Life and History. Hurston's assignment was to travel south to collect folklore. She failed miserably in her first attempt to gather data outside of Harlem. In her autobiography she compared the minuscule amount of material collected during her first visit with "not being enough to make a flea a waltzing jacket":

When I went about asking, in carefully-accented Barnardese, "Pardon me, do you know any folk-tales or folk-songs?" the men and women who had whole treasuries of material seeping through their pores looked at me and shook their heads. No, they had never heard of anything like that around there. Maybe it was over in the next county. Why didn't I try over there? I did, and got the self-same answer.[12]

Hurston made many trips to the South afterward.

Hurston's folklore collection records the action guides the Black community deemed appropriate within ineradicable systems of oppression. This rich body of accumulated data speaks of some of the ways that Black folk have tried to answer to the wills and whims of those in power, over whom Blacks have no control. The exigencies of circumstances often require Black people to cultivate as a virtue the ingrown capacity for meeting difficulties with fortitude and resilience. Even when daunted by tribulations, Black people are compelled to act in order to ensure their ongoing survival:

> You see we are a polite people and do not say to our questioner, "Get out of here!" We smile and tell him or her something that satisfies the white person because, knowing so little about us, he doesn't know what he is missing. The Indian resists curiosity with a stony silence. The Negro offers a featherbed resistance. That is, we let the probe enter, but it never comes out. It gets smothered under a lot of laughter and pleasantries.
>
> The theory behind our tactics: "The white man is always trying to know into somebody else's business. All right, I'll set something outside the door of my mind for him to play with and handle. He can read my writing but he sho' can't read my mind. I'll put this play toy in his hand, and he will seize it and go away. Then I'll say my say and sing my song." [13]

The central moral emanating from the Black community in such an exchange was an unequivocal call for human equality. The constellation of values that the community upholds taught its members to keep at bay Hurston or anyone else who seemed to disrespect their humanity. As moral agents in oppressive situations, Black people live with the haunting consequences of the involuntariness of life. When presented with even a glimpse of choice, oppressed people give answers and responses that allow them to maintain their dignity with all the resilience and strength they can muster.

The Black community's folklore, which Hurston collected, is the corporate story that enshrines the interlocking complexities of the beliefs, etiology, and practices of Black folk. It constitutes the community's understanding of, and response to, its own humanity. The oral stories are reappropriations of their past experiences. Br'er Fox, Br'er Deer, Br'er 'Gator, Br'er Dawg, Br'er Rabbit, and the devil always outsmart Ole Massa, his wife, and God.

In order for Zora Hurston to collect the much-desired folklore, she had to shed the superficial vestiges of privilege and voyeur status and stand in solidarity with the group of people who sat on the steps of Joe Clarke's store, exchanging lies and telling stories. Hurston had to let go of any hierarchical stance that subordinated, undervalued, or threatened the well-being of the teller or the tale. Black people did not want anyone tampering with the raw wisdom reflected and reinforced in their oral traditions:

> Men sat around the store on boxes and benches and passed this world and the next one through their mouths. The right and wrong, the who, when and why was passed on, and nobody doubted the conclusions. There were no discreet nuances of life on Joe Clarke's porch. There was open kindnesses, anger, hate, love, envy and its kinfolks, but all emotions were naked, and nakedly arrived at. It was a case of "make it and take it." You got what your strengths would bring you.[14]

It was while working as a folklorist and anthropologist that Hurston began combining the moral counsel that she had learned from her family (especially from her mother) with the folk wisdom of the Black community. Hurston grew to appreciate the genuine virtue of surviving the continual struggle and the interplay of contradictory opposites. Hurston knew that there could be no "perfectionism" in the face of the structures of oppression she experienced as a Black professional woman. From her work, she grasped an understanding of the moral quality of life being fulfilled, not as an ideal, but as a balance of complexities in such a way that suffering did not overwhelm and endurance with integrity was possible.

Zora Neale Hurston's own code of living forms a basis for the characterizations in her novels. Hurston and her female characters are Black women who learn to glean directives for living in the here-and-now. In their tested and tried existential realities, the majority of these women refuse to get caught up in the gaudy accoutrements of the middle-strata sham. Against the vicissitudes of labor exploitation, sex discrimination, and racial cruelties, they embrace an ingenuity that allows them to fashion a set of values on their own terms as well as to master, radicalize, and sometimes destroy pervasive negative orientations imposed by the larger society.

Hurston and her fictional counterparts are resources for a constructive ethic, wherein they serve as strong, resilient images, embodying the possible options for action open within the Black folk culture. Women who live in the circle of life must discern the genuine choices available or else they will be characterized by one or more of the following folk metaphors: mule, spit cut, rut in the road, chewed-up and discarded sugar cane, or wishbone.

As moral agents struggling to avoid the devastating effects of structural oppression, these Black women create various coping mechanisms that free them from imposed norms and expectations. The moral counsel of their collective stories accentuates the positive attributes of Black life. Through the mode of fiction, they articulate possibilities for decision and action that address forthrightly the circumstances that inescapably "color" and shape Black life. As the bodily and psychical representatives of the majority of the members of the Afro-American female population, Hurston and her characters serve as the consciousness that calls Black women forth so that they can break away from the oppressive ideologies and belief systems that presume to define their reality.

Ellease Southerland notes that Hurston's work brings together a religion of opposites, and when these opposites are made to coincide, there is the power of new life.[15] This transcendent spirit of new life provides a hard-won sense of self-understanding in the midst of extreme constraints and projects a positive valuation of the Black woman's humanity even when life itself is threatened. The reenactment of female experiences, "holding up proverbial mirrors" within the social fabric of the Black community, conveys moral wisdom to Black women. Hurston's character Mentu, in *Moses, Man of the Mountain,* describes the proverbial mirroring in this manner: "You are right to listen to proverbs. They are short sayings made out of long experiences."

Both in tone and in language, Hurston's characters look at the world with their own eyes, form their own judgments, and demythologize whole bodies of so-called social legitimacy. For instance, Hurston's most popular novel, *Their Eyes Were Watching God* (1987), is a drama based on the values of the community and the tension that arises when there is a conflict between what the community advises Black women to do and what, in fact, is done.

The high point of this novel occurs when Janie comes to the end of her search. She returns home after a two-year absence to tell her best friend, Phoeby Watson, the story of her struggle for full humanity. Her gratuitous retelling of her past, her stratagems, and her linguistic idioms all correspond to the existential reality of the Black community. After thirty years of looking, Janie finally finds spiritual freedom and a physically satisfying love. The tragedy is that Janie has to kill her lover in order to save her own life. However, Janie accepts this loss and all other losses as part of the truth that brings one to self-authenticity. Janie surmises, "If you kin see de light at daybreak, you don't keer if you die at dusk. It's so many people never seen de light at all. Ah wuz fumblin' round and God opened de door."[16]

It is important to see how Zora Neale Hurston prepared her heroine, Janie, for newly found identity and freedom. Janie's recounting of her experiences begins with her being weighed down with false images that say that as a Black woman she is not allowed to exist naturally and freely. Hurston contrasted these community values of one generation with the next.

Nanny Crawford, Janie's grandmother, is a freed slavewoman who understands marriage as a way to escape poverty and abuse, as a way to avoid the traditional fate of Black women. Nanny had suffered the sexual will and whims of the White slaveowner, which resulted in the birth of an illegitimate child. The baby resembled the White man so much that his wife violently attacked Nanny and threatened to have Nanny beaten with one hundred lashes of rawhide on her bare back, "till the blood run down yo' heels." Nanny then ran away and hid out in the swamp until her body had time to heal because she didn't want her baby to be sold away from her. "De noise uh de owls skeered me, de limbs of dem cypress trees took to crawlin' and movin' round after dark, and two three times Ah heered panthers prowlin' round. But nothin' never hurt me 'cause de Lawd knowed how it was."[17] Nanny's gallant action amid fear was the quiet grace of slavewomen, but Janie yearns for something more. The grandmother wants Janie to have all the material possessions and protective security she herself never had. She tells about her search for dreams and aspirations after Emancipation. "Ah wanted to preach a great sermon about colored women sittin' on high, but they wasn't no pulpit for me....Ah been waiting for a long time, Janie, but nothin' Ah been through ain't too much if you just take a stance on high ground lak Ah dreamed."[18]

Nanny's entire moral code has developed in relation to the ethical ambiguities in her experience. Functional prudence is the value center for self-fulfillment. As a slavewoman, Nanny at an early age learned to discern suitable courses of action. In order to follow the most ethical course, Janie's grandmother teaches Janie the critical forethought and discerning deliberation that Black women have mastered with an extremely delicate sense of balance down through the years.

More than anything, Nanny wants Janie to be spared the servile role of Black women in the society:

Honey, de white man is de rule of everything as fur as Ah been able tuh find out. Maybe it's some place way off in de ocean where de black man is in power, but we don't know nothin' but what we see. So de white man throw down de load and tell de nigger man tuh pick it up because he have to, but he don't tote it. He hand it to his womenfolks. De nigger woman is de mule uh de world so far as Ah can see. Ah been praying fuh it to be different wid you. Lawd, Lawd, Lawd.[19]

Hurston presented Janie as a woman who unmasked the conventional code of social behavior and created a new code of values more appropriate to her needs. Her success or failure is measured by the goal of self-actualization. Moral agency is exemplified each time Janie stands against critical dilution of her personhood. As Mary Helen Washington contends, "Janie has to resist both male domination and the empty materialism of white culture in order to get to the horizon."[20]

Moses, Man of the Mountain (1939), the longest fiction in Hurston's canon, is an allegorical satire concerning the affinities between Voodoo and Christianity. While Hurston's earlier novel, *Jonah's Gourd Vine* (1934), dealt with the common features of these two religions manifested in the life of a Black pastor, this novel delineates the same causal, coalescent relationship by retelling the biblical legend of Moses in the Black aesthetic tradition. Hurston provided somewhat greater depth for the values of the Black community by establishing Moses as an amalgam of the best features of magic art, "the secrets of the deep," and the practices in the inner and outer life of those who are called God's chosen people.

Just as Janie in *Their Eyes Were Watching God* is Hurston's most powerful female character, Moses in this novel is her most powerful male character. Jethro, his father-in-law, tells him, "The great I AM took the soul of the world and wrapped some flesh around it and that made you."[21] Even when Hurston tries to demystify Moses as a person with two beings, one that lives and flourishes in the daylight and stands guard, and one that walks and howls at night, she still describes him in universal terms.

Hurston used Black speech to codify in written form the subtle dynamics of the metaphorical and proverbial connections between the exodus of the Hebrews and the African American trek from slavery to freedom. She deflated the rigid seriousness of biblical rhetoric. Just below the surface of this drama is the collective wisdom revealed in the Black community, related to the discrepancy between professing Christian learnings and practicing a religious faith.

The basis for the dynamic structure in *Moses, Man of the Mountain* is that it allows us to see "how Hurston 'invents' a legend to demonstrate how the traditional legend of Moses might have been created."[22] Hurston discounted the biblical version of Moses' origin. She saw it only as a mythical concoction of Miriam, the daughter of a Hebrew couple. Instead, Hurston juxtaposed the biblical legend with modern-day reality. For example, the Hebrews working in Egypt refer to the overseer as "bossman." In the wilderness when they grow tired of manna and quail, they yearn for "the nice fresh fish...nice sweet-tasting little pan-fish" that they enjoyed in Egypt. Even the housing in Goshen resembles the living quarters of chattel slaves on southern plantations.

The resource for a constructive ethic in this novel is identified with Moses' call to emancipate the people of God. There is a shift from individualism to a search for truth in the context of community. Moses is involved in a difficult process, wherein he is "constructing a new identity from the ground up, with no blueprints to predict the final shape of the edifice. Moses' life will be *transformed* into something new when he comes to identify with the oppressed; he truly crosses over into a new and different land."[23] Eventually, Moses passes on this ethical idea in a remarkably prophetic passage:

> Now one thing I want you to get in your head: You can't have a state of individuals. Everybody just can't be allowed to do as they please. I love liberty and I love freedom so I started off giving everybody a loose rein. But I soon found out that it wouldn't do. A great state is a well-blended mash of something of the people and all of the none of the people. You understand. The liquor of statecraft is distilled from the mash you got. How can a nation speak with one voice if they are not one? Don't forget now. If you do, you encourage all the stupid but greedy and ambitious to sprout like toadstools and that's the end of right and reason in the state. Coddling and wheedling is not going to stop these destroyers. To a haughty belly, kindness is hard to swallow and harder to digest.[24]

Seraph on the Suwanee (1948), Zora Neale Hurston's last published novel, is the only one in which the main characters are White. Hurston changed the color of her characters in this novel, but she did not change the basic habits, attitudes, and mode of life: "All the characters in *Seraph* sound exactly like the Eatonville folks sitting on Joe Clarke's front porch."[25]

This last novel of Hurston's continues to follow the ethical resources established in the earlier works that deal with the search for self-actualization and love, with life-affirming rather than life-denying experiences. A review of the plot reveals Arvay, a poor White woman of Sawley, Florida, spending most of her life protecting the propositions that support her cherished false assumptions. At age sixteen, when her older sister marries the man with whom Arvay lives in "mental adultery," Arvay renounces the world to become a "foreign" missionary. At age twenty-one, Jim Meserve, a high-class Irishman, presents Arvay with a proposal of marriage. Arvay tries to discourage Jim with self-induced fainting spells. The more Jim pursues her, the more Arvay tries to discourage him. "Ah, no, this pretty laughing fellow was too far out of her reach. Things as wonderful as this were meant for nobody like her. This was first-class, and she was born to take other people's leavings."[26]

Finally after Jim initiates a violent sexual assault, Arvay submits and agrees to marry him. Together they prosper as citrus-fruit farmers in Citrabelle, Florida. When the first of their three children is born, Arvay believes that her child's deformity is punishment from God for her adolescent sin of "adultery in the mind." Incident after incident occurs, and Arvay continues to cling to a denial of reality. She wreaks havoc in the marriage, in her parenting, and in her life. "Arvay scorned off learning as a source of evil knowledge and thought fondly of ignorance as the foundation of good heartedness and honesty."[27]

Jim grows weary and exasperated with Arvay's patterns of denial. He walks out of the marriage. Soon after, Arvay returns home to Sawley to tend to her mother, who is terminally ill. It is during this visit home that Arvay comes to terms with her personhood. She finally breaks free of her shackling past.

The ethical resources in *Seraph on the Suwanee* are qualities that belong only to those who emerge as victors in the battle against self-centered fear. Whatever is "an evil, ill-deformed monstropolous accumulation of time and scum" must be destroyed. Whatever is "soaked in so much of doing-without, or soul-starvation, or brutish vacancy of aim, of absent dreams, envy of trifles, ambitions for littleness, smothered cries and trampled love," has to be destroyed. Whatever "caught people and twisted the limbs of their minds"[28] has to be burned to ashes so that real life can begin.

It is possible to conjecture that Zora Neale Hurston's explicit portrayal of sexism in this novel coincided with increasing gender discrimination in her own life during the 1940s. Sexism is dealt with in all of her novels, but it emerges in full scale in *Seraph*. Hurston fully delineated the propositions, attitudes, and behavior that men exhibit to support their belief in the inherent inferiority of women and their right to dominate them. Hurston's revealing commentary in *Seraph* is that Jim Meserve, a man blessed with admirable qualities — courage, honesty, loyalty — is also a chauvinist. Jim begins his tirade against women in this manner:

> Women folks don't have no mind to make up no how. They wasn't made for that. Lady folks were just made to laugh and act loving and kind and have a good man to do for them all he's able, and have him as many boy-children as he figgers he'd like to have, and make him so happy that he is willing to work and fetch in every dad-blamed thing that his wife thinks she would like to have. That's what women are made for.[29]

Joe Kelsey, the Black man who works for Jim, believes women are property. Joe spouts his invectives: "Make 'em knuckle under. From the very first jump, get the bridle in they mouth and ride 'em hard and stop 'em short. They's all alike, Boss. Take 'em and break 'em."[30]

About midway through the novel, Jim becomes irritated with his wife, Arvay, and orders her to strip naked. When she attempts to cover herself, he yells: "Don't you move! You're my damn property, and I want you right where you are, and I want you naked. Stand right there in your tracks until I tell you that you can move."[31] In one of Jim's protracted closing speeches to Arvay, he compares her to "an unthankful and unknowing hog under a acorn tree. Eating and grunting with your ears hanging over your eyes and never even looking up to see where the acorns are coming from."[32]

What is recognizable and familiar in all these comments is that gender discrimination is an immutable fact in women's existence. Ostensibly a social-literary critic, Hurston showed how both men and women are captives of their oppression.

Conclusion

Alice Walker, in introducing a collection of Zora Neale Hurston's writings, asserts that the fundamental thesis that Hurston embodied and exhibited as an ethical resource was that one "must struggle every minute of life to affirm black people's right to a healthy existence."[33] The work of Hurston is quite diverse. Some of her writings are purely satirical and entertaining. Other pieces are colloquial in style and avowedly persuasive. All reveal a fundamental truth: self-fulfillment in a situation of oppression requires hitting a straight lick with a crooked stick. In other words, all of Hurston's work is a type of ambiguous featherbed resistance.

Zora Hurston understood the elaborate facade of myths, traditions, and rituals erected to couch systems of injustice in America. Thus, the complexity of being a Black woman artist writing for the *Saturday Evening Post,* the *American Mercury,* and the *American Legion Magazine* caused Hurston to combine her private experiences with various linguistic modes, so that her writing at times appears fairly oblique and nonthreatening. Hurston used irony, wit, and humor to entertain White readers as she reported the Black community's understanding and manifestations of courageous living. In different ways of saying much the same thing, Hurston's writings are sometimes very belligerent. She took for granted the inseparability of words and actions. Her work is imbued with a conscious hope that language can expose "the weight that racism lays on the whole world."[34]

All in all, Zora Neale Hurston's life and work relate to the struggle for racial justice. Identifying resources for a constructive ethic was not her explicit goal but can be frequently explicated from the stance she took on various issues. Testifying to a vision of a just society, Hurston made particular claims on the moral agency of her audiences. She encouraged protest against the dehumanization of Black personhood. Across the boundaries of her own experience, Hurston wrote about the oppressive and unbearable, about those things that rub Black women raw. Her richness and chaos, her merits and faults witnessed to an ethic that can be lived out only in community.

Chapter 7

Unctuousness as Virtue

According to the Life of Zora Neale Hurston

It may surprise some readers that a study in virtue would focus on the life of Zora Neale Hurston. To be sure, Hurston did not write as a formal exponent of ethics, but she clarifies the moral values that are central in the Black community in the very life she lived. As a Black-woman-artist, who was subjected to the violence of White supremacy, of male superiority, and of economic poverty, Zora Neale Hurston offers a concrete frame of reference for understanding the Black woman as a moral agent. Hurston's life serves as a prophetic paradigm for understanding the modes of behavior and courses of action that are passed from generation to generation by the most oppressed segments of the Black population.

Hurston, like Black women generally, understood suffering not as a moral norm or as a desirable ethical quality, but rather as the typical state of affairs. Virtue is not in the experiencing of suffering, nor in the survival techniques for enduring. Rather, the quality of moral good is that which allows Black people to maintain a feistiness about life that nobody can wipe out, no matter how hard they try.

Even though suffering is all but universal, Black women establish a relationship with suffering in their lives in order to endure. Due to Black women's widespread intimate acquaintance with suffering they do not assess suffering as the chief end of creation. It is not a natural condition. Nor is it a spiritual accompaniment of their life story that supposedly causes them to grow to maturity. Instead, suffering is the normal state of affairs.

The Black female community connects the entire range and spectrum of Black suffering to the history of this country, a history grounded in slavery, a history whose purpose and intent is denying Black people their full humanity. Suffering primarily arises from the inevitable trials and

This chapter was first published in the *Zora Neale Hurston Forum* (Fall 1987): 38–48.

tribulations that come with being Black and female in a society that despises both. Such suffering occurs in many degrees of intensity, from that
which is specifiable to that which constitutes an unimaginable anguish.
Black women have suffered in fields and kitchens, their bodies freely
used, their children taken from them, their men castrated before their
eyes, "and yet in the mind of white America this abuse, this outrage,
was somehow not serious, was in fact justified."[1]

In light of such suffering, what counsel of action is central for Blacks?
Very specifically, the primary ethical principle or action guide is "unctuousness."[2] What Hurston makes clear is that it is the quality of
steadfastness, akin to fortitude, in the face of formidable oppression
that serves as the most conspicuous feature in the construction of Black
women's ethics. My thesis is that Hurston portrays this moral quality
of life not as an ideal to be fulfilled but as a balance of complexities
so that suffering will not overwhelm and endurance is possible. The
moral premises and assumptions that are inherited from the Black community's oral tradition, accentuated by Hurston's life, emphasize the
continual struggle and interplay of contradictory opposites as the highest good. Creatively straining against the external restraints in one's life
is virtuous living.

After her brief research fellowship expired in 1928, Zora Neale Hurston returned to New York City with the little bit of folklore she
had collected, no money, and no job. She was able to continue her
data-gathering for several more years under the auspices of Charlotte
Osgood Mason, a White Park Avenue dowager of enormous wealth and
influence. Some of Hurston's critics mercilessly discredited her as a re-
spectable artist because she "got money from white folks." More often
than not, these same critics, who caricatured Hurston as a charming,
manipulative minion, "who lived up to the whites' notion of what a
'darky' should be," were financially backed by the same White patrons.

In spite of the ridicule, Hurston acted with unctuousness in this
racist financial arrangement. Implicit in her contract, as in all of Mason's contracts with Black artists — Alain Locke, Langston Hughes,
Richard Wright, Miguel Covarrubias, Aaron Douglas, Raymond Barthe
and Louise Thompson — was an understanding that their work ought to
reflect unalloyed primitivism. Mason wanted her protégées to "slough
off white culture — using it only to clarify the thoughts that surge in
your being." Mason also insisted that her Harlem beneficiaries never
mention her name to others. They were only to refer to her as "Godmother." Mason had strict control over all of Hurston's work. She
forbade Hurston to display in revues or publish any of the information, data, or music transcripts she gathered without her permission.
Hurston knew that she needed Mason's financial sponsorship in order
to preserve the Black cultural heritage, and at the same time she was

aware of the razor-blade tension between obsequious accommodation to "Godmother" and fidelity to her own values.

A Black woman writer who was never able to make a living from her craft, Hurston experienced her situation as a moral dilemma and as a yoke around her neck. On the one hand, she celebrated the value of the rich reservoir of materials passed along in the oral tradition of her parents, neighbors, and common everyday people. On the other hand, Hurston had to confront the almost universal understanding outside of the context of Black culture itself: that of Black folkways as inferior, comic, and primitive.

During this period, Zora Neale Hurston coined the term "Negrotarian" for Whites such as Charlotte Mason, Carl Van Vechten, Fannie Hurst, Florenz Ziegfeld, Clarence Darrow, Pearl Buck, and Amy and Joe Springarn, all of whom specialized in "uplifting" all areas of Negro life. Negrotarians not only patronized Blacks and socialized with them, but sometimes used their White privileges to lionize Black artists in the most elite social circles. They would feature Black writing in leading national magazines, invite Blacks to participate in lecture series at Ivy League institutions, and publish Black manuscripts through the most notable publishing houses.

Karla Holloway described this type of WASP and Jewish philanthropy as New York's own form of the "peculiar institution." Holloway contends that the criteria for defining Black art, literature, and music as "truly Black" were determined by the economic imbalance between the wealthy White patrons and the poverty of the struggling Black artists. Thus, Black culture was commercialized and perverted. David L. Lewis, who described and analyzed the Negrotarians in significant detail in *When Harlem Was in Vogue,* said that the premise for the uplift mentality among Whites was a combination of "inherited abolitionism, Christian charity and guilt, social manipulation, political eccentricity and a certain amount of persiflage."[3] Jeanne Noble's comment on this "peculiar institution" within the Harlem Renaissance is that even though Black writers were inspired by the Black experience, they were almost completely dependent on Whites for public exposure and financial help, a dependency that sucked the vitality and creativity from Black artists. Whites either co-opted Black writers' ideas and style in an attempt to transfuse new and vigorous creativity into their own culture, or when awareness struck that what Black writers were communicating was not all fun and games they repressed the literary movement.[4] Harold Cruse suggests that the Black intellectual "must deal intimately with the white power structure and America's cultural institutions while dealing as a spokesperson for the inner realities of the black world at one and the same time."[5]

Hurston had to deal intimately with the White power structure while dealing with the inner realities of the Black world. She was constantly caught between the rock and the hard place, accepting financial assistance from wherever it was offered so that Black culture would survive. Considering the implications of accepting the financial backing of Negrotarians, Hurston concluded that it was more important to uncover Black folk culture in all its rare beauty than to reject the financial support. Hurston understood the rich resources in the Black cultural heritage for her ongoing process of determining who she was and who she would become.

Gender discrimination as a complex social force had a profound negative impact in Zora Neale Hurston's career as well. Black men, such as Alain Locke, the leader and chief interpreter of the cultural revitalization in Harlem during the 1920s, believed that by virtue of their gender they were in charge of the infrastructures in the Black community. As the prime movers of the Harlem Renaissance, Claude McKay, Countee Cullen, Langston Hughes, Arna Bontemps, and W. E. B. Du Bois used their privileged positions and monopoly of power to identify, nurture, and promote the artists who best represented their interests. As "godfathers" of the Black Art Movement, these men used their eminence to give a rubber stamp to some and to filter out other young artists. As males, subtly socialized to perpetuate superiority over females, most of these men were unaware of the pervasive ideologies they harbored that subordinated, distorted, and devalued Black women. Zora Neale Hurston, both in the life she lived and in the writings she produced, challenged the assumptions of men. Hurston tapped her inner strength and pushed against the structural limits that did not adhere to her own standards of self-fulfillment. Hurston's modus operandi of unctuousness was a genuine threat to her male colleagues.

Hurston was twice stigmatized — once for race and once for gender. Yet Hurston refused to fit into a male mold. She would not succumb to the subtle, debilitating pressures to conform to the norms and values of the Black male literary tradition. While some of Hurston's contemporaries were busily proving that well-bred, intelligent Blacks could mimic the attitudes, behavior, and standards dictated by well-bred, intelligent Whites, Hurston invested her energies into entertaining Whites, and all who would listen, with vivid, metaphorical stories of the Black oral tradition. While Hurston's colleagues focused on White antagonism as the cause for the poverty of the masses who supposedly languished in despair, anger, and defeatism, Hurston was trekking through the South collecting the Black classics in music, art, dance, and literature with hopes of eventually correcting dominant misconceptions about the quality of life in the Black context.

The moral wisdom that Hurston received from her all-Black southern context encouraged her to "jump at de sun," not to bend to the demanding will of her critics, most of whom were members of a self-selected male sanctioning body. Thus, Hurston's behavior was seen as an "unnatural" anomaly. The more successful she became as a writer, researcher, and critic, the more her motives were subjected to misinterpretation.

The men in the literary guild had difficulty accepting the seriousness Hurston brought to her work. She made it clear to everyone that her writings were an integral part of her life. She was unwilling to be defined by others or limited in exchange for male endorsement and support. Hurston fought hard. She faced rigorous demands and obstacles. Her professional aspirations posed such a threat that in her obituary she was attacked by a male writer for "shuttling between the sexes, the professions and the races as if she were a man and a woman, scientist and, creative writer, white and colored."[6] Hurston's "unctuousness" trespassed on something that her critics felt was exclusively theirs. The Black male literary guild picked apart Hurston's person and viciously satirized her work.[7] Hurston, the most prolific Black woman writer in the United States between 1920 and 1950, was "lauded by the white world, but suspiciously regarded and often lampooned by the black."[8]

When Zora Hurston wrapped her hair in beautiful cloth turbans, her critics charged that she was trying to pass for an African queen.[9] when she dared divorce, not one, but two husbands, with rumor alluding to the possibility of a third marriage, her critics portrayed her as indecent.[10] However, Hurston refused to take a defensive posture about acting in ways that were not acceptable for women until decades later.[11]

In 1938, while working with the Florida Federal Writers Project, Hurston was described as "flighty" because she loved to show off, refused to cooperate with her co-workers, and hated to stay inside at her desk. Carl Van Vechten, a White critic and one of her closest friends, assessed Hurston not as "flighty" but as a woman with a "magnetic" personality:

> What it comes down to is the fact that Zora was put together entirely different from the rest of mankind. Her reactions were always original because they were always her own. When she breezed into a room (she never merely entered), tossed a huge straw hat (as big as a cart wheel) on the floor and yelled "I am the queen of the 'niggerati,'" you knew you were in the presence of an individual of the greatest magnitude.[12]

One of the most damning and damaging charges against Hurston focused upon her fight against integration. When most Black leaders were organizing around integration as a goal, Zora Hurston was a lonely frontrunner who saw the implementation of integration as an affront and threat to the Black community. Hurston believed that the integration of schools was needed only if "some residual, some inherent and unchangeable quality in white schools were impossible to duplicate anywhere else."

> The Supreme Court would have pleased [her] more if they had concerned themselves about enforcing the compulsory education provisions for Negroes in the South as is done for white children.[13]

Hurston, busy affirming Black values and Black life, saw no benefit in forsaking the Black reality under the pretense of being bleached into acceptance in a so-called superior White world. Hurston wrote in that same article:

> The whole matter revolves around the self-respect of my people. How much satisfaction can I get from a court order for somebody to associate with me who does not wish me near them....It is a contradiction in terms to scream race pride and equality while at the same time spurning Negro teachers and self-associations.

Hurston personally believed in the principle of an integrated society, but she did not support the invidious comparisons that implied that Black people were divergent deviants from the "norm."[14] She did not believe that Black people were a negligible factor in the thought of the world. Instead, her life was committed to redressing ignorance about Black culture. Her work was an affirmation of the Black race as one of the great human races, inferior to none in its accomplishments and in its ability.

Hurston's social relationships put her in close contact with her male colleagues. Her apartment was always open, with a communal pot on the stove. Zora entertained entire parties with stories, group singing, and stand-up comedy routines mimicking snobbish Park Avenue Whites who she called "Astorperious." Discovering that there was to be no support when these peers put their critic hats on to review her work, Hurston refused to behave in ways that conformed to the status quo.

Hurston's emphasis on "the Negro farthest down" brought criticism from many quarters. Richard Wright condemned Hurston for being unconcerned with racism, class struggle, and the revolutionary tradition of Black people. Roy Wilkins, after reading Hurston's article on Jim Crow, went so far as to say:

> Now is no time for tongue-wagging by Negroes for the sake of publicity. The race is fighting a battle that may determine its status for fifty years. Those who are not for us, are against us.[15]

Lester B. Granger of the *California Eagle* responded to some of Hurston's articles in this manner:

Miss Hurston has written seldom in recent years and so far as her public is concerned, when she has come out with a production it has been readily evident that she "shoulda stayed in bed."[16]

In 1932, Wallace Thurman wrote an elaborate satire on himself and his colleagues of the Harlem Renaissance entitled *Infants of the Spring.* Unfortunately his "bas-relief" caricature of Zora Hurston as Sweetie May Carr, "a short story writer, more noted for her ribald wit and effervescence than any actual literary work," has haunted the authentic Hurston up to the present time.[17] As recently as 1971, Black men like Darwin Turner still depicted Zora Neale Hurston as

superficial and shallow in her artistic and social judgements.... Always, she remained a wandering minstrel. It was eccentric but perhaps appropriate for her to return to Florida to take a job as a cook and maid for a white family and to die in poverty. She had not ended her days as she once had hoped — a farmer among growing things she loved. Instead she had returned to the level of life which she proposed for her people.[18]

While the *Saturday Review* was praising Hurston's autobiography as a significant contribution to the field of race relations, Arna Bontemps denounced her life story:

Miss Hurston deals very simply with the more serious aspects of Negro life in America — she ignores them. She has done well by herself in the kind of world she has found.[19]

Harold Preece, writing for *Crisis,* dismissed Hurston's autobiography as no more than

the tragedy of a gifted, sensitive mind, eaten up by an egocentrism fed on the patronizing admiration of the dominant white world.[20]

Hurston's scientific study of folklore in novelistic form, *Mules and Men,* was of such quality that it resulted in invitations for her to become a member of three prestigious organizations: the American Folklore Society, the American Ethnological Society, and the American Anthropological Society. By direct contrast, Sterling Brown's review of this work found the characters "naive, quaint, complacent and bad enough to kill each other in looks, but meek otherwise, and socially unconscious."[21]

Some critics lauded Hurston's third novel: "If Hurston had written nothing else she would deserve recognition for *Moses, Man of the Mountain,*" but Alain Locke called it "a caricature instead of portraiture."[22] Ralph Ellison claimed that "for Negro fiction, it did nothing."[23]

Robert Bone, a White critic of Black literature, heralded Hurston's *Their Eyes Were Watching God* as a "classic of Black literature, one of the finest novels of the period,"[24] while Richard Wright reviewed this work and found it to be a "shallow romance, lacking in protest value."[25]

Poor reviews also shut down in fast order the song-dance revues *Fast and Furious, Jungle Scandals,* and *Spunk,* which Hurston had arranged from her exclusive collection of folklore material. Hall Johnson, of *Run Little Chillun* fame, summed up the popular sentiments toward Hurston's colorful revues among the Renaissance artists:

> The world was not ready for Negro music unless it was highly arranged. The barbaric melodies and harmonies were simply not fit for musical ears.[26]

George Antheil, a U.S. composer known internationally for his ultra-modern music, attended one of the revues Hurston had arranged, *The Great Day,* when it was performed at the New School for Social Research in 1932. Antheil insisted that the quality of Hurston's revue was so superb that she would be the most plagiarized Black person in the world for at least a decade.

> This sort of thievery in unavoidable. Unpleasant, of course, but at the bottom a tribute to one's originality.[27]

In 1948, Zora Neale Hurston was falsely charged with sexually molesting a ten-year-old-boy. Hurston was able to prove that she was not in the country when the alleged crimes were supposed to have happened. The charges were dropped but not before the Black press in Baltimore, Chicago, and New York had exploited the scandal to the hilt. This was the straw that broke Hurston's back. In a letter to Carl Van Vechten dated October 30, 1948, Hurston described the devastating catastrophe in this manner:

> The thing is too fantastic, too evil, too far from reality for me to conceive it.... One inconceivable horror after another swept over me. I went out of myself, I am sure, though no one seemed to notice. It seemed that every hour some other terror assailed me, the last thing being the Afro-American filth. I care nothing for anything anymore. My country has failed me utterly. My race has seen fit to destroy me without reason, and with the vilest tools conceived of by men so far. A society, eminently Christian, and supposedly devoted to super-democracy has gone so far from its announced purpose, not to protect children, but to exploit the gruesome fancies of a pathological case and do this thing to human decency. Please do not forget that this thing was not done in the South, but in the so-called liberal North. Where shall I look in the country for justice?
>
> All that I have ever tried to do has proved useless. All that I have

believed in has failed me. I have resolved to die. It will take a few days for me to set my affairs in order, and then I will go.... No acquittal will persuade some people that I am innocent.

I feel hurled down a filthy privy hole.[28]

As we have seen, Zora Neale Hurston captured the integrity of Black people who buttressed themselves with the community's moral wisdom in her effort to hold on to the essence of her humanity. Hurston lived out of a Black consciousness and political/social awareness that provided realistic assessment of the nature of virtuous living in situations of oppression.

So the question now before us is, What caused this creative, vibrant, and astute Black woman to acquiesce into neurotic passivity after the false sodomy charges of 1948? Why did she let go of everything she previously valued? What was missing in the Black woman's wisdom tradition that caused Zora Hurston to sink into unreboundable brokenness when the sex slander was circulated by, to, and through the Black community?

Hurston's entire life had been grounded in an uncompromising struggle to fulfill her human capacity against incredible odds. In all of her work she adamantly opposed a defensive, reactionary posture for Black people. Yet Hurston assumed such a stance as her only recourse in her fight to reclaim her dignity and self-worth. Since the politics of justice was not on the horizon for her and the experience of community was denied to her, were there any resources that would have helped Hurston recover from this traumatic attack against her personhood?

There are two main criticisms lodged against Zora Neale Hurston: political conservatism and obsessive individualism. I believe that both of these criticisms are valid and highly accurate when they are evaluated within the context of Hurston's own time. In the throes of betrayal, Hurston responded in opposite ways from her previous approach of unctuousness.

However, much of the critical commentary tends to minimize the devastating impact of the false charge that she had committed an immoral act with a ten-year-old-boy. Hurston was an intensely proud woman. Her whole life was committed to a defiant affirmation of the cultural practices manifested in the Black community. Hemenway's biography documents how Hurston's professional career was spent "trying to show that normality is a function of culture, that an Afro-American culture exists, and that its creators lead lives rich with ideological and esthetic significance."[29] And yet it was a Black court employee who peddled the inaccurate and sensationalized story to the Black press, which, in turn, circulated lurid coverage to the Black community. Hurston referred to this betrayal of her as "the Afro-American sluice of filth." In the prime of her career, she felt that her world had collapsed, unfairly, unreasonably, in the ugliest possible way.

After the case was dropped and the indictment dismissed, Hurston commented that she didn't think that she could even endure the sight of a Black person. Dispirited and broken, Hurston was occasionally suspicious and paranoid. Questioning the motives behind her moral and intellectual lynching, Hurston even wondered if the charges against her in 1948 were part of some kind of Communist frame-up. Always struggling to remain solvent, Hurston sold articles and essays to White magazines, knowing that they would be heavily edited. She also campaigned for conservative Republicans such as Taft.

Barbara Christian provides a critical analysis of Hurston's situation:

> One cannot help but note the similarities between Larsen [Nella] and Hurston's disappearances from the world. Although very different writers, they were both assaulted by the prejudices of the other society. Larsen's writing ability was challenged and Hurston's sex life was used, consciously or unconsciously, as a means of diminishing her effectiveness as a writer and as an anthropologist. Both charges are indicative of the vulnerable position of black women writers. Their sexual morality and intellectual capacity are seen as tentative, not only by their fellow countrymen but by members of their own race as well. Both writers fell prey to the racial and sexual stereotypes inflicted upon the black woman.[30]

I maintain that this virtue of unctuousness was directly responsible for Zora Neale Hurston's brief periods of professional notoriety and also for her professional demise. Living under a system of triple oppression, Hurston's unprecedented strength to endure could not ward off the precedented assaults on her as a Black woman. The defeat of Hurston's "unctuousness" was not due to its importance as a virtue in Black women's lives, but to the viciousness of the assault on her. Without communal recognition that *unctuousness is a virtue,* even it is not enough to sustain Black women. In other words, if the Black community cannot recognize and celebrate its Zora Hurstons more in their ongoing struggle against race, sex, and class oppression and if Black women are forced to embrace the conventional morality of middle-class American ideals, which twists their virtue into a vice, then Black women face the gravest danger yet.

Chapter 8

"The Wounds of Jesus"

Justification of Goodness in the Face of Manifold Evil

Twenty years ago, a minister friend of mine, Dr. G. Murray Branch, posed the question that captures the essence of the problem of evil as it has resounded down through the ages from the African American pulpit: "Can God create a rock that God can't pick up?" Without doubt the African American sermon is the earliest form of spoken religious art wherein the Black church community wrestles with how evil can occur in a world created by a benevolent God.[1]

Put another way, this inquiry — "Can God create a rock that God can't pick up?" — is the fundamental query that deals with the traditional theological problem concerning transgressions that proceed directly from human sin — structures of domination, subordination and constraints that reinforce and reproduce hierarchies based on race, sex, class, and sexual orientation. These sermons sometimes address those ills suffered because of physical and natural calamities and the immense human suffering that follows in their wake — disease, tempest, fire, famine, flood, tidal wave, earthquake, drought; but African American preachers in my church community have been particularly interested in framing and arguing the question of moral evil, seen in the fact that two-thirds of the human family are hungry, have no homes, have no schools or medicine for their children, no pure water to drink, and no work.

African American sermonic texts have been the most vital factors in explaining moral evils such as chattel slavery, economic impoverishment, wars, and the atrocities they involve.[2] The sacred rhetoric produced by African American preachers validates and makes coherent the yearnings of Black Christians to explain moral evil inflicted by human agency.[3] Yet many of these texts have been passed over, basically unnoticed. The

This chapter was first published in Emilie M. Townes, ed., *A Troubling in My Soul: Womanist Perspectives on Evil and Suffering* (Orbis Books, 1993), 219–31.

substantial omission of African American sacred rhetoric from theological discourse on the nature, explanation, and remedy of evil flows quite naturally from scholars using analytical frameworks that take the Euro-American religious experience as the norm.

In broad outline the dominant tradition poses the problem of evil like this: If God is omnipotent, omniscient, and omnipresent, then God would prevent evil if God wanted to. And if God is a perfectly good God, then of course God would want to prevent evil if God could. Thus, if God is all-powerful, all-knowing, and ever-present and is also perfectly good, then God *could* prevent evil if God *wanted to,* and God would *want to* prevent evil if God *could.*

My primary goal in this essay is threefold: (1) to examine theodicy as it is presented in the ecclesiastical texts embedded as distinctive rhetorical units in Zora Neale Hurston's canon; (2) to critique Hurston's sermon "The Wounds of Jesus,"[4] as a sketch of the problem of evil in Afro-Christian sacred rhetoric; (3) to construct, even in the barest outline, my own composite womanist matrix for the corpus of sermons in the African American women's literary tradition.

Numerous African American novelists have included sermons in their work.[5] I do not want to suggest that the Afro-Christian teachings espoused in this text constitute the whole of the preaching tradition in African American literature. "The Wounds of Jesus" in *Jonah's Gourd Vine* by Hurston deserves special attention, however, because it reproduces certain Afro-Christian ethical conventions and cultural patterns concerning theodicy. By placing this sermon in a context where its worth and value can be reassessed and redefined, I am naming some of the preferred meanings, values, and interpretations of evil — those favored and transmitted through Afro-Christian religious rhetoric. Thus, this essay addresses the many issues connected with a womanist interpretation of the African American church community's justification of divine goodness in the face of manifold human experience of evil.

Hurston's Ecclesiastical Texts

I first became interested in examining the problem of evil as it is embedded in the ecclesiastical rhetoric of African American women's novels while completing research for my dissertation, "Resources for a Constructive Ethic for Black Women with Special Attention to the Life and Work of Zora Neale Hurston."[6] The personal joy of studying Hurston's canon comes from the sheer fact of being able to read about the familiar world of the African American church community that I know most intimately. Hurston included explicit theological materials in her work, ranging from full-length sermons, prayers, and proverbs to the passing acknowledgment of religious persons, places, and things. In her work my Afro-Christian culture is mirrored and writ large.

Even though Hurston was not, at least in the traditional sense, a religious novelist, contestable ethical issues and religious imagery pervade her work. Hurston's writing preserves, like forms embedded in prehistoric ore, traces of her Baptist upbringing. Her characterization of Rev. John Buddy Pearson and his sermon "The Wounds of Jesus" in *Jonah's Gourd Vine* draw heavily upon her own experiences. As the daughter of a southern Black Baptist preacher and, therefore, a direct heir to the worshiping Christian community, Hurston expressed the creative spiritual force around which the Black church is organized and from which the Black community draws its prophetic nourishment. For Hurston, preaching in the Black idiom is an essential creative aspect of African American culture. Black preaching is not theoretical, factual reporting of Afro-Christian theological doctrines and dogmas that vindicate God in the face of evil.[7] Instead, these sermonic texts are pastorally engaged writings that reflect the teachings of the Black church community concerning God's redeeming love.

An outstanding novelist, cultural anthropologist, folklorist, and critic, Hurston was extremely close to the sensibilities of her unlettered characters. Along with her meticulous collection of folklore, legends, superstitions, music and dance of the common people, this identification with her people enables her work to serve as a rich repository of resources helpful in delineating the moral counsel cultivated by African Americans. Working both as a collector and a systematizer, Hurston collated and classified various Afro-Christian expressions and theological themes that help us understand the religious vernacular that dominated African American Christian culture during the first half of the twentieth century.[8]

For instance, all four of Hurston's novels are packed full of exemplifications of independent actions of the Black community expressing our loves and frustrations in the context of our faith or lack thereof. *Jonah's Gourd Vine* (1934) is a literary allusion (Jonah 4:6–10) to various ways that the protagonist has great and sudden growth and, after an act of malice, withers and experiences a tragic end.[9] *Their Eyes Were Watching God* (1937), her second novel, is a drama based on the values of the community and the tension that arises when there is a conflict between what the community advises Black women to do and what, in fact, is done, especially when the mirror in the Black woman's soul (her eyes) is focused on God. According to Hurston's biographer Robert Hemenway, the novel *Moses, Man of the Mountain* (1939) is nothing less than Hurston's attempt to kidnap Moses from the Jewish-Christian tradition, claiming that Moses' true birthright is African and that his true constituency is African American. *Seraph on the Suwanee* (1948), Hurston's

last novel, has a title that suggests winged celestial beings, possibly an-
gels or flying serpents of uncertain identity. The plot is filled with ironies
and ambiguities regarding self-improvement and self-extension, not with
a world of earthly victims whose survival and transformation depend
upon a change of heart of their antagonists.

Three of Hurston's short stories, "The Fire and Cloud," "The Sev-
enth Veil," and "The Woman in Gaul," include biblical imagery that
allows Hurston's stories to produce a particular representation of Afro-
Christian theological understanding of God's gift of freedom to act
rightly or wrongly. These fictional narratives do not obscure or deny
the existence of the ugly dimensions of human nature, circumstances,
and conduct, but rather through the full, sharp, and inescapable awareness of them they show the meaningfulness of Black existence. By
confronting and contending with the internal absurdities and ever-
impending frustrations in the reality of African Americans, Hurston sets
before us the problem of evil and the possibilities of endurance.

Between 1926 and 1944 Hurston wrote, alone or in collaboration,
eight plays.[10] "The First One" (1927), which is a one-act mythic drama
of the legend of Ham, won the 1927 *Opportunity* magazine award. In
"Mule Bone" (1930), a folk comedy in three acts,[11] Hurston dramatized
the religiosity that exists outside the traditional ecclesial boundaries of
mainline Protestantism, disclosing the factions in a town divided between Black Baptists and Black Methodists. "The Fiery Chariot," a
one-act comedy, focuses on a slave's nightly prayer for deliverance from
bondage; the God of Western Christianity is indicted as an ineffective
liberator. The characters in these plays draw on the wisdom of their
personal strengths and determination to protect themselves from the
brutality of dehumanizing situations. These texts function as indices
and theoethical messages for African Americans; they use the symbols
of the curse of Ham's son, Canaan, a mule bone, a fiery chariot, and
the conflicts between light-skinned and dark-skinned people to provide
some means of balance, an equilibrium that makes suffering bearable.
By ironic juxtaposition and emblematic situations, Hurston counters existing myths to present African Americans as complex human beings
who have survived and prevailed in racist/sexist/capitalist constellations.

In all of these writings, Hurston presented sacred rhetoric that rep-
resents the diverse ways that African American people of the working
poor social strata bring our folkways to the experience of the Christian gospel. Hurston described the various ways that Black Christians,
particularly of my social location, use biblical symbols and images to
neutralize the brutality of oppressive and exploitative systems, in our
struggle to maintain our humanity, our integrity, and our sanity. Hurston portrayed Black protagonists lifting up aspects of the biblical legend
in order to validate the deep religious bent manifested as a major sus-

taining power in the church community. Such Afro-Christian religious symbolism is integral to the unique character of Hurston's texts.

In essence, Hurston portrays the Black preacher as one of the most colorful and dynamic figures in American literature. She recognized, with W. E. B. Du Bois, the eminent sociologist who wrote about the survival of Black religious culture at the turn of this century, that the Black preacher was "the most unique personality developed on American soil."[12]

"The Wounds of Jesus"

Hurston's most famous religious narrative is the sermon I singled out earlier, "The Wounds of Jesus," wherein Hurston recognized the sermon as a critical cultural phenomenon of African American culture. Hurston's sermon on the crucifixion of Jesus is a pivotal text in Afro-American letters. With notable skills and sensibilities she captures in writing the distinctive style of Black oratory and gives evidence of a previously spoken-only understanding of certain religious truths. Hurston's sermonic eloquence can be judged as equal, if not superior to, the very best masters of the oratory art in any age. Hurston's sermon was disclaimed by the *New York Times* as "too good, too brilliantly splashed with poetic imagery to be the product of any Negro preacher." On May 8, 1934, Zora Hurston wrote to James Weldon Johnson expressing her disappointment with the White critic's ignorance of the place and power of the sermon in Afro-Christian culture:

> He means well, I guess, but I never saw such a lack of information about us. It just seems that he is unwilling to believe that a Negro preacher could have so much poetry in him. When you and I (who seem to be the only ones even among Negroes who recognize the barbaric poetry in their sermons) know that there are hundreds of preachers who are equalling that sermon weekly. He does not know that merely being a good man is not enough to hold a Negro preacher in an important charge. He must also be an artist. He must be both a poet and an actor of a very high order, and then he must have the voice and figure. He does not realize or is unwilling to admit that the light that shone from *God's Trombone* [sic] was handed to you, as was the sermon to me in *Jonah's Gourd Vine*.[13]

Hurston was very upset with the review from the *New York Times* because she knew that "The Wounds of Jesus" was an exemplary text.

Like the genre of Black preaching it reflects, "The Wounds of Jesus" must be understood within a particular Afro-Christian cultural context at a particular time. As a sermon set in the first quarter of this century, it is wedded to the prophetic traditions of Amos, Hosea, Isaiah, and Micah and is divorced from the brand of Euro-American homiletics that shaped preaching as linear, bland, and formally speculative.[14] "The Wounds of Jesus" is a recital of God's dealings with people in times past, as well as a proclamation of the relevance of God's message in relation to the particular pain and anguish of contemporary church folks. The sermon is saturated with Bible verses. Thus, a knowledge of Scripture comprises the foremost requisite for the Black preacher's proposition that God could create a universe containing evil.

In other words, this sacred rhetoric, originating in Zechariah 13:6 and Isaiah 53:5, serves both as a reflection of the liberative reality about which Afro-Christians speak and as a clue and allusion to the oppressive reality under which we live. The problems and issues explored in this sermon show us how African American people understood every believer in Christ as a friend of Jesus and how every sin committed in the house of friends is a wound to Christ. What is indisputable in this sermonic text is the existence of a strong religious imagination that formed and substantiated belief in the goodness of God, who vouchsafes a liberating redeemer whose potency eases the burden of Black people's afflictions.

The preacher of Hurston's sermon, the Reverend John Buddy Pearson, is well acquainted with biblical texts that explain why a perfectly good God permits human sin to occur. He says that when God said, "Let us make human beings in our image, after our likeness," the elders who were members of the heavenly court adamantly cried out, "No, No, No," arguing that if God decides to make human beings, humans will sin. Rev. Pearson then asserts that it was at this point in the creation of the world that God promised to send a redeemer. For him, the incarnation of Jesus Christ was God's forethought, God's remedy for human sinfulness, a part of the God's original intention. To make this theological point another way is to say that evil is not sidestepped or explained away as the absence of good but instead it is exposed as an essential element in the completion of human history, a presupposition for the fulfillment of the divine purpose in creation.

Rev. Pearson is not bothered by the chronological distance between the biblical era and the present. Operating with a sense of sacred time, he extends time backward so that the congregation can experience an immediate intimacy with biblical characters as faith relatives. The trials and triumphs of Zechariah wounded in the house of his friends, Isaiah's measure of the sea in the hollow of his hand, Mark's worms that never die, Ezekiel's fire that is never quenched, Matthew's secrets kept from the foundation of the world, John's bread of life, and the Psalmist's mountains that skip like lambs are all interwoven throughout this sermon as the preacher interprets the crucifixion of Jesus against a wider narrative of atonement and redemption. In other words, Hurston aligns Rev. Pearson with earlier Black preachers whose sermons rehearse the biblical stories in the language and culture of the people. Pearson's sermon is full of analogies and parables that compare and juxtapose contemporary problems of evil with ancient dilemmas in the biblical text.

Second, this sermon utilizes the medium of metaphorical adornment in order to make the sacred discursive narrative visible to the listeners. As a storyteller and a mythmaker, the Black preacher combines a disciplined imagination with realistic reflection, converting the sermon into a genuine art form. This sermon reiterates the macrosigns of suffering and evil in a White supremacist, patriarchal society by signifying African American Christians' understanding of how God is greater than all instances of evil. This ethical value operates in the church community and promotes a life-sustaining faith praxis. Such rhetoric functions to restore self-confidence, giving Black believers back our nerve, especially when we are confronted by the morally repugnant White supremacy.

Articulating in rhythmic fashion, the Black preacher presents a word picture of problems created by morally offensive actions that humans perform. Images are not merely hinted at in Black preaching; symbols and metaphors become alive to the listener, taking on fixed character in the tradition of their origin and past adventures.

Again, using "The Wounds of Jesus" and Hurston's character, Rev. Pearson, we are presented with a concretized dramatization of how Jesus loved us before the creation of the world. Dispersed throughout the sermonic text is Jesus' declaration that if and when we do evil that he will go our bond before God's mighty throne. Rev. Pearson says that Jesus left heaven with all of its grandeur, disrobing himself of his matchless honor, yielding up the scepter of revolving worlds, clothing himself in the garment of humanity in order to rescue his friends from the clutches of evil and damnation. Thus, like his preaching forebears, Rev. Pearson's sermonic text moves from an ardent apprehension of a theological image, figuratively expressed, to more and more precise comprehension, until the hearers are able to make the connections between the metaphorical statements and their real-lived situations.

The third and final theme at the core of this text is a dominant Christocentrism. Black preaching is concerned with the revelation of God in Jesus Christ. This sermon exposes the dialectical tension of those who have suffered not only the pain of evil perpetrated by so-called Christian friends but also alludes to the structural differences that exist in political rights and economic realities for African American people. The "Wounds of Jesus" text provides a framework that gives substance and reality to Afro-Christianity's ethical understanding of reconciling evil to the active morality of Christians. This sermon brings together theological assent wherein the existence of Jesus as Redeemer is embraced prior to any rational consideration of the status of evil in the world. Rev. Pearson preaches that the damnation train pulled out from the Garden of Eden loaded with cargo going to hell, running at breakneck speed all the way through the law, the prophetic age, the reigns of kings and judges, plowing through the Jordan on her way to Calvary. Jesus stood out on the train track like a rough-backed mountain and shed his blood in order to ditch the train of damnation. "He died for our sins, wounded in the house of His friends." This fundamental religious lore embodying African American people's understanding of evil and suffering implies that human sins committed against humanity are in flagrant opposition to Divine Goodness. The evil that we do to each other not only inflicts wounds on Jesus but causes suffering to all of creation. The mountains fall to their rocky knees and tremble like a beast. The veins of the earth bleed. The geological strata fall lose and the chamber of hell explodes. In "The Wounds of Jesus" the redemption story begins with creation and ends with consummation at Calvary.

Womanist Queries for the Black Preaching Tradition

Since completing my dissertation on Hurston, I have continued to research sacred rhetoric in African American women's writings. I have found that sermons, prayers, and proverbs as religious events continue to make their way from the substratum of church life and religious activities into literary form in the work of Black novelists such as Nella Larsen, Jessie Fauset, Margaret Walker, Alice Childress, Sarah Wright, Toni Morrison, Alice Walker, Paule Marshall, and Gloria Naylor. These women do not write as exponents of the African American religious tradition, but they convey religious sensibility central to the Black community throughout their work. As creators of literature these women are not formally historians, sociologists, or theologians, yet the patterns and themes of their writings are reflective of historical reality. They are sociologically accurate and describe the religious convictions that undergird the ethical practice of my church community.

In other words, Black women novelists give me a way to look at Afro-Christian thought outside of the institutional and traditionally articulated expressions of faith. As participant-interpreters of the African American experience, Black women novelists coalesce their sociocultural perspectives with their intimate knowledge of Afro-Christians' words and colorful ways of speaking. By presenting widely used cultural forms of sermons, prayers, and proverbs that deal with *what is,* these writers enable me to do ethical analysis concerning *what should be* — beyond the limits of the parochial situation of my denomination as well as propositional identities such as creeds, theologies, and books of order.

For example, Nella Larsen's Reverend Mr. Pleasant Green in *Quicksand* (1928), Margaret Walker's Brother Ezekiel in *Jubilee* (1966), Alice Childress's Reverend Mills in *A Short Walk* (1979), Paule Marshall's Reverend Morrissey in *Praisesong for the Widow* (1983), and Gloria Naylor's the Right Reverend Michael T. Hollis in *Linden Hills* (1985) all use the poetic style and fixed forms of speech that are characteristic of the Black preaching experience. In order to illuminate the charismatic and ecstatic forms of expression as well as the rational medium of Black preaching, these novelists blend the sophistication and savvy of the urban church with the earthiness and mother wit of the rural tradition. Their sermons are consistent with the framework, structure, and organizing principles that have emerged from within the Black church and conform to the general rules of preaching in the Black idiom. The sermons in these novels are not just fictional tools but cultural truths, which in turn allow me to investigate whether or not these texts are normatively appropriate to mobilize a non-patriarchal Black Theology for today.

Thus I contend that Black women writers add an important voice to the discussion of the sermon as genre and preaching as process. For more than two and a half centuries Black religious thought has been expressed in a variety of forms, mainly nonliterary. However, the sermons of the preliterary oral tradition are explicit in these novels. The Black women's literary tradition allows me to get behind the verbal compositions of the Afro-Christian experience to decode, question, and challenge the givens of patriarchal consensus contained therein. I maintain that if one wants to turn to a body of writings that incorporate the seminal experiences of evil, suffering, and God's goodness in Black lives, it is to African American women's novels that one turns.

It is not possible to discuss and analyze the texts of male ministers without recognizing the gender dimension, that the majority of the faithful who heard and who continue to hear these sermons are women. Since women outnumber men in church congregations, we need to address, on the basis of our experiences, how the sacred rhetoric reflects and mirrors the social, cultural, and religious realities of the Black church patriarchy. We need to evaluate these sermons historically in their own time and assess them ethically in terms of a womanist scale of value.

For instance, when we turn to the experience of Black churchwomen to establish criteria for interpreting and determining the worth of sermonic texts, we need to ask what difference it makes that African American women hear sermons, like the ones embedded in this literary tradition, in which the feminine pronoun is used to refer to the sun, the moon, lightning, and long-legged faith, who has no eyes. The linguistic sexism of Rev. Pearson results in nouns with feminine pronouns all having form without substance. Using gratuitous expressions, the preacher paints a picture of creation with the sun gathering up her fiery garments and wheeling around the throne of heaven while the moon grabbed up the tides of the ocean, dragging a thousand seas, as the lightning zig-zagged across the sky licking out her fiery tongue. At the most crucial moment in history, when Jesus is crucified, an angel who stands at the gate with a flaming sword pierces the moon and she runs down in blood while the sun bats her fiery eyes, puts on her judgment robe, lays down in the cradle of eternity, and rocks herself into sleep and slumber.

What do we do with sexist paradigms and negative female imagery included and promoted in such sermons as "The Wounds of Jesus" — in which the female damnation train that is carrying people to hell at breakneck speed throws her cow-catcher and murders Jesus? As womanist theologians, what are we doing to counter negative real-world consequences of sexist wording that reinforces sexist cultural realities? How disruptive are such gendered-biased language and androcentric sermons for social relations within the African American family?

This theoretical frame of questions is at once a comparative and an ideal construct. It employs a critical and interpretative apparatus of selection and evaluation to gain knowledge about the judgment and criticism of women in relation to systemic evil and inevitable suffering. A womanist ethical critique helps us delegitimize the patriarchal teachings of the Black church. By disentangling the textual marginalization of women, we can find clues to Black churchwomen's moral agency and restore, as much as possible, the rich traditions of women's contributions to African American theological thought. This matrix serves as a model for understanding the silences, limitations, and possibilities of cultural patterns and forms that are unique and peculiar to the Black church community. It also enables women to see the constraints and limitations of male-defined and male-dominated religious ideas that have been fed to Afro-Christian women for hundreds of years in the name of naturalness. By using womanist ethical questions to measure the worth of sermonic texts, we become aware of the ways in which widely accepted patriarchal beliefs and cultural practices dictate Black theology.

My womanist queries for the Black preaching tradition ask new questions of these ecclesiastical texts in order to unmask both linguistic and material reality. By combing Black sermons for womanist meaning, I want to show how this genre functions as an essential Afro-Christian theological resource with ethical impact that can be calculated politically. Sermons are conduits for many of the theological and intellectual preferences within Afro-Christianity because they keep certain theological ideas and social habits alive in the Black community's mind.

I contend that a womanist liberation matrix can break the silence of Black sermons because it places African American women's history and pastoral praxis in dialogue with the androcentric interests and perspectives that function as inclusive concepts in Afro-Christian patriarchal culture. By looking at when and how the feminine is mentioned in these texts, I am analyzing the Afro-Christian sacred canon for the ethical "stuff" that can give contemporary Black churchwomen a greater sense of being, that can validate, make coherent, and give meaning to the dailiness of life as it relates to risk-and-security, weakness-and-strength, death-and-life. Furthermore, a womanist methodology critically analyzes social-cultural conditions and contexts in order to burst asunder the dominant understandings of theodicy and produce new archetypes that release the Afro-Christian mind and spirit from the manacles of patriarchy so that Black women might emerge and discern just what kind of moral agents we really want to be.

Conclusion

Womanist liberation ethics and the Black women's literary tradition have much to contribute to one another. The fruitful interaction between these two fields of inquiry enables me as an ethicist to examine the patriarchal apparatus of African American Christian sacred rhetoric to assess whether these cultural treasures reinforce dehumanizing images or produce liberating paradigms for churchwomen. By critiquing the modes of religious expression and theoethical systems of representation that emerge, my intent is to unmask the Black church community's uncritical connections to the dominant traditional theological "worries." The point of much African American women's spirituality as expressed in the literature is that it does not begin with questions about the omnipotence, omniscience, and omnipresence of God and then move to justify God's goodness in the face of evil. Rather womanist protagonists contend that God's sustaining presence is known in the resistance to evil.

My hope is that this essay serves as one of the vehicles for weaving and shaping the liberating sacred rhetoric of the Black church community. In order to assess the ongoing value of Afro-Christian sermons, Black liberation ethicists must continue creating modes of critical inquiry that allow African American women, and others who cast their lot with us, to evaluate sermonic texts from a womanist perspective. When we exegete the established canon of intellectual Afro-Christianity,[15] we break with specifiable social, structural, and cultural constructs that mock, demean, and exclude Black women. Those who form and maintain the patriarchal apparatus of Afro-Christianity must realize that the Black church is in crisis and that the African American church community has to respond to womanist theological interests and concerns if it wants to survive. Thus, our task as liberationists is to continue debunking, unmasking, and disentangling the messages in African American sacred rhetoric, so that together we can expose the various ways that their representations affect the well-being of us all.

Chapter 9

Womanist Interpretation and Preaching in the Black Church

A new and significant connection is beginning to exist between the new modes of critical inquiry created by African American women in the theological academy[1] and the central role that preaching plays as a cultural phenomenon in the Black church community.[2] It is new because until recently Black preaching has not asked questions about womanist interpretation and womanist theological studies have not included homiletics. It is significant because the majority of the faithful who have heard and continue to hear Black preaching are women.

While the majority of these churchgoers have little trouble testifying that a good sermon is a many-splendored art form, the articulation of an analysis by which we elucidate and delegitimize patriarchal teachings is not as easily arrived at. When sermons are written and presented in the interest of men, the categorical definitions of theoethical concepts lend an evidently weighty authority to androcentric conclusions about male preachers and masculine-centered culture.[3] It is therefore important to analyze sermonic texts in terms of their socioecclesial locations and theological interests, with special attention to their gender dimension. Such methodological analysis of sermonic texts needs to be the task of womanist interpretation.

My own proposal for the form this womanist interpretation should take lies in the convergence of a feminist liberationist theoretical interpretation inspired by Elisabeth Schüssler Fiorenza's groundbreaking scholarship[4] and the seminal work of Isaac R. Clark, Sr., on Black homiletics.[5] These two dynamic areas of interpretative discourse offer a challenging nexus for womanist scholars concerned with radically rethinking and revisioning "how duties and roles are advocated, how

This chapter was first published in Elisabeth Schüssler Fiorenza, *Searching the Scriptures,* vol. 1 (Crossroad Publishing Co., 1993), 326–37.

arguments are constructed and how power is inscribed"[6] in the Black church community.

A womanist critique of homiletics challenges conventional biblical interpretations that characterize African American women as "sin-bringing Eve," "wilderness-whimpering Hagar," "henpecking Jezebel," "whoring Gomer," "prostituting Mary-Magdalene," and "conspiring Sapphira." A womanist hermeneutic identifies the frame of sexist-racist social contradictions housed in sacred rhetoric that gives women a zero-image of ourselves. This analysis deconstructs biblically based sermons that portray female subjects as bleeding, crippled, disempowered, objectified, purified, or mad. It enables us to ask hard questions about the responsibility of Black preachers to satisfy the *whole* congregation's spiritual hunger with their intellectual grasp, mastery of Scripture, social analysis, and constructive homiletical skill. Both areas of research, feminist liberation interpretation and preaching in the Black church, reinforce each other by raising questions, clarifying problems, and amplifying issues that shape our collective consciousness about "the survival and wholeness of an entire people."[7]

Feminist Liberationist Interpretation

Following Schüssler Fiorenza's methodology, I would argue that the essential task of a womanist hermeneutic consists in analyzing Black sermonic texts with regard to how they "participate in creating or sustaining oppressive or liberating theoethical values and sociopolitical practices."[8] Womanist analysis provides an interpretative framework that holds together the spiritual matrix of Black religious culture while exposing the complex, baffling contradictions inherent in androcentric language. I am arguing for a critical evaluation of sermonic texts, including an analysis of when and how women are mentioned and whether these sermons adequately reflect African American reality.[9]

Schüssler Fiorenza's methodology can be likened to detective work, which does not rely solely on historical "facts" nor invent its evidence. Instead, it engages in an imaginative reconstruction that rests upon observation and inference; it employs a critical analysis of whether scriptural texts in sermons mention women only as problems or as exceptions. The task of womanist homiletics is to unearth what Black preachers are saying about women and what we are saying about men.

A critical study of Black sermons shows that African American church traditions and redactional processes follow certain androcentric interests and perspectives that do not reflect the historical contributions of African American women's leadership and participation in the life of the church. By showing the detailed and numerous androcentric injunctions about women's nature, place, and behavior in Black preaching, we are able to identify and critique sermonic texts that express and maintain patriarchal historical conditioning. We are also able to highlight those sermons that reproduce and shape the liberative reality for all members of the worshiping community.

A womanist adaptation of Schüssler Fiorenza's integrative heuristic model seeks to provide a means of ethical assessment that can help the Black church community look at the practices and habits, assumptions and problems, values and hopes embedded in its Christian cultural mind-set. It does so with the hope of renewing and reforming the faith-justice praxis in the Black preaching tradition. It is essential that womanist interpretive practices be employed not only in the critique of androcentric preaching with its references to patriarchal relationships of inequality. We must also use womanist methodology at the constructive stage of sermon preparation and delivery.

Preaching in the Black Church

The history of Black preaching begins with the emergence of the Black church as an invisible institution in the slave community during the seventeenth century.[10] Utilizing West African religious concepts in a new and totally different context and blending them syncretistically with orthodox colonial Christianity, Black women and men developed an extensive religious life of their own.[11] The Black church was the only social institution in which African Americans could exercise leadership and power, and the preacher and preaching were held in the highest esteem in the Black church community. Preaching was one of the principal instruments used by enslaved Black leaders. They preached what they knew about the progression from patriarch to priest to prophet to Jesus to Paul and testified to what they had seen, exalting the Word of God above all other authorities. The preacher sought close, empathetic, communal identification with the congregation. Holding forth in the pulpit on Sundays and throughout the week as one of God's earthly representatives, the preacher was the dominant, influential spokesperson for the community at large. The Black preacher served as the arbiter of intellectual/moral life and the principal *interpreter of* canonized sacred writings.[12]

The continued self-inventiveness of Black preaching is inescapably bound up with gifted orators gathering Bible stories, accounts of deeds, and sayings from their given theological contexts and transposing these words of faith into patterned episodes in clear, "gettable" language, i.e., language accessible to listeners. Black preaching is a running commentary on Scripture passages, showing how the Bible is an infinite thesaurus that provides hearers with resources in word and deed for overcoming oppressive situations.

Due to the oral proclivities of African American Christian culture, a written sermon cannot be understood apart from its delivery. The sermon is a combination of serious exegesis and imaginative elaboration of the stories in the Pentateuch, the sayings in Wisdom literature, the prophetic writings, and the New Testament. It is an unhampered play of theological fantasy and at the same time an acknowledgement of the cultural maturity and religious sophistication of traditional themes.

The homiletical explorations of Isaac R. Clark penetrate to the soul of Black preaching, providing us with insight into the way in which oral religious thought is organized and conceptualized. To be sure, Clark speaks of Black preaching in the broadest sense, as a fundamentally creative, artistic cultural form of African American Christian speech that exhibits a distinct expressive style and flavor for communicating religious beliefs and theoethical considerations in an articulate oral pattern. According to Clark, preaching as the spoken representation of the dimensions of the holy is *"divine activity* wherein the *Word of God* is *proclaimed* or *announced* concerning *contemporary issues* with a view toward *ultimate response to God."*

Black preaching is a narrative that exhibits all of the formal structures of rhetorical prose, such as a text, title, introduction, proposition, body, and conclusion. It is the major medium for making scriptural proclamation relevant to our times. By figuratively dramatizing biblical conflicts of dominance and submission, assertion and deference, the righted and the outlawed, the propertied and the dispossessed, the Black preacher calls into question "the social network of power/knowledge relations."[13] In each preaching event, the religious practices and deepseated theoethical beliefs of the Black church are reinvented in and through specific scriptural interpretation. Investigation of the integral connection between the preacher who creates the sermon, the sermon's internal design, the world that the sermon reveals, and the religious sensibilities of the congregation that are affected by the sermon invites us to a higher degree of critical consciousness about the invisible milieu in which we worship.

Divine activity refers to the customary three-tiered configuration that places the Black preacher in the mediating position between God and the congregation. With one ear on the ground hearing the cries and longings of the people and the other ear at the mouth of God, the preacher has a special obligation to instruct the hearers in defining, interpreting, and solving problems related to the life we live, the life we dread, and the life we aspire to live. The preacher has the power and privilege to determine precisely what biblical text will be used and whose experiences are central and endowed with force and continuity in the encoding of norms and values for the Black church community. Throughout the sermonic delivery the preacher must communicate that the authority for the sermon emanates from a guiding force beyond the preacher, from God.[14]

Word of God focuses on the Word that becomes flesh and dwells with us as the living God; it does not simply apply to the "words" of canonized Scripture that we read and hear. The God-self is present as the content of the preached word. The Holy Spirit must work through the critically conscious preacher to present the person and work of Jesus Christ as recorded in the Bible to the body of believers.[15] Jesus, the kerygmatic Christ, pulsates with a quality of "isness," a particular contemporaneity that identifies the sacredness spoken of during the sermon with recognizable aspects of the congregation's everyday raw material of existence.[16] Preaching in the Black church is a dynamic process that matches the scriptural texts with temporal sequences, provides etiological explanation for evil and suffering inflicted by human agency, and emphasizes the close union of heaven and earth, God and people.

Black Preaching concentrates a lot of attention upon Jesus who acts decisively and speaks with pointedness.[17] The gospel stories about Jesus are linked back to quite definite events of the Greco-Roman world and to the life of the present-day community. However, in the final analysis it is not the historical Jesus who occupies the central place, but the divine power that holds sway over him as the Word Incarnate.

Proclaimed or *announced* is the preacher's indicative mode for declaring the biblical ideas, beliefs, and systems of thought in the vernacular of the hearers. To be most effective and efficient the preacher artfully amplifies sacred referencing in a language that includes the idiomatic and colloquial forms most recognizable to Black churchgoers. The exposition of the scriptural text must be delivered with vigor and vitality in order to bear witness to the preacher's enthusiasm for being called to this sacred task. Parishioners participate in a call-and-response dialogue with the preacher that subjects biblical preaching to dynamic, in-the-moment expressions of resurrection.

The narrative strategies of Black religious lore recapitulate the lives and decisive action of biblical ancestors who are not thought to belong merely to the past, but are considered also to be living, in, with, and beyond their faith descendants. Black preaching takes great liberty in tapping into the inexhaustible treasures of wisdom and spiritual power lodged in the biblical canon.[18] Black preaching encourages proclamations of the "good news" Bible stories in ways that are interactive, memorable, and commonly public.[19] Anthropomorphism in the Black preaching tradition transforms biblical characters, adventures, and behavior into a larger context of experience so that the finite mind can grapple with the eternal creative act.

Contemporary issues are determined by gifted communicators transforming and reinterpreting their divine call as it interfaces with Scripture and the existential circumstances of the hearers. Clark's study of sacred rhetoric suggests a number of intriguing approaches that open up windows to the biblical concepts structured into the imaginative core of the Black worship experience. By communicating with gestures, facial expressions, and chanted deliveries, the Black preacher builds a compelling sermon by preserving and "making plain" the stories of the Bible that have been handed down through the years.[20] Equilibrium is maintained by sloughing off memories that no longer have relevance while proclaiming the religious inheritance of ancestral mothers and fathers that enhances narrative variation for audience responses in new situations.

The Black sermon is more than a mere tangent to social history.[21] It has a special affinity with contextual reality insofar as it connects the experience of finitude with the transcendent dimensions expressed with the biblical culture of bygone days. It encompasses vivid descriptions, colloquial diction, and concrete imagery drawn from both the Bible and daily life that symbolize liberating possibilities between actuality and hope, real and ideal, earth and heaven. In other words, Bible stories are relived, not merely heard; the preacher gives enough details and embellishes the actions with metaphors to keep the story moving so that the hearers stay abreast of their present-day identification with the biblically based narratives.

Given the complexity of and ambiguity in the Black church community, preachers verbalize their homilies with more or less close reference to the African American lifeworld, assimilating the abstract world of theology to the more immediate, familiar world of everyday life and struggle. Homiletical proclamation is enmeshed with historical and social events in the African American community, engaging knowledge in the arena where human beings struggle with one another.

The overall objective and purpose of preaching is to call the worshiping congregation to an *ultimate response to God*. According to Clark, the Black preacher's primary activity is to inform, engage, and point out contradictions within situations of complacent security in order to invite the congregation to make a decision for or against emancipatory praxis. Preaching not only helps us to know what we believe and why, but it is the medium through which events of transformative understanding shake up creeds, question social power, and transform traditions. The preacher thinks through complex problems and articulates solutions by verbalizing a "why crisis" that motivates the listeners to contemplate the complicated series of theoethical assertions. The constant exposure to the abounding iniquity in the world opens the congregation to a gracious message of deliverance.

Clark's rhetorical methodology shows why Black preaching has acquired a particular and unique physiognomy, why certain theoethical themes and motifs are present and others absent, why certain stylistic treatments are accepted and others rejected. In other words, this signifying process enables us to see how theoethical canons, standards, and conventions are produced and maintained in African American homiletical texts. Black sermons are characterized by the combination of biblical retrospect and exhortation in which the worshiping community is called forth to be among the chosen, fully grasping and proclaiming the character of Yahweh as the liberating God of history. Black sermons have a great deal to teach us concerning the congregation's call to redemption through the fullest imaginative response.

Clark effectively solves the problem of intellectually organizing the data of text and context by developing a rhetorical methodology of *definition, elaboration, exemplification,* and *justification,* thus establishing a line of continuity inside the mind. The syntax, rhythm, and balanced patterns in repetition of these four formulary essentials help implement rhythmic discourse that act as retention and ready recall aids in their own right. Also, they form the substance of thought itself. Clark's coordinated homiletical structure, through which the syntactic and theological ideas are generated, expands the aesthetic dimensions of Black preaching, achieving the most effective, consistent, innovative "telling of the old, old story."

Womanist Queries

My particular concern is how a womanist critical evaluative process, understood in its contextual framework, can suggest possibilities for eliminating the negative and derogatory female portraiture in Black preaching. An intensive examination of sermonic texts shows how preachers follow certain androcentric interests in objectifying and commodifying Black women. Even in "text-led" biblical preaching, where the representation of woman may occupy a central place in the expository structure, women are often occluded. By unmasking those detailed and numerous androcentric injunctions, womanist hermeneutics attempts to expose the impact of "phallocentric" concepts that are present within Black sacred rhetoric.

For instance, when we turn to the experience of Black churchwomen to establish criteria for interpreting and determining the value of sermonic texts we need to ask what difference it makes that African American Christians hear sermons full of linguistic sexism, in which images of and references to women are seldom positive. As womanist theologians, what can we do to counter the negative real-world consequences of sexist wording that brothers and sisters propagate in the guise of Christian piety and virtue? How disruptive are such gender-biased androcentric sermons for social relations within the African American family? What is the correlation between what is preached in church on Sunday and what Abbey Lincoln describes as the African American woman's social predicament?

> Her head is more regularly beaten than any other woman's, and by her own man; she's the scapegoat for Mr. Charlie, she is forced to stark realism and chided if caught dreaming; her aspirations for her and hers are, for sanity sake, stunted; her physical image has been criminally maligned, assaulted, and negated; she is the first to be called ugly, and never yet beautiful.[22]

As clergywomen committed to the well-being of the African American community how are we refuting gender stereotypes that are dehumanizing, debilitating, and prejudicial to African American women?[23] Can we change male supremacist attitudes by prescribing alternatives to discriminatory word usage? What happens to African American female children when Black preachers use the Bible to attribute marvelous happenings and unusual circumstances to an all-male cast of characters? The privilege, power, and prerogative in developing such sermons are in themselves significant. The marginalization of women from the cast of characters constitutes a significant choice within these larger patterns of decision.

What are the essential liberating strategies that African American clergywomen use in our own sacred rhetoric that will continue to encourage an ethic of resistance? What are we doing that will allow a womanist interpretation to emerge, an analysis that shows how Black women underneath patriarchal teachings and relations of domination are complex, life-affirming moral agents? I maintain that a womanist analysis provides the internal analytical categories of the valuation system for this genre of sacred rhetoric.

The sensibilities of a womanist interpretation of preaching in the Black church require sacred orators to be responsive to the emotional, political, psychic, and intellectual implications of our message. We anticipate and embrace both power and subsequent actions in the creation and in the delivery of our sermons. Therefore, we must identify the qualities of an "ideal" Black churchwoman and a "realized" Christian woman. In appreciating the complexity of the genius of Black preaching, we must be able to analyze how this genre is both sacred and profane, active and passive, life-giving and death-dealing. Womanist interpretation calls for a balanced tension between the accuracy of the spoken word — organization, language, fluidity, and style — and the expressed political aim of our sermonic content. In order to present co-equal discipleship the preacher must reflect upon the sacred words that underrepresent and truncate women in the creation of African American women's image, voice, and agency.

A womanist hermeneutics seeks to place sermonic texts in the real-life context of the culture that produced them. The basic premises of sermonic development aim to operate inside the boundaries both of canonized Scripture and the circumstances in which the sermon is written and delivered. Images used throughout the sermon can invite the congregation to share in dismantling patriarchy by artfully and deftly guiding the congregation through the rigors of resisting the abjection and marginalization of women. A womanist interpretation requires each component of Black homiletics to adhere to the emancipatory practice of a faith community. The preacher is obliged and expected to show the listeners how to "trace out the logic of liberation that can transform patriarchal oppression."[24]

Womanist hermeneutics regards sociocultural context as an important component of the sermon. The preacher's testimonial function is necessarily looked at within a personal-existential framework. The utterances of the preacher must be examined in the situation in which they are produced and delivered to the hearers, that is, in terms of the preacher's and congregation's own experiences. Nothing prohibits us from asking questions about the role of social factors in shaping sermonic texts and what part the preacher's gender plays in selecting the kinds of biblical stories and sayings that she or he uses in preaching. Womanist analysis of sermons inquires into the depictions of women's experiences, missionary circles, mothers and female saints of the church, and the women officers and leaders in the ecclesiastical community. This practice removes men from the "normative" center and women from the margins. It leads to the alteration of prevailing masculine models of influence. To avoid perpetuating traditional, binary assumptions, womanist theory offers a helpful strategy for focussing on the oppression of women while simultaneously providing visions of liberation. Using Clark's tools and methods on preaching in the Black church and relating them to Schüssler Fiorenza's most recent writings on feminist liberationist criticism, we can provide precise answers to the questions of (1) how meaning is constructed, (2) whose interests are served, and (3) what kind of worlds are envisioned in Black sacred rhetoric. Every choice that a preacher makes in constructing a sermon will have certain connotations, inherited from its forebears among the sermons that preceded it. Preaching in the Black church is as much affected by issues of misogyny, androcentricity, and patriarchy as by homiletical form. Within this complex discursive construction of sacred rhetoric, women and men who cast their lot with us must make an intervention, no matter how slight, in the dominant religious discourse of our time.

Chapter 10

Hitting a Straight Lick with a Crooked Stick

The Womanist Dilemma in the Development of a Black Liberation Ethic

To be a Black womanist ethicist places me in a most precarious predicament. On the one hand, my task as a *Christian social ethicist* is to transcend my blackness and femaleness and draft a blueprint of liberation ethics that somehow speaks to, or responds to, the universality of the human condition. On the other hand, my task as a *womanist liberation ethicist* is to debunk, unmask, and disentangle the historically conditioned value judgments and power relations that undergird the particularities of race, sex, and class oppression. Zora Neale Hurston described this dilemma as trying to hit a straight lick with a crooked stick. In essence, my role is to speak as "one of the canonical boys" and as "the noncanonical other" at one and the same time. These two tasks stand in opposition to each other.[1] The question that has evolved from wrestling with this dilemma is the following: What importance do race and gender have as meaningful categories in the development of a Black liberation ethic?

Black Woman Ethicist as One of the Canonical Boys

Even though there is no clearly written statement among Christian social ethicists regarding the nature of scholarship, enough areas of agreement do exist within the guild to make reasonable generalizations regarding the ethicist as scholar. Most of these have nothing to do with the realities of Black women. For instance, membership in this highly complex fraternity means investigation of abstract metatheory, traditional

This chapter was first published in the *Annual of the Society of Christian Ethics*, 1987, 165–77.

philosophical thought, and the established canon of ethical inquiry with supposedly calm and detached objectivity.[2]

To prove that she is sufficiently intelligent, the Black woman as Christian ethicist must discount the particularities of her lived experiences and instead focus on the validity of generalizable external analytical data. The dilemma she faces in joining the canonical boys is that of succumbing to the temptation of mastering only the historically specified perspective of the Euro-American masculine preserve.[3] In order to be a respected scholar in the discipline, the Black woman is placed under a double injunction. She has to face a critical jury, primarily White and male, that makes claims for gender-neutral and value-free inquiry as a model for knowledge.[4] The Black female scholar will have little opportunity to expand her creative energy in the direction of liberation ethics if she concentrates on searching for universal truths unhampered by so-called incidental matters such as race, sex, and class differences. In other words, there is an unspoken informal code within the guild that the Black woman academician must engage in this type of abstract moral discourse or else she runs the risk of being misunderstood, misinterpreted, and frequently devalued as a second-class scholar specializing in Jim Crow subject matter.[5]

What is important to grasp here is that both the inclusion of Black women and the inclusion of Black women's moral reasoning within the structure of traditional ethics are pioneering endeavors.[6] Black women's experience has been overlooked, neglected, or distorted in most of the existing ethical scholarship. For instance, Black women as subjects for scholarly research have been given little attention. Little writing in ethics focuses on the moral agency of Black females. Unfortunately, this situation is not peculiar to ethics; Black women as worthy subjects of study are ignored in most areas of scholarship.

From behind the veil of race and sex neutrality, the Black female scholar understands that the metaphysical and ethical issues are mutually connected. The accepted canonical methods of moral reasoning contain deeply hidden biases that make it exceedingly difficult to turn them to the service of the best interest of Black women.[7] Universality does not include the Black female experience.

Why does the discipline of ethics have so little to say about Black women's role in church and society? What value does the academy place on the history, culture, and traditions that Black women have created? Do we see Black women's moral wisdom as making a poor virtue of survival?

In scanning the canon in ethical studies, one finds that this omission of Black women provides continuing ideological support for conditions and public policies oppressive to Black women. The White masculine orientation that characterizes the field of study leaves Black women out.

This type of academic invisibility reinforces racist/sexist stereotypes and justifies misapprehensions that lock Black women into marginal status. In other words, the concepts used by the majority of White male ethicists to discuss moral agency implicitly devalue Black women's contribution. Chanzo Tallamu argues that as long as current research methods do not reflect or pay enough attention to the needs of Black women, the policies and programs that result may benefit White women or Black men but not Black women.[8]

When ethical discourse provides truncated and distorted pictures of Black women, the society at large uses these oppressive stereotypes to define what it is to be Black and female in America. An even more basic manifestation of this trivialization of Black women has been the traditional practice of generalizing about Black women on the information gathered from White women or Black men.[9] The emphasis has to be placed on information derived from Black women talking about their own lives and religious experiences.

Until the advent of the civil rights movement in the 1960s and the women's movement in the 1970s, Black women were virtually ignored and their questions reduced to marginal absurdity as a result of sexist/racist assumptions. Black women's contributions to the academy have been considered incidental to the substance of theology and ethics — mere asides, insignificant to the conceptual framework that defines the body of thought as a whole.[10] The moral agency of Black women must be understood on their own terms rather than being judged by essentially abstract external ideological norms and squeezed into categories and systems that consider White men the measure of significance. Lives of Black women cannot be fully comprehended using analytical categories derived from White/male experience. Oftentimes such concepts covertly sustain a hierarchy of White supremacy, patriarchy, and exploitative power.[11]

Black Woman Ethicist as Noncanonical Other

The dilemma of the Black woman ethicist as the noncanonical other is defined as working in opposition to the academic establishment, yet building upon it. The liberation ethicist works both within and outside the guild. The Black womanist scholar receives the preestablished disciplinary structures of intellectual inquiry in the field of ethics and tries to balance the paradigms and assumptions of this intellectual tradition with a new set of questions arising from the context of Black women's lives.[12] The tension is found in the balancing act of simultaneously trying to raise the questions appropriate to the discipline while also trying to understand what emphasis ought properly to be placed on the various determinants influencing the situation of Black women. In order to work toward an inclusive ethic, the womanist struggles to restructure the categories so that the presuppositions more readily include the ethical realities of Black women.

The womanist scholar identifies the pervasive White and male biases deeply embedded in the field of study. As a liberationist, she challenges and reshapes the traditional inquiry and raises candid questions between the two locales of whiteness and maleness. She insists that new questions guide the research so that Black women's moral wisdom can provide the answers. In essence, she seeks to determine why and how Black women actively negotiate their lives in a web of oppression.[13]

The Black woman's ethical analysis distinguishes between "possibilities in principle" and "possibilities in fact." She extends Black women's existential reality above the threshold of that frustrating and illusory social mobility that forms the core of the American dream. That is, she strips away false, objectified conceptualities and images that undergird the apparatuses of systemic oppression.

The intersection of race, sex, and class gives womanist scholars a different ethical orientation with a different ideological perspective. The experience of being both the participant from within and the interpreter from without results in an inescapable duality to the character of womanist ethics. Beginning with her own historical, socio-ethical situation, the Black woman scholar cuts off what is untrue and adds what is most urgent. In other words, she refutes what is inimical and coopts the positive. This task is difficult since Black women in general are dealing with vague, amorphous social ideals, on the one hand, and with the long-standing effects of American racism, sexism, and class elitism on the other.[14]

For example, Black female ethicists endure with a certain grace the social restrictions that limit their own mobility, and at the same time they demand that the relationships between their own condition and the condition of those who have a wide range of freedom be recognized. They bring into clear focus the direct correlation of economic, political, and racial alienation. As participant-interpreters, they have direct contact with the high and the lowly, the known and the unrecognized, the comic and the tragic that makes them conscious of the myriad value systems that are antithetical to Black survival. To demystify large and obscure ideological relations, social theories, and, indeed, the heinous sociopolitical reality of tridimensional oppression is a moral act. To do ethics inside out and back again is the womanist norm.

In other words, as the noncanonical other, these women rightly recognize how family life, cultural expression, political organization, and social and economic roles shape the Black community. Furthermore, they identify the way Black women as moral agents persistently attempt to strip away the shrouding of massive dislocation and violence exacerbated in recent years by the nation's fiscal crisis.[15] Under extremely harsh conditions, Black women buttress themselves against the dominant coercive apparatuses of society. Using a series of resistance modes, they weave together many disparate strands of survival skills, styles, and traditions in order to create a new synthesis that, in turn, serves as a catalyst for deepening the wisdom-source that is genuinely their own.[16]

Black women ethicists use this framework of wisdom to compare and contrast Black female moral agency with the agency of those in society who have the freedom to maximize choice and personal autonomy. The womanist scholar focuses on describing, documenting, and analyzing the ideologies, theologies, and systems of values that perpetuate the subjugation of Black women. At the same time, she emphasizes how Black women are shaping their own destines within restricted possibilities, resisting and overthrowing those restrictions, and sometimes, in the interest of survival, acting in complicity with the forces that keep them oppressed.[17]

To make this point clearer: Black women ethicists constantly question why Black women are considered merely ancillary, no more than throwaway superfluous appendages in a society that claims "life, liberty, and the pursuit of happiness" as "inalienable rights." What theological systems relegate Black women to the margins of the decision-making mainstream of American religious, political, and economic life? And what qualitative judgments and social properties establish a chasm between the proposition that Black women, first and foremost, are human beings and the machinations that allow glaring inequities and unfulfilled promises to proceed morally unchecked?

The womanist scholar stresses the role of emotional, intuitive knowledge in the collective life of the people. Such intuition enables moral agents in situations of oppression to follow the rule within, and not be dictated to from without. Untrammeled by external authority, Black female moral agents' intuitive faculties lead them toward a dynamic sense of moral reasoning. They designate the processes, the manners, and subtleties of their own experiences with the least amount of distortion from the outside. They go below the level of racial, sexual structuring and into those areas where Black people are simply human beings struggling to reduce to consciousness all of their complex experiences. Communion with one's own truths makes one better able to seize and delineate with unerring discrimination the subtle connections among people, institutions, and systems that serve as silent accessories to the perpetuation of flagrant forms of injustice.[18]

Intrigued by the largely unexamined questions that have fallen through the cracks between feminist ethics and Black male theology, the womanist scholar insists on studying the distinctive consciousness of

Black women within Black women's institutions, clubs, organizations, magazines, and literature.[19] Appropriating the human condition in their own contexts, Black women collectively engage in revealing the hidden power relations inherent in the present social structures. A central conviction is that theoethical structures are not universal, color-blind, apolitical, or otherwise neutral. Thus, the womanist ethicist tries to comprehend how Black women create their own lives, influence others, and understand themselves as a force in their own right. The womanist voice is one of deliverance from the deafening discursive silence that the society at large has used to deny the basis of shared humanity.

Conclusion

In order to move toward a Black liberation ethic, attention must be paid to an ethical vision that includes Black women. The substantial omission of Black women from theological discourse flows quite naturally from male theologians using analytical concepts and frameworks that take the male experience as the norm.[20] An inclusive liberation ethic must focus on the particular questions of women in order to reveal the subtle and deep effects of male bias on recording religious history.[21] As scholars, we must demonstrate the hidden assumptions and premises that lie behind our ethical speculations and inferences. Our task is to change the imbalance caused by an androcentric view, wherein it is presumed that only men's activities have theological value. If we are willing to unmask the male assumptions that dominate religious thought, we will discover whole new areas of ethical inquiry.

Second, in moving toward a Black liberation ethic we must examine Black women's contributions in all the major fields of theological studies — Bible, history, ethics, mission, worship, theology, preaching, and pastoral care. The Black male biases operate not so much to omit Black women totally as to relegate Black church women to the position of direct object instead of active subject.[22] Too often Black women are presented in a curiously impersonal dehumanizing way as the fused backbone in the body of the church.

A womanist liberation ethic requires us to gather information and to assess accurately the factual evidence regarding Black women's contribution to the Black church community.[23] Black women organized voluntary missionary societies, superintended church schools, led prayer meetings, took an active part in visiting and ministering to the sick and needy, and raised large amounts of money to defray the expenses of the Black church. Black women are conscious actors who have altered the theological picture in significant ways. Furthermore, this second area of research does more than increase our understanding of Black women in the church community; it also elicits reinterpretation of old conclusions about the church universal.

Finally, the development of an inclusive ethic requires us to recognize and condemn the extent to which sex differences prevail in the institutional church, in our theological writings, and in the Black church's practices.[24] A womanist liberation ethic directs critical attention not only to scholarship in the fields of study but also to its concrete effects on women in the pews. The work has to be done both from the basis of church practices and from the basis of continuing academic investigation. For instance, we need to do an analysis of sexist content of sermons in terms of reference to patriarchal values and practices. Particular attention needs to be given to the objectification, degradation, and subjection of the female in Black preaching.[25] At the same time, we need to analyze the social organization of the Black church — curricula, music, leadership expectation, pastor-member interactions — as well as outright sex discrimination.[26] Far too often, the organization of the church mirrors male dominance in the society and normalizes it in the eyes of both female and male parishioners.

Whether the discipline of ethics has almost completely neglected Black women (as in White male scholarship) or treated them as incidental to central issues (as in Black male scholarship) or considered gender as the important factor for research (as in White feminist scholarship), the cumulative effect of womanist scholarship is that it moves us toward a fundamental reconceptualization of all ethics with the experience of Black women at center stage.

Chapter 11

Appropriation and Reciprocity in the Doing of Womanist Ethics

"Christian Ethics and Theology in Womanist Perspective," by Cheryl J. Sanders, served as the lead article in the "Womanist Roundtable Discussion" published in the *Journal of Feminist Studies in Religion,* in 1989.[1] Sanders's "Final Rejoinder" became the catalyst for my interest in the controversy concerning appropriation and reciprocity. Sanders's closing remarks and assessment of the roundtable discussion articulated a contestable issue similar to the ethical crisis that Cecil W. Cone advanced in 1975.[2]

Cone charged that Black theology failed to recognize the irreconcilability of Black Power and established Eurocentric academic theology. He argued that the failure of major Black liberation theologians was the inability to create Black theology from the essential core and essence of Black religious sources. In fact, Cone objected to the way African American theologians succumbed to the conservative theoretical concerns of the received European traditional standards in order to achieve academic respectability within the structure of predominantly White seminaries.[3]

> The problem with theological standards can be stated generally as an undue sensitivity on the part of black theologians to the opinions and working conventions of white theologians. Because theology, like other fields of western intellectual activity, was developed by white people, it ignored black religion. It is not surprising, therefore, that a large part of its methods and results are inappropriate for black theologians. When black theologians write about black religion, they will inevitably depart in large measure from matters that have concerned the white majority and have therefore been labeled "good" theology. This will, of course, create a question of "acceptability" for the black scholars. Although the

This chapter was first published in the *Annual of the Society of Christian Ethics,* 1993 (Georgetown University), 189–96.

black writers have often shown considerable courage in resisting the pained outcries of white colleagues, the former have sometimes compromised in the interest of "dialogue" or "reconciliation." While this may sometimes be appropriate in informal encounters, it confuses and retards Black Theology when carried into formal writing.[4]

Furthermore, Cone reasons that as long as African American scholars allow Euro-American analytical concepts to serve as the point of departure in Black Religious Studies, then there will be a distortion in the essence of what is intended to be analyzed. He concludes that contemporary writers of Black theology cannot probe the depths and scope of Black religion if they use the academic tools of White theologians.

Cheryl Sanders expressed Cone's concern in relation to womanist scholarship in the following way:

> The fact that almost all of their footnotes are derived from the writings of black women sends the important signal that we are appreciating, analyzing and appropriating our own sources, and also those of black men, without appealing for the most part to white sources for sanction and approval of what we ourselves have said. This observation is especially significant in view of the fact that in a racist society, self-hatred manifests itself as unmistakably in the academy as in the ghetto when we are pressured to employ our oppressors' criteria to evaluate our own work and worth. To see black women embracing and engaging our material is a celebration in itself.[5]

After reading and analyzing the above statement by Sanders I realized that of the four other respondents in the roundtable discussion (Emilie M. Townes, M. Shawn Copeland, bell hooks, and Cheryl Townsend Gilkes) I made more references to and cited more sources by White women scholars than any of the other womanist respondents.

Yes, this was my irrefutable ethical crisis: Am I, Katie G. Cannon, who boldly stated my anger with Sanders's treatment of "womanist" as a secular terminological issue and who proudly proclaimed myself as "a self-avowed, practicing, Black-Womanist-Liberationist-Christian Ethicist," guilty of misappropriation? By using the scholarship of White feminist liberationists to frame and substantiate the theoretical requisites for rejecting patriarchal intrusions in the predicament of African American women, am I running the risk of lobotomizing womanist ethics and diminishing both Black women agents and agency? Within the terms of the controversy, we need to ask: Is it appropriate for Black women to use analytical modes of exposing and criticizing domination and exploitation created by women with different social identities?

In other words, what are the pros and cons of modeling our right to meaningful and constructive self-determination on paradigms created by non-Black women?

The implied accusation in Sanders's rejoinder was a shocking and terrifying disorientation for me. I knew that I had fashioned an original, concise, and powerful critique of Sanders's essay, and yet her closing statement suggests that my response was somehow bogus relative to her criterion of womanist accountability. Did using quotations from the writings of Beverly W. Harrison and Elisabeth Schüssler Fiorenza to shape and substantiate my theoretical argument manifest self-hatred, or did it make me a fraud?

It was at this moment that I felt I had no choice but to do everything I could do to confront this challenge. Every reflective and well-intentioned African American scholar who is consciously concerned with "the liberation of a whole people" must work to eradicate the criterion of legitimacy that implicitly presumes an absolute incompatibility between womanist critical scholarship and White feminist liberationist sources. As one of the senior womanist ethicists, I am issuing advance warning to new womanist scholars, both actual and potential, that Sanders's devaluation of credibility consequent on such a conservative framework of Black-sources-only encourages guesswork, blank spots, and time-consuming busy work, the reinvention of the proverbial wheel over and over again. Having struggled so long and hard at the intersection of race, sex, and class, African American women scholars cannot allow the suspicion of fraudulence to spread and contaminate the creative horizons in womanist research and writing. Staying open-minded as heterogeneous theoreticians may prove to be the most difficult ethical challenge in securing and extending the legacy of our intellectual life.

In my experience as a Black woman in a racist and misogynistic society, tremendous pressure is continually exerted on me to choose between my racial identity and my womanhood. Black women are repeatedly asked to cast our lot of identifying loyalties in one or the other competing camp. Either we are Blacks or we are women. Despite womanist scholar's best efforts in arguing that this is a conceptual impossibility because we embody both realities as Black women, the full force of the punitive and damaging effects of binary categories remains intact. When African American women defy the traditionally accepted race and gender niches of where others think we and our work belong, our essential worth and competence come into question.

In light of these concerns, let us consider a working definition for appropriation in the doing of womanist ethics. Generally speaking, one would have to say that the concept of appropriation has to do with the act of preempting, usurping, confiscating — possessing the power to seize and control a people's resources without authority or with questionable authority. Within the terms of this critique, the social process of appropriation means the taking over of someone else's culture and, I would add, someone's educational capital or discourse, more or less with desire beforehand to convert the thing taken over to one's own use.

One may question how operative is this working definition of appropriation when I, an African American woman, study in an in-depth way the body of feminist liberationist literature created by Beverly W. Harrison, Elisabeth Schüssler Fiorenza, and Letty M. Russell in order to lay bare the underlying realities of Black women's lives. Is it merely self-evident that a person or a group is guilty of appropriation only when they have power to co-opt, seize, and control? Is it reasonable to assume that any process of appropriation is also a process of confiscation?

Yes, this is the ethical dilemma: What is the appropriate relationship between women of color, who only in the past decade have been able to enter the learned societies of the theological guild, and senior women scholars of European and Euro-American ancestry who have exercised their legitimate right to shape the essential nature and foundations of feminist liberationist discourse? Or, is authentic womanist discourse an unprecedented phenomenon, representing not just progress in our collective struggle to transform invasion and conquest to revelation and choice, but total innovation in cultural, ideological, and ethical preferences? As African American womanist ethicists, how do we evaluate the content of White feminist ethics and its relevance to the lives of the majority of Black women who live under radically different circumstances? In essence, can there be appropriation without intellectual domination?

Next, let us consider the concept of reciprocity. The assumption has been that in a reciprocal process one recognizes the validity of sources and origins in the development of one's own discourse. For me it means giving back in kind and quality, mutually exchanging and being changed by each other's data and resources, paying back what I have received from working with some of the keenest formative feminist intellectuals of our time. There is indeed a collaborative moving to and fro between my work and the work of White feminist liberationists as we each return something given, done, or said from a place of mutual dependence, action, and influence.

Even more obvious and troubling is the question that emerges at this point in the debate. Is the politics of citation determined solely by who befriends whom? The vast majority of African American women have not had trusted White women mentor-friends who consistently show commitment and belief in our capabilities and motivate us to work to our full potential. Only a few of us have received genuine invitations into the exclusive inner circle of European and Euro-American feminism. Can there be reciprocity among womanist and feminist scholars without the prior acceptance of unguarded camaraderie and close friendships?

The intellectual and political currents within the feminist movements determine whether or not African American women will respond yea or nay to these strategic overtures of friendship. The invitations by White women are not unintentional nor are the responses by Black women insignificant.

In order to address some of these emerging questions concerning heterogeneous perspectives and critical modes of assessment that ignite, inform, and help establish the parameters of appropriation and reciprocity in womanist discourse, I sent out fifty questionnaires focusing on "Epistemological Sources for Critical Womanist Scholarship."[6] The number of questionnaires answered indicates what is at stake for "the essential core and essence of womanist religious sources."

Over and over again, African American women responded that the starting point for womanist epistemology is the oral culture bequeathed to us by our grandmothers, mothers, aunts, and sisters. Examples from the womanist questionnaire illustrate this:

I attribute the origins of my womanist voice to my grandmother, a strong, articulate women who was deliberate in nurturing my sense of who I am and what I could attain in life.

The origins of my womanist voice are from my great-grandmother, grandmothers, mother and aunts and the kitchen-table conversations I heard and participated in from the time I was four or five years old. That is as far back as I can remember really *understanding* the stories and values they passed on to me. I inherited my voice from them and the richness of their conversations.

My womanist voice comes from deep within myself. It rests in my innate God consciousness present in the breath of my ancestors from the Motherland. Scripture inspires it to speak. My womanist voice is strong because of my mother's strength and resilience, attributes which I choose to embrace. My womanist voice is the legacy of Wisdom passed over to me through the lives of African American women, living and dead; kin women, women of the church, women activists and friends near and far.... My womanist voice is deep speaking into Deep!

My voice originates in the personal voices of my mother and grandmother and sister whose voices sound like my own when it comes to personal survival and the survival of family members, as well as the community.

The origins of my womanist voice are from my reflections on my life as a black woman, a daughter, a sister and a spiritual sojourner. The origins seem to arise from the flowing waters of the "life river" within me. When I retreat with myself I find myself sitting at the banks of my life river, listening to the constant, continuous, flow of river water, calling me to flow with it, to stir it up, or simply lie in it. The voices of women, black women, that I have known and have read about, call to me from the river.

Through inventive expressions, womanists are finding opportunities to model in our writing the traditional intimacies of our historical-social context. Our goal is to acquaint others with the distinctive dynamics of the orally constituted thought forms of African Americans so that the stream of Black women's proverbial sayings and wisdom stories flows naturally into our academic life. By linking the ironies, frustrations, and ambiguities of the spoken wisdom from mouth to ear to the visible but silent thoughts written on the page, we import the codification of our ancestors' lore.

It is a fact, to be sure, that as we engage in the scholarship of interpreting, particularizing, and reproducing the life, power, and meaning of the spoken wisdom, the appropriation question changes. The new question is how do we remain both beholden to our inherited religious culture materials as well as responsible in favoring the extension of oral texts for posterity? In other words, what are the trade-offs in our movement from orality to textuality?

Another distinctive feature of epistemological sources for critical womanist scholarship is the intersecting of medium and message. As African American scholars, our effort is to transpose the essential experiential elements of racism, heterosexism, and class elitism into a written medium, as a way of affirming Black people's ethical equilibrium against the odds. Responses from the questionnaire bear this out. Womanist respondents note:

> My upbringing in the Black Church and the racist, sexist, homophobic culture of life in the USA are the experiences that shape the womanist voice I have.

> The two important experiences that shape my voice consist of being one of the first Black children to attend an all-White school (my siblings and I might have integrated it) and coming out as a lesbian at age 19. As the daughter of a middle-class Black woman and a poor Black man from the South, who struggled his way into the middle class, my commitment to race, gender, sexual orientation and gender justice comes from my experiences in this context.

> My voice is shaped by the personal experience of racism and other forms of oppression, particularly the elitism of class oppression in the African American community (sometimes manifested as re-

gionalism, North/South). My voice is also shaped by experiences of sexism and, finally, by seeing others oppressed and exploited.

Living, being exposed to white culture at an early age — the demystification of it, Black culture, and seeing and feeling first-hand the destructive power of alcoholism are the experiences that inform my womanism.

The womanist writing consciousness does not obscure or deny the existence of tridimensional oppression but rather through full, sharp awareness of race, sex, and class oppression we present the liberating possibilities that also exist. Our womanist work is to draw on the rugged endurance of Black folks in America who outwit, outmaneuver, and outscheme social systems and structures that maim and stifle mental, emotional, and spiritual growth. Repeatedly, in light of the stated task, womanist thinkers raise the question of reciprocity in this way: How do we bring to the forefront the unity of knower and known?

Hence, we have come full circle. The origin of the idea dictates the claims of accountability. Whether we begin with paradigms created by mentors of European and Euro-American ancestry or with theoretical constructs emerging from the oral traditions in the African Diaspora or with a dialectical, syncretistic interplay between the two, we must answer the inescapable questions of appropriation and reciprocity. To decline the ethical labor of wrestling with the questions I have raised throughout this essay is to cede our future scholarship to conventional either-or dichotomies. It is to play the game of androcentric, heteropatriarchal academese without understanding it.

Chapter 12

Metalogues and Dialogues

Teaching the Womanist Idea

Metalogues: highly organized or specialized forms of logic, designating new but related disciplines that can deal critically with the nature, structure, or behavior of the original discourse, talk, performance, or recital.

— Katie G. Cannon

"Wheels in the Middle of Wheels"

Over the past two decades, an alternative theological pedagogy has been evolving in this country. It can be found in all the disciplines of theological study that African American women, once locked out, have been able to enter. The notion of womanist pedagogy can probably be traced to those moments in Black women seminary training when two or three of us gathered together to share our observations of classroom dynamics, to question the weighty authority of male-canonized texts and interpretations, and to contemplate meaningful research projects of our own design. We dreamed of inscribing what Black women really think, see, and do upon a small section of the large tabula rasa of genuine inclusivity in theological education.[1]

Twenty years ago when I began seminary there were fewer than thirty-five African American women enrolled in master of divinity programs and only one African American woman registered in a doctoral program in the two hundred accredited seminaries in North America.[2] As Black women pursuing advanced theological degrees in a predominantly male setting, alienation, isolation, and maginalization were our

This chapter was first published in the *Journal of Feminist Studies in Religion* 8, no. 2 (Fall 1992): 125–30. It was originally presented at a session of the Womanist Approaches to Religion and Society Group at the 1991 Annual Meeting of the American Academy of Religion.

daily fare. Even with the requisite credentials for matriculation in hand, we were constantly barraged with arrogance and insults, suspicion and insensitivity, backhand compliments and tongue-in-cheek naiveté. The worlds of divinity school, denominational headquarters, regional judicatory offices, and local parishes, between which we negotiated, demanded different and often wrenching allegiances.[3] But we continued to study, struggling for our rightful places in the church and in the academy.

From time to time the paths of African American women seminarians crossed and a sisterly solidarity started to form. We talked about how we entered every situation knowing that we were "the sister outsider."[4] We entered every class discussion with a developing awareness that the indisputable norms of established truth would not be the norms of our daily existence.[5] We engaged with others across all kinds of barriers, and most of those with whom we dialogued were not even aware such obstacles existed. In order to crack open the patriarchal traditions that underlie and generate oppressive Christian practices, particularly against women of color, we worked with our sleeves rolled up, busily sharpening our oyster knives.[6]

In 1978 Delores Williams published an essay that I think identifies the foundations of womanist pedagogy. This is what she said:

> If I were asked what we black women students need to make the Union [Theological Seminary] experience meaningful, I would say we need what every other student needs. We need role models. We need competent scholars who are black women. We need black women to provide input into selection processes. We need to select our own voices to represent us in those processes. We need mature black women scholars who are actively committed to the task of welding together the theological and the ethical, the theoretical and the practical dimensions of the theological enterprise. We need black women in the support and counselling areas.... We need spiritual, community and financial support to structure whatever it takes to make our academic experience here compatible with our vocational objectives and with our personal needs as students. We need the facilities to enter into those self-definition processes which help us understand more fully our ministry to the world.[7]

I suggest that womanist pedagogy emerges out of this experience of Black women challenging conventional and outmoded dominant theological resources, deconstructing ideologies that led us into complicity with our own oppression. Seminary-trained African American women began inventing opposable-thumb processes by problematizing the "obvious" to create alternative ways of conceptualizing the "natural." In other words, African American women scholars created new modes of inquiry for dealing critically with the tradition, structure, and praxis of our fields. These modes invite women and men of contemporary faith communities to a more serious encounter with the contribution African American women have made — and continue to make — to theological studies. The imperative suggested by this pedagogy is an engaged scholarship that leads us to resist domination through mindful activism and helps all of us to live more faithfully the radicality of the gospel.[8]

For instance, as a womanist ethicist I have created seven graduate courses in Christian social ethics, and each course is a metalogue, three courses in one. Each course consists of three concentric circles of discourse. Hence, womanist liberation ethics is very much like the vision of the prophet Ezekiel — "wheels in the middle of wheels way up in the middle of the air." One wheel is the intellectual predisposition of traditional male thinkers, usually dead and of European ancestry, whose very language of objective universality masks our existence, forces us to persist in binary oppositions, and looks at Black women as superfluous appendages, saddled with odd concerns about race, sex, and class oppression.[9] The second wheel is the specificity of Afro-Christian culture, systematic accounts of the history and achievements, perspectives and experiences of members of the Black church community. And a third wheel is the experiential dimensions of women's texts and interpretations. In this part of each course we listen to women of the African Diaspora speaking our mothers' tongues, as we refine and critique our own realities across time and space through the written word.[10]

The theory that informs my womanist pedagogy imaged as wheels in the middle of wheels can be summed up in the definition of liberation ethics that I created in 1981 when I was a tutor in the Introduction to Christian Ethics class with Beverly Harrison at Union Theological Seminary in New York. When asked by students to define the special nature of "liberation ethics," I wrote the following on the chalkboard:

Liberation ethics is debunking, unmasking, and disentangling the ideologies, theologies, and systems of value operative in a particular society.

How is it done?

By analyzing the established power relationships that determine cultural, political, and economic presuppositions and by evaluating the legitimating myths that sanction the enforcement of such values.

Why is it worth doing?

In order that we may become responsible decision-makers who envision structural and systemic alternatives that embrace the well-being of us all.

This metalogic understanding of liberation ethics defines my purpose for each course and serves as the standard against which to evaluate the full participation of seminarians and professor. The "what," "how," and "why" give me perspectives for how best to design a syllabus, select required texts, compile bibliographies, prepare instructional strategies, choose reference materials, organize the sequence of assignments, and create pre- and post-assessment questionnaires.

My particular locus for doing womanist pedagogy is that of a Black woman who defines graduate theological education as my lifework and who for a variety of reasons worked diligently to earn tenure and become chair of my department by the time I reached the age of forty. I was tenured as an associate professor in Christian ethics at the Episcopal Divinity School in Boston shortly after my thirty-ninth birthday, and as the only full-time ethicist at EDS I hold department-meetings-of-one each day. Being a member of a seminary community that has both master of arts and doctor of ministry degree programs in feminist liberation theology and ministry inspired my creation of womanist ways of teaching. Also, it was particularly encouraging to work with and among White women colleagues who are feminist liberationist scholars in their own fields of study. As the only African American woman with a full-time position among the nine seminary faculties in the Boston consortium known as the Boston Theological Institute (BTI), I was the womanist that seminarians studied with if they wanted to give sustained theological articulation to both the transcendent moments and the usable truths from the everyday life of African American women.

Thus, the challenge for me as a womanist ethicist in a graduate school of theology (as I realized within my first semester of teaching) was that there would be a core of students who would enroll in every course I taught. In order not to be redundant or risk becoming a bore, I decided to create a different procedure and working concept for each of the seven courses, originating from the seven wheel spokes radiating from the hub of Beverly Harrison's "dance of redemption" (see the diagram on p. 140). These seven methodologies enable seminarians to teach themselves what they need to know about ethics. Hence, the heuristic nature of womanist pedagogy means that students use cognitive, self-educating exploratory processes to discern mechanisms of exploitation and identity patterns that must be altered in order for justice to occur (see the two sample course assignments on pp. 141–43).

The students generate the energy that moves the three-level wheel of discourse by actively seeking and naming the cognitive dissonance they experience in their belief systems, lifestyles, and/or behavior. This type of pedagogy is designed to make seminarians self-conscious and deliberate learners who continually confront the contestability of life's contradictions. The emancipatory historiography requirements — which

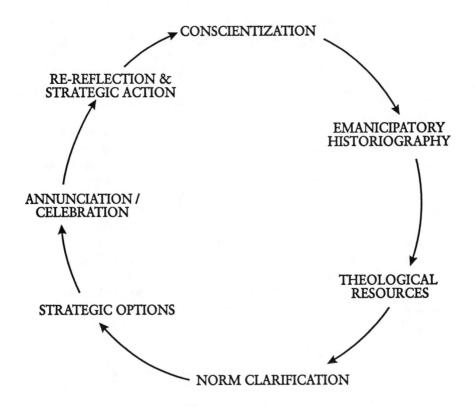

encourage students to question whose experience is validated, what
groups are left out, what ideology accompanies the analysis, and what
framework provides meaning and holds conflicting elements together —
sharpen their analytical skills so that they see how particular death-
dealing situations arose and how they affect our lives and the life of our
communities. By consistently applying an ever-developing liberationist
rationale to classroom discussions, we do not waste time rehashing what
is already known. We begin with those concerns about God, the world,
and neighbor that are genuinely problematic and confusing. The refec-
tory as well as the library are alive with the hum of erons[11] as students
reflect on their work of demystifying the dominating and chauvinistic
Christian heritage in order to act more effectively as empowered agents
of faith.

It is essential that class discussions be structured so that the dialectic
of metalogue can be apprehended. I use the data gathered in assessment questionnaires and in the race, sex, class inventories to design my
lectures and to facilitate class discussions. The trick is to encourage a
certain movement toward conscientization without squelching others.

Like Ann Berthoff, I too have learned to come to class not thinking of a territory to be covered but with a compass to point the metalogical direction for a community of critically conscious ethicists.[12]

Womanist teaching is interactive. I read students' papers the way I read letters: to learn. I conduct a running dialogue in the margins of each paper, suggesting supplemental readings, challenging students to find their ethical voice and to develop a method of moral reasoning that will stand them in good stead in any situation. The chief pedagogical value of weekly community announcements, lecture-note handouts (students have called them "opaque transparencies"), conscientization exercises, written course requirements, and an end-of-each-course annunciation/ celebration ceremony is to encourage seminarians to see how they can embrace what Beverly Harrison calls a faith praxis that transforms life in the direction of nonalienating experience. The overall objective of this work implies moral notions about obligations, values, and virtues characterized by benevolent cohumanity and sacred power.[13]

If we were to do mathematical calculations of the womanist pedagogy I am describing, the numbers would compute this way: first, I compress a minimum of twenty-one subjects into seven courses taught over a two-year cycle, with two courses during each fall semester and one course each spring. Next, I teach each course at least three times before I am able to work out all the kinks and, after the sixth time, I start the pedagogical process all over again. Finally, we arrive at the sum that there must be one hour of preparation for every lecture minute and a minimum of three hours of study time for every unit of course credit.

I conclude that liberation ethics is something we *do;* epistemology is accepting the findings we come to *know;* womanist pedagogy is the process by which we bring this kind of knowing about African American women into relation with a justice-praxis for members of our species and the wider environment in which we are situated in order to resist conditions that thwart life, arriving at new understandings of our doing, knowing, and being.

Sample Course Assignment I
DEMYSTIFYING DOMINATION

1. Construct a cognitive map of the "logic" that sets the perimeters for the intelligibility and legitimacy of race, sex, and class oppression. In other words, describe the hierarchical mechanisms of race, sex, and class exploitation to identify the patterns that must be altered in order for justice to occur.

2. Identify a benchmark of deviation from the "logic" of White supremacy. Give an example of how acts of resistance of women and men vary.

3. Unmask the theological rhetoric, especially around issues of clericalization, that supports the complex interstructuring of patriarchal domination in women's lives.

4. Using the list below, assess the ethical rationale for the prevailing means of production.

    - *Deontology:* Divine Will Deontology; Rational Intuitional Deontology; Rule Deontology; Act Deontology; Rational Prescriptivism.

    - *Teleology:* Classic Utilitarianism Teleology; "Good Society" Utilitarianism; Agape Utilitarianism; "Ideal" Consequentialism; Divine Purpose or Utopian Consequentialism; Eschatological Vision.

5. On the basis of surprises in the reading, name the race, sex, and/or class contradictions that deform your life. What new forms can your resistance to these contradictions take?

6. Propose a research topic related to critical theorizing and reflective action that will transform human life in the direction of non-alienating experience for members of our species and the wider environment in which we are set.

Sample Course Assignment II
MODEL FOR ACTION

1. *Problem, hypothesis, or question* (clearly state the focus of your "model for action").

2. *Rationale for the "model for action":* Why is it worthy of responsible action?

3. *Significant prior research:* Mention the success and failure rate of others who have tried similar models; include at least three sources and three book reviews of texts from the recommended bibliography.

4. *Limitations and key assumptions:* This section is useful in defining how much you will undertake; it will also govern your building of the model.

5. *Methodology:* This step-by-step outline should explain the "model for action" as precisely as possible.

6. *Budget:* Plan the coordination of resources and expenditures.

7. *Evaluation:* What tools will you use to explain the conclusions that can be drawn from your data and the implications of your model for the eradication of race, sex, and class oppression?

Chapter 13

Racism and Economics

The Perspective of Oliver C. Cox

My work as a scholar in Christian ethics took a decidedly new turn when I became aware of the White academic community's flourishing publishing monopoly of the writing of Black history, Black thought, and Black worldview. Black scholars did not abdicate their roles in these fields to White academicians. Blacks have written monographs, theses, conference papers, proposals, and outlines for books on various aspects of Black reality since the 1700s, but White publishers did not give them serious consideration until the 1970s.[1]

For years I had concentrated on mastering the spate of books, articles, and pamphlets written *by* Whites *about* Blacks. Suddenly, I was reading in rapid-fire the writings of Black scholars whose biases favored the victims and the survivors of racism.[2] These Black scholars corrected the racist ideologies that assessed a Black person as "three-fifths of a White man." They refused to allow the polarization of information and interpretation of the history of Black people to continue. Instead, they provided data that heightened my sensitivity to *what has been* in direct relationship to the viable possibilities of *what can be*.[3] This research cleared away much ambiguity, revealing an autonomous development of Black cultural traditions, value systems, ideas, and institutional forms.

This turn in my scholarship led me to focus carefully on the varying social theoretical perspectives developed by Black scholars on the dynamics of racism. Not all theories of racism agree as to how to act against it. For instance, Carter G. Woodson (1875–1950), a distinguished Black historian who popularized the field of Black studies, had a nineteenth-century faith in education as the major strategy against racism.[4] He believed wholeheartedly that race relations would improve through increased knowledge. Woodson defined racism as the logical

---

This chapter was first published in *The Public Vocation of Christian Ethics* (New York: Pilgrim Press, 1986).

result of faulty education. Racism, he argued, is the socialized indoctrination of systematic lies that exploit the imperfections of the Black race. It was the inevitable outcome of the tradition of chattel slavery that had become institutionalized through instruction.

For Woodson, racism as mis-education is a conscious and deliberate manipulation of falsehood. Black people are presented as negligible contributors to the substantive interpretation of the world, whereas Whites are depicted as the source of all the worthwhile intellectual accomplishments. Such twisted education presumes that Blacks are not oppressed, but inferior. Brutality and criminality against Blacks are appropriate to their meager talent and limited intellect. For Woodson, racism abounds in assiduous propaganda based on untested opinion and distorted arguments to justify Black exploitation.

Woodson argued that people in the United States are taught from cradle to grave that Blacks are inferior. The assumptions of racist dogmas forcibly handicap Blacks in every walk of life. Whites, as well as Blacks, are imbued with the alleged inherent superiority of Whites and presumed inherent inferiority of Blacks in order to perpetuate White racial power and control. Woodson's numerous writings redress ignorance about Blacks, marshal irrefutable evidence concerning Black life and culture, and restore the most luminous achievements of Blacks as great African people within human civilization. Carter G. Woodson's life and work were dedicated to the affirmation of the Black race as one of the great human races, inferior to none in accomplishment and ability.[5]

George D. Kelsey, a Drew University professor of Christian ethics, developed a theological theory depicting racism as an idolatrous religion and an abortive search for meaning.[6] According to Kelsey, racism emerged as an ideological justification during slavery so that powerful entrepreneurs could continue their political and economic control. The idea of the superior race has been heightened and deepened so that now it points beyond the historical structures of slavery to the conviction that race superiority is ordained by God.

Kelsey contends that racism poses the problem of idol worship in a unique way. The faith character of racism within organized religion divides human beings as human beings. The racist glorifies in the *being* of Whiteness. What the racist scorns and rejects in Black people is precisely their *human beingness*. Millions of men and women gain their sense of power of being from their membership in the so-called superior race. Kelsey pointed out that the fundamental presupposition undergirding racism is that the White race is glorious and pure in its essential being and the Black race, defective and depraved in its essential being. Racism teaches the superior race that the place of Blacks is fixed in the basic *order* of reality. The so-called inferiority of Blacks is not a matter of historical victimization, but is held to be determined in the divine order of creation.

Kelsey argued that racism as idolatrous religion calls into question the nature of divine action itself. God made a creative error in bringing the inferior race into existence. The theological assertion is that God condemned Blacks to be "the hewers of wood and drawers of water, now, henceforth and forever under the curse of Ham."[7] A variation of this doctrine is that Black people share in the universal condemnation of the human race in Adam but bear the added condemnation of God in a special, racial fall as descendants of Cain, the first criminal. Because no promise of renewal and redemption is ever correlated with this second, special fall, racists maintain that Black people are permanent victims of history and ultimately without hope.

The central purpose of this essay is neither to assess Woodson's understanding of racism nor to elaborate Kelsey's thesis of in-group/out-group relations. Rather, I propose to weigh carefully the thesis of another major but little-known theorist, Oliver C. Cox, whose contribution was to relate racism to the economy of U.S. society. Cox maintained that racism must be understood as a historical reality embedded over time specifically in a capitalist mode of political economy, a mode that now has come to control the world. Because he criticized capitalism, Cox has been quickly dismissed and little understood. He was charged with selling out to Karl Marx. Because so many postcapitalistic regimes such as Cuba and Nicaragua have not fully transcended racism, many refuse to reconsider his work. Yet Cox did not believe that social ownership of the means of production would, per se, eradicate racism. He did believe, however, that moving beyond capitalism would be a necessary step in the eradication of White supremacy. I share Cox's conviction that once chattel slavery and White supremacy have become interstructured through capitalist political economy only the elimination of a capitalist mode of production can open the way to making racism dysfunctional. The goals of the chapter, then, are to introduce Cox's perspective and demonstrate dimensions of racism as economic reality that would not be identifiable if this historical interweaving were neglected.

Oliver C. Cox as Social Theorist

Oliver Cromwell Cox, born in Port of Spain, Trinidad, on August 25, 1901, was a premier social theorist, the most systematic expositor of the relationship of economics and race of his era. At age eighteen he came to the United States to work and complete his education. After graduating from the YMCA High School in Chicago, he earned a law degree from Northwestern University in 1928 and two advanced degrees from the University of Chicago, a master's degree in economics in 1932 and a Ph.D. in sociology in 1938. Cox taught for several years at Wiley College in Marshall, Texas, and at Tuskegee Institute in Alabama before joining the faculty at Lincoln University in Jefferson City, Missouri. His position at the time of his death (1974) was at Wayne State University in Detroit.[8]

Although Cox was a prolific writer, he received little of the public recognition he deserved. This was due in large measure to his theoretical and ideological approach as a sociologist. Cox's primary orientation was not toward the reigning paradigm of empirical sociology. Rather, he used a historicocomparative research method that he contended could provide opportunities for genuine theoretical advance. Cox engaged only in hands-on structural observation. He rejected a focus on isolated, observable phenomena. For him, using questionnaires and interviews to assemble opinion and statistical data was helpful only insofar as these methods illumined basic structures for social change. Cox regarded the value of social research to rest in clarifying conceptual definitions that aided in identifying the basic social dynamics operating in society. He was influenced by Karl Marx's contention that only a careful critical historical/structural analysis was genuinely "scientific."

Unlike many social theorists, Cox explicitly spelled out the role of ethics within his own methodological process. He affirmed the duty of the sociologist to unmask views of society that render some as victims. The sociologist must aim to burrow through the complexity of factual material, to discover the actual social process at work, to define these social processes as clearly as possible, and to point to the factors and derive the theory involved in their development. The cogency of his analysis rested on his conclusion that all these responsibilities were aimed at a sociology that was fully historical. The sociologist must remain a maverick historian who gains *critical* historical understanding of how human oppression develops.[9] This is the true goal of social science. Cox summed up his sociological philosophy this way:

> Clearly the social scientist should be accurate and objective but neutral; he should be passionately partisan in favor of the welfare of the people and against the interest of the few when they seem to submerge that welfare. In a word, the reason for the existence of the social scientist is that his scientific findings contribute to the betterment of the people's well-being.[10]

Cox was ostracized by his colleagues because early in his career he challenged not only the method, but also the conceptual formulation of Gunnar Myrdal, the Swedish economist, and his numerous respected Black assistants, such as E. Franklin Frazier, St. Clair Drake, Charles S. Johnson, and Horace Cayton.[11] Cox disagreed with the underlying thesis of *An American Dilemma.* He argued that the crux of racism is not analogous to caste, but to class, that is, to relationships created by how the production of wealth is organized. Racism cannot be reduced merely to prejudice, ancient bigotry, and the strangeness of ethnic differences that the idea of "caste" suggests; rather, racism must be viewed as an inherent part of the basic political economy — the capitalist system.[12] To be sure, racism provided the moral rationale for the subjugation and exploitation of Blacks as "inferior" people, but it was their labor power that had made chattel slavery an irreplaceable necessity to Whites.

> Slave trade did not develop because Indians and Negroes were red and black, or because their cranial capacity averaged a number of cubic centimeters, but simply because they were the best workers to be found for the heavy labor in the mines and plantations across the Atlantic.... *Race relations was not an abstract but rather a practical exploitative relationship with its socioattitudinal facilitation.*[13]

Because Cox stressed the concrete material sources of racism, he was treated as an outcast.

According to Gordan D. Morgan, Oliver C. Cox was all but disbarred from the fraternity of "promising" Black sociologists of the first generation.[14] He was not only highly critical of the race relations hypothesis of Myrdal, but also disagreed vehemently with the noted sociologist Robert E. Park.[15] Morgan contends that Cox paid a high price for this independence of thought because Black peers who worked within the approved theoretical frameworks of White scholars were often given grants. In his earlier years, Cox never received financial support from any foundation for the pursuit of his research. Despite the lack of financial support, Cox continued his work prodigiously and authored four books and numerous articles.[16] With Morgan, I believe that Oliver C. Cox was probably the soundest, most rigorous thinker of the first generation of Black sociologists.

Cox's Central Thesis

It was Oliver C. Cox's thesis that the capitalist mode of political economy is the essential structural problem of contemporary society. As the most powerful and dynamic form of social organization ever created, the capitalist political economy generates a political order that is ostensibly democratic but that leaves economic power unchecked. It also generates a suitable religion to nationalize and loosen all social restraints rooted in mysticism and cultural ritual. In other words, Cox argued that capitalism is a form of social organization in which the distinctive economic

order slowly shapes government and religious structures into a neutral-
ized network of national and territorial units wherein commercial and
exploitative economic relationships can flourish. A body of international
law, traditions, and rules develops that is increasingly weighted in favor
of the most economically powerful individuals and nations. The "mirac-
ulousness" of capital culture, declared Cox, rests in its seeming capacity
to create wealth from nothing. In such a culture, existence comes more
and more to be based purely on the acquisitive instinct. To fill out the details of this thesis, Cox identified eight historical dynamics of a capitalist
society.

    1. *The development of the national-state as sovereign republic.* Cox
pointed out that capitalism creates a political economic order in which
the totality of relationships among groups and individuals is drawn into
interdependence. Such a society comes to have enormous capacity for
cultural assimilation because social interrelations are increasingly conditioned and mediated through the national, political, and economic
order. The people in the society depend significantly on this unified system to teach them their fundamental behavioral patterns and thought
processes. Cox insisted that this learning usually occurs with such fa-
cility and speed from infancy onward that members of the society are
likely to be unaware of their cultural origins outside the system and thus
come to think of their social relations as natural and instinctive. For
instance, "Race prejudice, from its inception became part of the social
heritage, and as such both exploiters and exploited for the most part are
born heirs to it. It is possible that most of those who propagate and defend race prejudice are not conscious of its fundamental motivation."[17]
"Civilization," then, comes to mean one's ability to adjust and integrate
oneself consistently into these patterns and processes.

    2. *The perpetuation of the dominant ideology of the ruling class.* Cox
recognized that power in capitalist civilization tends to be associated
with wealth that is acquired by the economic ingenuity of those who
best exploit relations with foreign peoples. The tendency here is toward
more and more cooperation of the owners of wealth in pursuit of oppor-
tunistic foreign transactions. According to Cox, capitalists must trade or
perish. Foreign commerce and territorial expansion are indispensable to
a capitalist nation, which must expand or collapse.

    In Cox's view, cooperative expansion abroad, together with the con-
flict of interest of economic groups within the domestic economy, calls
for "rules" and so-called impartial leadership. The president of the
United States supposedly embodies power as the head of state "of, by,
and for the people." Yet ultimate power in capitalist political economy actually resides increasingly in a ruling class.[18] Cox contended that
this ruling class has openly taken over the national legislature. It has
achieved such a degree of consistency between economic power and the

law that it has won outright government protection of and assistance to private economic interests. The welfare of the state is now fully identified with the interests of the wealthy class. Everything else is subordinate to the prosperity of the wealthiest business people and to the welfare of the commercial class as a whole. Contrary to ideology, Cox notes, this group has assumed the unquestioned leadership of the nation. Their control of taxation, judiciary, and the armed forces gives them free access to all political processes so that capitalist power grows commensurate with the capitalist control of wealth. Cox contends that the changes made from time to time in government increasingly support the aspirations and power of business-oriented families. The consensus of business executives *becomes* national policy in a capitalist system, with the result that the interest of the ruling class becomes de facto the interest of the "public."[19]

In terms of Cox's economic analysis, capitalist political economy necessitates a relatively elaborate system of civil, criminal, and international law. The laws regulating property and commerce set the direction of all other relationships. The sanctity of property predominates, with the result that severe penalties always are attached to thefts but not always to crimes of violence against persons. Individuals may gain rights but only in relation to the rules of business transactions, e.g., child labor laws, sanitary and food inspection laws. Cox observes the ways in which the judicial system is administered so that there is no appreciable participation of the masses in the administration of justice, to say nothing of revolt or serious objection to laws that disadvantage them.

Nor do all citizens have the same status in a capitalist society. Participation at the top is a valuable privilege controlled by an elite who makes room only for the social mobility of a few. Cox claimed that only those who emerge as active, self-seeking, "responsible" individuals with a direct material interest in the state and a passionate allegiance to the country and its dominant ideology come to be granted access to mobility. Such in-group identification and the privileges that it affords are selectively lavished on a small portion of the population. It is maintained by an invidious controlling attitude that is exclusive, proud, and defiant. Cox argued that the heart of racist privilege is sustained by the reality that the control of wealth and profits (not merely wages) from capital is for White citizens only.[20]

Cox argued that the economic structure of a culture tends to have a prominent role in the attribution of social status. It was his thesis that a salient trait of capitalist culture is the way in which honor is distributed or denied by this system of wealth control. Because wealth acquired through commerce is *the* fundamental status-giving factor, capitalist societies have the persistent tendency of making rich families richer in order to reinforce upper-class status as an exclusive coterie of privileged participants. The appearance that prosperity is widely shared by all the people is one of the features of capitalism that reinforces loyalty to it despite growing control by a few.

Cox argued that there is a close relation between the continual need for news and information and the development of the capitalist system. Thus learning, in all its forms — especially the arts and sciences — is readily available for privileged citizens in capitalist society. The extension of education enables more people to gain access to information about social conditions, changes in various trading areas, war, famine, deaths, births, marriages, and weather conditions, but education and information are shaped by the ideology of the dominant groups.

3. *Integrated diplomacy — the new institution of capitalist society.* Cox identified a third characteristic of the evolution of capitalist political economy: the development of integrated global diplomacy. One of the prime necessities of capitalist commerce is the maintenance of order in international relations so that economic activity is not impeded. Because capitalist nations reap their greatest harvests in stable political environments, a capitalist political economy evolves toward diplomacy as a permanent formal institution. Cox's explanation of integrated diplomacy as a new institution implies that diplomatic bureaucracies — ambassadors and consulates — function chiefly to tie countries of the world into a web of commercial relations, defined by treaties centered in the sovereign republic that they represent. The fine art of diplomacy becomes more and more important to foster the industrial and commercial interests of nation-states. U.S. ambassadors, he noted, deal on the highest level with foreign rulers concerning matters of broad economic scope, but they also take care of practical matters, including the detailed adjustment needed to carry out the terms of treaties.

Cox located the basis of capitalist control of foreign people not in the need to facilitate exchange, but in the need to sell goods abroad. Profit-making, commercial exploitation, business practices not tolerated at home work better abroad, and weak nations are virgin soil for the capitalist, providing a relatively noncompetitive market and lack of experience in resisting the commercial organization that produces goods to be consumed. Because the entire domestic economic structure depends on the success of foreign trade, ambassadors and consuls function to bring other nations under the exploitative hammer of national corporations. A careful observer of the activities of our diplomatic service, Cox concluded that it was regularly overhauled and reorganized to support business more efficiently.

4. *The necessity of religious tolerance.* Cox also emphasized that capitalist society requires a nationally oriented church, one unmastered by foreign power or cultures not Americanized. Religion must become

virtually inseparable from capitalist philosophical assumptions, science, and economic thinking. In other words, religion must be subordinated to economic interests so that nothing challenges the dictum that "wealth in a capitalist society should be made to produce more wealth."[21] Religious scruples against wealth and worldly activity must cease to interfere with the unconstrained enhancement of material welfare. Cox insisted that under capitalism the separation of church and state comes to *mean* that the state subjects the church to conditions friendly to our national political economy.

Cox stressed that capitalism must be extremely tolerant in religious matters. There is no problem in permitting divergent sects to worship in relative freedom, and, in fact, religious tolerance is helpful in attracting the best laborers from other countries who are fleeing religious persecution. Such tolerance has been a principal means of gaining a nation populous in labor resources. However, whenever the religious practices of a group prove to be inimical to capitalist economic welfare, the system is quick to show displeasure and to discriminate. The "civil utility of tolerance,"[22] is rooted in economic need, which also means that, historically, pressure accelerates to assure that religious teachings become consistent with national economic purpose.

In Cox's view, a capitalist nation seeks order for commercial expansion but expects war. Peace is espoused as a primary value, but the ruthless processes of foreign relations shaped by economic penetration inevitably create hostilities that lead to war. Both diplomacy and a willingness and capacity to fight to open up new markets, to keep markets accessible, to eliminate serious competitors, or to quell the resistance of weaker nations must be maintained. "Besides wars for the protection of 'the life line,' all sorts of territories have to be acquired by the capitalist on terms which are seldom if ever fully congenial to the natives. Ultimate settlement ordinarily relied upon force."[23] The perennial obsession of capitalist nations, so Cox maintained, is monopoly of commercial opportunities. Supremacy in military power determines dominion in world markets, and such supremacy becomes a preoccupation.

Thus militarism is a consequence of the system of commodity exchange that must be defended from the sporadic moral attacks on it, attacks that arise principally from the church. In Cox's view, capitalism largely has succeeded in deflating and harnessing the intractable cultural forces of religion that oppose military expenditure and war. It is also of the utmost importance to recognize that in a capitalist culture welfare institutions emerge in abundance. Many presume that "big business" society deserves credit for providing pure water, a clean city, care for the sick and poor, an organized system of inspectors and police, protection from dishonest merchants, attention to the wounded in time of war and peace, pensioning of retired civil servants, provisions for widows and orphans, free legal aid for the defenseless, and permanent health offices. In Cox's view, these are all pretentious manifestations of humanitarianism or, at best, concessions to domestic discontent, aimed to adjust conditions to make capitalist political economy appear to provide a respected way of life. Most capitalists believe that decent working conditions and humane treatment of workers are incompatible with optimal profit-making. Business people use the ingenious manipulations available to finance and industry to seduce the church into serving as an indispensable component of the legitimating structure of the dominant political economy. The ideology of capitalism, in which profit often is maintained by force, manipulation, and fraud, is usually couched in some form of Christian teaching, appealing to the Bible as its apparent source of inspiration.[24] The expansion of capitalism is portrayed as virtually assuring the expansion of Christianity and vice versa.

Cox was further convinced that religion increasingly serves as a primary instrument of social control. The church, Cox noted, is where common people are disciplined: there they are taught in the name of God to obey and respect authority and to accept the society as they find it. The church functions to encourage members to transfer faith to greater reliance on the efficacy of science and engineering. Thus capitalists come to consider Christianity a priceless cultural possession.

5. *Capitalist "freedom": the right to choose capitalist values.* Since the Industrial Revolution, Cox argued, there has been an increasing dependence under capitalism on new and improved modes of production. The urge to invent new technology is a strong and persistent dynamic of this mode of economy. Technology also reduced the dependency of the economy on humans, animals, seasons, and geography. Cox insisted that accelerated exploitation of resources on a worldwide scale enhances the unconstrained freedom and power of the dominant capitalist community. Capitalist economy is a congenial milieu for inventive activity and treasures the reservoir of industrial know-how. In short, it aims to carry out the exploitation of both workers and machines as systematically and efficiently as possible. "Freedom" in society is chiefly of the sort that serves the efficiency of production.

Cox recognized that the greater the dependence of a society on its industrial sector, the greater the likelihood of resistance to such exploitation, chiefly through the appearance of determined resistance of labor and its organization. He judged that unionization stemmed from a growing consciousness among workers that their interests differed fundamentally from those of owners and that status as workers would be permanent. The principal goals of trade unions needed to be increasing wages and bettering conditions of work on one hand and gaining governmental power for political leaders supportive of labor on the other.

Union "freedom" would be curtailed, he thought, whenever the success of organized workers seriously interfered with maximizing profits.

6. *The inevitable dynamics of Third World imperialism.* Cox was among the first to stress that the emergent structure of the capitalist world market system had its indispensable anchor in Third World countries. Cox conceived imperialism as being grounded in economic subservience. Defined by the degree of their economic value, Third World peoples are considered appendages in reference to labor, raw materials, and the requirements of manufacturing. To this system, the most valuable people of color are those most completely and contentedly exploitable. In Cox's estimate, commerce is not only a less costly means than war to ravish a people, but it is also regarded by capitalists as being far more effective in that it brings the world's peoples within the orbit of the dominant capitalist nations, bringing them "civilization."

Cox long argued that it always would be considered a cardinal offense to capitalist nations for Third World people to withdraw from the system of capitalist political economy. Cox claimed that, in fact, the most ferocious and spectacular capitalist wars have been and would continue to be fought out as a struggle for leadership in African, Asian, and Latin American countries. To bring the argument down to particulars, Cox maintained that when Third World nations tried to extricate themselves, violence was brought to bear and that this attests to the vital importance of their resources and markets within the global system. It is clear that Cox regarded the stakes of war to be the control of the economic life of the world.

Cox argued that the only remedy yet discovered by capitalist democracies for unemployment was *total war.* Only in war and the preparation for war could capitalists secure full employment by socialization of demand without socialization of production.[25] Everything relates, here as elsewhere, to exploitation for profit. Government spending for military purposes, usually referred to as national security, increased consumption but did nothing to distribute wealth. The profits went to private producers. The threat of war, Cox asserted, provided a capitalist rationale for stockpiling. Because no one knows the moment when maximum military danger may occur, the nation must perpetually engage in military buildup and live in a state of military emergency. Many domestic industries come to rely on government protection and military spending, believing that the state should underwrite their success. Aircraft and automobile production, shipbuilding, mining, and even watchmaking and agriculture are secured by government purchases and supports, especially in the interest and name of national defense.

The linkage between capitalist economy and national emergency was characterized by Cox in several ways. First, defense industries are used to stabilize the domestic economy, for example, by shifting spending to economically depressed areas or by purchasing from private enterprise services that traditionally were rendered by military personnel. Globally, the government uses military aid to bolster its economy by selling productive facilities, including war industries, to Third World countries. For Cox, military outlays assume strategic economic significance.

Cox believed that the United States had become the most powerful and incontestable national leader to emerge from centuries of capitalist development. The United States now stands at the center of an international structure, resting on a broad base of economically underdeveloped countries. The U.S. internal economy is inseparably tied into this world system not only through its progressive dependence on military expenditures, but also in its ever-growing exploitation of Third World people.

Linking past and present, Cox traced the way in which the United States emerged as the world leader in technological innovation and mechanical production. He contended that by 1914 the United States had made its superb national resources accessible to extensive exploitation, stimulated foreign trade outlets, established a flexible system of protective tariffs, received financial assistance from older nations, and developed a magnificent network of transportation and communication.[26] Cox documented the way in which American businessmen during World War I moved quickly into areas of weakened competition to sew up postwar control of markets. Latin America was a major target, especially attractive because it would never be a U.S. competitor in iron, steel, and kindred industries; nor would it be able to satisfy its domestic demands for such products.[27] After World War I, Cox insisted, capitalist leaders embarked on a more complete and pervasive integration of U.S. domestic production with production in Third World countries, thereby continually increasing U.S. reliance on foreign economic relations for stability of its own economy. Cox insisted that certain indispensable imports were provided by Africa, Asia, and Latin America: wool, silk, fibers, cotton, rubber, hides, ores (including copper, manganese, tin, and nitrates), sugar, coffee, tea, cocoa, and fruits. He argued that imperialist greed was reflected in U.S. control of these major raw materials in the world market.

Cox also documented the manner in which U.S. control of important markets for manufacturing goods was secured through large investments in the very foreign projects calling for use of those goods.[28] The United States purchased essential raw materials from Third World countries and returned them as semi-luxury or nonessential manufactured goods. The more debt Third World countries incurred by borrowing from the United States, the greater was the sale of U.S. products abroad. Cox observed that to enhance the purchasing power of its customers, it was necessary to grant loans to enable them to make further purchases of

U.S. commodities. "If you want our money, you must buy our goods."[29] The "capitalist mind," he claimed, required indoctrination of the public in the principles of international commerce. A convinced public, psychologically invested in commerce, influenced Congress to give more direct aid or loans to enlarge opportunities for foreign investment and commerce.

This pattern of economic dependency was also reinforced by militarism. Military expenditure constituted an essential part of the national budget, and military consignments to Third World countries were seen as a form of economic aid. To receive such aid from the United States, Third World countries had to encourage the flow of production and foreign investment. Governments might use such aid for public services — health, education, sanitation, and agricultural techniques — but could not use it for industrial development. The U.S. military programs gave large grants for equipment and training in Third World countries, and our government induced these countries to make strenuous contributions for "defense" from their limited resources. All such economic aid serves as a brake on social transformation. The thrust of Cox's insight lies in his perception that defense spending is the central thrust and urgent concern of the United States, not of Third World peoples themselves. For Cox, then, the very act of enhancing the war machine of Third World nations was designed to keep capitalist nations technologically and commercially ahead.

7. *Racism as justification for continuing capitalist control.* Cox's elaboration of these dynamics of economic control are of utmost significance, both for understanding the subsequent development of his thought and for grasping his contribution to economic and race analysis. Cox's theses have been sustained again and again since the end of World War II. Since then, American political economic elites have acted as if they believed themselves authorized to arrange, order, and guide the destiny of the global system — a duty that has even included responsibility for the internal stability of the European nations. "Never in modern times has the economic destiny of the peoples of the world so rested within the hands of one nation."[30] Nearly all the world's primary natural resources now serve the needs of the central capitalist economy.

Cox's goal was to demonstrate how the reality of Third World self-development and self-determination would run counter to the notion of development conceived as an auxiliary to expansion of the core capitalist system. Cox focused on the fact that a concentrated attempt must be made by the core system to breed universal contempt for those people exploited by the system.[31] The constant theme in Cox's work was that racist ideology is the ingredient that assured a favorable climate for capitalist development, a pattern of "development" that must be congenial to capitalist interest. The heart of Cox's analysis of racism is that capitalist-imperialist penetration of the world must use racist ideology to assure that "backward peoples" will "allow" themselves to develop gradually under the continued tutelage of private business enterprise.[32] Cox's most penetrating insight is that what this system requires is the belief that capitalists have the right to hold people of color in subjection until they are "civilized." They do not use their power to expedite the process of Third World people's capacity to govern themselves because aspirations for self-determination lead to unrest and demands for further emancipation. Against this background, Cox added that the United States invests money and effort to demonstrate to Third World nations that racism is *not* an intrinsic attitudinal component of capitalism.[33]

Cox recognized and emphasized that a major challenge for the United States was to hold Third World countries within the orbit of the existing political economic system. It was incumbent that they develop according to the processes of private enterprise. The newer form of capitalist development now being encouraged, Cox recognized, is subtler and more poisonous than the old colonialism because it masquerades under the guise of nationalist self-development. In the name of national independence, Third World peoples are persuaded to surrender their desire for freedom to their own emerging national security states and to economic "progress." U.S. policy presumes that the ultimate desire of Third World countries is to become miniatures of the United States and that their people could want or deserve nothing more.

In order to keep the threat of self-government at a minimum, Third World rulers are amply rewarded for their collaboration. In exchange for providing labor and land, the primary production processes are now moved to some Third World countries, which also become markets for finished products. In exchange for what these nations provide, native rulers receive an extraordinary return, which allows them to maintain the services of large retinues of servants and police. This arrangement is reinforced by the vastly superior military might of the United States.

8. *The accelerating exploitation of Black people and people of color.* Finally, we must focus on and critically assess Cox's view of the meaning of racism within this structural dynamic. For this social theorist, race relations in a capitalist society must be understood basically as an aspect of labor relations. Cox's unshakable conclusion is that Blacks have always occupied and will continue to occupy the lowest rungs of the labor hierarchy. Racism cannot be eliminated *unless* this division of labor is broken. Domestically, employers will work to depress Black wages, to restrict Blacks to poor working conditions, and to limit job opportunities. Globally, African populations will remain the poorest of the poor.

The central and basic issue is that under a capitalist political economy, Blacks cannot achieve more than second-class citizenship. Capitalists are critical to the spread of racial antagonism. The rich do not overtly suppress the development of the masses of non-White people because the belief that there is room for social mobility must be sustained. Nevertheless, the biological difference of color provides the dominant class with a concrete symbol to which fear of failure and projective hate can be anchored. The dominant group's control of the media enables a subtle, but direct, derogatory and discriminatory propaganda against Black people to continue. At the same time, a paternalistic relationship toward the masses of Black people has come to be the traditional pattern of dealing with Black life and culture. In light of this analysis, it is no mystery why Cox believed that the aristocracy of the capitalist system preserved its interests in cheap, tractable Black labor by establishing control over a single, provincial political party dedicated to perpetuating that system.[34] Cox reiterated the point by citing the many ways in which the capitalist political economy abrogated the fundamental citizenship rights of Blacks, ways that leave Black people brutalized, slanderized, and peonized, virtually helpless both socially and economically.

He insisted that the more that Black laborers are used within the capitalist productive system, the greater is the opportunity to "seize" surplus value and maximize profits because Black wage labor is easily exploited. Black workers have always been paid lower wages than their White counterparts. The surplus produced by their labor has been appropriated without giving Blacks even the limited return that White workers receive. Exploitation results from the demand for harder work, from lowering wages paid to Blacks, or by enhancing productivity through technological change that can easily be imposed on vulnerable Black workers. The Black worker can be subjected to the full force of entrepreneurial exploitation even more ruthlessly than the White workers. The maximum use of Black labor as a factor of production enhances the employer's welfare, not the welfare of Black people. Black exploitation indeed makes capitalism profitable for owners of the means of production.[35]

The insight at the heart of Cox's social theory is that an ideology of White supremacy bolsters and reinforces America's leadership of the world capitalist system.[36] Racial superiority is fundamental to the wiser capitalists ethos wherein White citizens may identify with the system by looking down with ill-disguised contempt on people of other races. Racism, race antagonism, and the illusion of mobility are not only compatible with but also contribute to the successful functioning of capitalist society. Cox's work abounds with statements that capitalist historical development shapes a specific, distinctive, and *virulent* modality of racism.

Racial exploitation and race prejudice developed among Europeans with the rise of capitalism and nationalism and because of
the worldwide ramifications of capitalism, all racial antagonists
can be traced to the policies and attitudes of the leading capitalist
people, the white people of Europe and North America.[37]

Elsewhere he claims:

The stability of color and inertness of culture together with effective control over firearms, subsequently made it possible for whites
to achieve a more or less separate and dominant position even in
the homeland of colored peoples.... It is probable that without
capitalism, a cultural chance occurrence among whites, the world
might never have experienced race prejudice.[38]

Chattel slavery was an extreme institutional expression of capitalist
exploitation. The frightful principle of capitalism — private ownership
of the means of production, including labor — dictated that the greater
the need for Black labor, the greater would be Black subjugation. Black
people not only had to be kept poor, but they had to be themselves
owned by Whites. As slaves, they received no pay. To assure their "happiness" under these meanest of circumstances, Blacks had also to be
kept ignorant. Laws were passed making it illegal for Blacks to read
and write. Cox's genius is reflected in his recognition and insistence that
racism is always nurtured by economics and cannot be separated from
relations of economic dependency.[39]

Cox's interpretation was that after slavery was formally ended,
Southern Whites gradually regained monopoly power over the constitutionally freed labor supply and relegated Black people to non-
citizenship. Cox traced the way in which Whites controlled Blacks
chiefly by extralegal mob violence, by intimidation, by distortion of
truth, by cheating, by economic boycott, by undermining efforts by and
for Black education, and by total control of political processes. No room
was left for debate.

In 1957, Cox pointed out that not a single piece of civil rights legislation had passed the U.S. Senate for more than eighty years. Southern
demagoguery reigned supreme. He reminded his readers that Senator
James Eastland had pledged support for White supremacy throughout
eternity.

Stressing that racism was a structured dimension of modern capitalist
political economy, Cox nevertheless was not at all reluctant to denounce
the virulent power of racism as a social force. For Cox, democracy for
Blacks was always an anti-capitalist movement.[40] The equation of capitalist exploitation and racism offered him a way of making sense of
basic sociohistorical facts. He flatly predicted that economic elites and

their political allies would invariably identify every attempt to secure citizenship rights for Blacks as Communist activity. If Cox's thesis is correct, then seeking human rights for Blacks is always to engage in "cold war" activity against the reigning class that controls society.

Conclusions from Cox's Analysis

Oliver C. Cox understood racism to be a dynamic historical structure — an intrinsic economic reality that enabled Whites to monopolize economic power through demagoguery and to use military power, laws, and ideology to assure the dependency of the majority of humans. Thus manifest destiny required that the leaders of capitalist nations control and guide the people of color, still too "backward" to be allowed self-determination, for the good of the whole.

The virulence of modern racism gets its distinctive shape from the capitalist structure of labor exploitation. The suppression and mistreatment of Black people is maintained despite its malevolence and its moral dubiousness because it serves the needs of this system. Racism rationalizes the enslavement and oppression of people of color. The racial supremacy of Whites is a lie that keeps its legitimacy because it has been used, widely and profitably, to justify the subjugation of people of color on grounds that they are inherently inferior.

Oligarchic economic power uses racial inferiority as justification for cruelty, discrimination, even wholesale murder. The U.S. political economy has always denied Blacks full access to the democratic process because genuine democracy is incompatible with the best interests and highest profits of business entrepreneurs. Self-aggrandizing social choices, including increased investment of profits in high-yield ventures, always have the result of further entrapping the Black community in poverty and disease. Racism supports the belief, conscientiously held, that poverty and ignorance sustained by force and fraud are desirable for people of color and that White power and prestige must remain at any cost.

The form of Christianity shaped by obeisance to economic interests of a capitalist system is a new form of Christianity, one that legitimates exploitation. This type of exploitative religious rationale accommodates to all sorts of social ruthlessness so long as profits increase. Christianity conflated to the dominant system invariably rejects the claim that the essence of the gospel mandate is liberation of the oppressed. Instead, a form of capitalist Christianity combines defense of the sanctity of the economic system with racial and theological conformity. Such Christianity separates the spiritual person from the bodily person and calls on people to be spiritual and avoid politics. The freedom and radical human equality professed in early Christian proclamations are assimilated into the propagation of a capitalist worldview. In Cox's formulation, the implicit liberating power of religion is supplanted by the more profitable social principal of fundamental racial difference. Thereby the church sanctions and stabilizes the mundane interests of the ruling class. The dominant churches continue to be the ominous symbol of White dominance.

Oliver C. Cox insisted that racism becomes an unquestioned dictum of history and literature to assure the persistence and expansion of existing economic arrangements and to give continuous reign and recognition to White supremacy. The myth of racial inferiority enables capitalist governments, economic organizations, and financial structures to penetrate the world. The hatred and fear of people of color now has developed into a global system of ideological subjugation, justifying the legitimacy of control of Third World countries through massive debt, monopoly industry, and direct military imperialism.

Exposing My Home Point of View

All the Black people lived together in Fishertown. It was named after a man who used to get drunk all the time and the White people would say, "Well, let's take Fisher home. Let's go over to Fishertown." Everybody in the community is kin to the Cannons. They had been sharecroppers all in Mecklinburg County when they moved off the Cannon plantation and then came to Kannapolis and eventually went to work in Cannon Mills. My mother's family took pride in being house servants and the Cannons were field hands, so that whole slave tradition carried over, and still does to this day — the part of the uppityness and her marrying beneath herself when she married these field people who didn't want much more than a good time, a good party, and good food. Eat, drink, and be merry. My daddy could not read or write except his name, which he practiced all the time. My mother's people were all in the church and thought of themselves as educated.

When I was growing up, there was only one paved road and that was our road, Charlie Walker Road. White people lived at one end and all the Black people lived in the middle. At the other end of the road, a White man lived in a big house right in the curve. His name was Charlie Walker. So they said, "Well, what we going to name this road?" Charlie Walker Road, that's what they called it. He used to walk down his road all the time. We'd say, "There goes Mr. Charlie Walker." Our house had a fence around it, between it and the other houses on each side. Daddy's baby brother, Uncle Sam, lived next door to Grandpa across the street, who lived next door to Aunt Emma. So you had a whole row of families and everybody went back and forth running between yards all the time. Fishertown had about thirty families in it. That was the Cannons and their offsprings.

My grandmother's name was Cora Witherspoon Cannon. I loved my Grandmother Cora. She was a sharecropper and had married a man by

This chapter was first published in Victoria Byerly, *Hard Times Cotton Mill Girls: Personal Histories of Womanhood and Poverty in the South* (ILR Press, 1986), 26–39.

the name of Dan Cannon. His family had been slaves on the Cannon cotton plantation, which later became Cannon Cotton Mills. They had twelve or thirteen kids. She had one by the sharecropper so there was one White child in the family. Grandma Cora was a tall woman, like an African queen, and tenderhearted.

Grandma Cora Cannon lived right across the road from us, and because my father, Esau, was an identical twin with his brother Jacob, they were like the favorites. They were the only ones that didn't drink. Several of my aunts and uncles have died of alcoholism. The twins were the favorites and so their children were the favorites, and we were the only ones on the whole Cannon side of the family who went to Scotia Seminary.

Grandma Cora didn't believe that we had to share every stick of chewing gum like my mother did, so going to her house was always like a splurge. She had bottled drinks and she'd have two or three kinds of meat at one meal, while we only believed in having one chicken. We'd have one chicken for nine people. She believed that nobody should ever be hungry. She didn't stress style or education; she stressed the way you shared your love and wealth with people. Who you are, your status, was shown by having food, good food. She always had three meats and always had googobs of dessert, and you didn't have to share. To share was to show poverty. Everybody could have their own, and that was totally against my mother's teachings. I just loved Grandma Cora, and because we were Esau's kids she had a great deal of respect for us too. We didn't get to go over there often even though she lived just across the road from us. My mother kept saying we were different from the rest of the Cannons. We were the educated side. She wanted us to be more like her side of the family.

Grandma Cora would say to Grandpa Dan, "Dan, go upstairs and knock Rufus down three times." So he'd go upstairs and you'd hear BOOM, BOOM, BOOM. Then he'd come back downstairs and say, "Cora, what did I do that for?" Rufus was my daddy's brother and he was always getting into trouble, stuff like stealing meat out of the brothers' and sisters' freezer. See, my grandmother was taller than my grandfather, and whenever she didn't get her way then she'd fake a heart attack. Then we'd call the White doctor, Dr. Nolan, to come out to the Black community, and try to coax him to come. Everybody would be on alert. "Well, is she living or dying?" She always lived, just hadn't got her way. She was spoiled. My family took care of her until she died when I was eight.

My mother lived with the Cannons when she and my daddy first got married. They never liked my mother. They didn't think she was good enough for my father. He being so special to his brothers and sisters, Mama wasn't light-skinned enough. Uncle Jacob married a high-yellow woman, so three of his kids are very light-complexioned. Then we came along dark-skinned with nappy hair. That wasn't the way it was supposed to be. Whenever Daddy and Mama would argue about something, he would always go over across the street to his mother's and that would upset my mother so much.

The Cannons partied a lot and two of my aunts were bootleggers. The Cannons were always carousing and driving into ditches on Saturday night, cutting up, and my mother just had greater dreams for us. Our county was totally dry, so you had to go up to Rowan County, and they'd get about four or five cases of beer to sell. They'd get it for thirty-five cents a can and sell it for seventy-five cents a can. People would come to my aunt's house and buy beer, chitlins, pickled eggs, and hot sausages. She'd have this food all cooked up and so people would buy food and drink all night long. They'd have liquor too. The whole house became a juke joint on Friday night. This was Aunt Tot's and Aunt Sis's houses. Their houses were spotless during the week, and Aunt Tot's house was the homeplace; that's where Grandpa and Grandma Cannon lived. Everybody was always over there, all the grandkids, all the brothers and sisters and sisters-in-law. You'd come home and eat and you'd have to go over by the house and see about the folk. It was a big house with a lot of cushion chairs in the living room and in the den. Then, it was the biggest house I knew. The house would stay the same when the different clientele came. There was an upright piano and there were these big overstuffed arm chairs like World War II furniture. In every space in the house there was a couch or a chair. Lots of pictures that had a blue and green tint to them of family people, but I never knew who they were. Later on there were always pictures of Martin Luther King, Jr., and the Kennedy brothers. A lot of knickknacks, glass horses, glass chickens, ashtrays, and vases. Everywhere there was a place to sit and a table top with doilies. Now Aunt Sis had a serious juke joint. Hers was down in the basement with tables, a juke box, and a bar and stools, and there would be cushion chairs down there too. I always wondered why my mother never had scars. They all had scars where people had cut them, and I thought these scars were like African tribal marks. I used to think Ma was deprived because she didn't have any scars.

I loved my aunts. They were so kind to us. They were both heavy set, brown-skinned, and cuss, oh God, they could cuss. Go worship on Sunday though and put beaucoup money in the church. They were so proud of us because we were Esau's kids. When we came around they would try to put on their best manners and they were always trying to feed us. "Eat, eat. We gon' get these little skinny kids to eat. Eat!" We weren't used to people shoving food at us like that. Most of the time, we'd get sick 'cause we'd overeat. Egg custard, pecan pie, pound cake, all the fried chicken you wanted, all the potato salad you wanted, all the green beans, pork chops, homemade biscuits all the time, butter, butter, butter, and buttermilk and cornbread with cracklin'. Always ate high on the hog. My mother was always into nutrition and had gone to the clinic and learned how to eat prunes and oatmeal, and that kind of food at my aunts' houses wasn't supposed to be good for us. My mother was very body conscious and she didn't want us to be fat. When we reached adolescence, she said, "Why can't y'all be petite? Why'd I have to have these big old grown girls?"

My other grandmother, Grandma Rosie, was born in 1882. She lived with us all my life until she died. Her name was Rosa Cornelia White Lytle. She had one sister named Anna. Because her mother, Polly, had died when Rosie was an infant, she was passed from relative to relative. Grandma Rosie was the smartest one in her class. She loved education, she loved reading, she loved writing and making things. One of her greatest prides was that she had never worked for a White person. Never in her whole life. She was ashamed that my mother worked as a domestic and that we were being trained to be domestics. She was just a very thrifty, ingenious woman who believed in her home. She crocheted, she sewed, made things from scratch — made her patterns out of newspaper — and all the curtains in her house had to be starched. Booker T. Washington and George Washington Carver had stayed in her home. When famous Black people would come through, they would have to stay with Black people. Because she was Mr. Manuel's wife — that's what she always called her husband because he was seventeen years older than her — then her home was the centering place.

My grandfather's name was Emmanuel Lytle and my aunt described him as a Martin Luther King. He had worked and saved until he got his land. When the Whites took his land he had a nervous breakdown. It was good bottom land and they wanted it so they just took the deed and said he didn't own any land. So he came home one day and said, "I'm done for." And that was it, he broke. He couldn't fight it. He couldn't get his land back, so he had a breakdown, got pneumonia, and died. My great-grandmother Mary had instilled in him how much it meant that he was her only free child, so to lose that land was to lose his freedom. He couldn't deal with it. That was in the 1920s when that happened.

My grandfather had ten children by his first wife and then he married Rosa and they had ten children. Five of hers lived. His first ten children were almost as old as she. Rosa was a kind mother who mothered these stepchildren as well as her own.

After all her children had left home, my mother brought her back to our house, where she lived until she died. She was the one who greased our faces everyday with Vaseline and combed our hair. She was a very gentle woman. She had a hump on her back, a wind is what they called it. She had always had it. She had crippled hands from arthritis, but I didn't even know they were deformed until sometimes children wouldn't take candy from her. She'd scratch her hair, "Oooh," she'd say, "it's like lice up here." So we'd all of us get in there and be scratching her head. She would let me comb her hair until it was real soft. I've gotten the comb tangled in her hair so many times and we'd have to cut that part out. She'd never get upset. She'd say, "It's all right, it's all right." It would do us such an honor to comb her hair, put her stockings on when she got out of the bed, grease her legs, and walk her to church. I learned a lot about patience, a lot about just what it means to be a human being.

My Grandma Rosa was a thinker, and she used to make us pronounce words correctly. If we said, "I wone some mo'," "Mo'?" she asked, "Morrre!" She was always correcting us. She had this little proverb, "Be in the ring if it don't mean a thing, just be there." She cited poetry all the time and she was interested in our dreams. I would sit and read the Bible with her every night and she taught me how to pray. I used to do all my reciting with her, for Mother's Day, Easter, Christmas, all the holidays at the church. She'd say, "Don't singsong, Kate, don't singsong." I'd go in and recite and she'd say, "Now slow down and say it like this...." She was an artist in that sense; she really believed in poetry. She read *Guideposts* religiously, *Ideal Magazine,* and *Reader's Digest Condensed Books.* She had this long prayer that she'd pray after all the food was on the table. We always knew she was getting to the end when she said, "And when waste and age and shock and strife shall have sapped these walls of life, take this dust that's earthly worn and mold it into heavenly form."

She was a very religious woman and she didn't believe in anger. She'd say, "It's nice to be important but more important to be nice." Christianity and niceness were synonymous for her, so she got pushed around a lot and exploited a lot. We couldn't laugh at anybody, never poke fun at any kid. There was a man in our neighborhood who looked like the elephant man with warts all over him. All the kids would run from him. She'd sit us down and say, "God made everybody." Sometimes kids would be poking fun at other kids because they had raggedy clothes and raggedy shoes, and she'd say, "No, you don't do that." I'd feel so cheated because I couldn't be like a normal kid, that I had to be this damn Christian all the time. But I'm so glad she gave us that, because even when the tables were turned and I was the poor one and the raggedy one, I still knew I was somebody.

My grandmother gave us a sense of stability. When she died, the hardest thing was calling home and realizing nobody was home. As long as she was alive, there was always someone home.

Our house changed over the years. What I first remember is that you walked in the front door and that was my parents' bedroom and there was always a baby crib in there. To the left was the dining room with an oil stove and a buffet and a china cabinet. Then there was a kitchen and another bedroom. There were nine of us and we kids slept in the back room. All the rooms were painted green. Our house expanded over the years and another bedroom and a bathroom were added on eventually. When I was growing up we had an outhouse out back. Our yard had a garden, pear trees, a plum tree, apple trees, cherry trees, muscadine, a grapevine, and a big hollow in the back where we dumped our garbage and burned it. The hollow led all the way back to the hog pen, the smoke house, and a coal house, a garage and a chicken coop. The front yard had hedges all around, grass, and a walkway. The back yard didn't have grass so we swept it and kept it nice and clean. We had a clothes line out there. One of the ways we knew we were upwardly mobile is when we moved the clothes line so that you couldn't see the underwear from the road.

My mother's name is Corine Emmanuelette Lytle Cannon. She was named for her father Emmanuel. She was the nineteenth child of twenty. She loved her mother. Grandma died in her arms. She always wanted to be a schoolteacher or a businesswoman. She had so many dreams. When she realized that she couldn't fulfill her dreams, she just gave those dreams to us. Most people think she is a teacher or something because of the way she carries herself, proud-like, a real survivor. If there was an opportunity to go somewhere for the church, "I'll go, I'll go do it." So some of the older schoolteachers and people in the church exposed her to things that normally one without an education would not get exposed to. She wanted to go to business college, and we had one of those real old typewriters in our house.

She is a very shapely woman and dresses very well. The house was hers and she let us know that. Her husband was hers too and she let us know that. I never knew my father because he was off limits to us. That was her man. "He's mine, get your own man," she'd say. We were appendages to their marriage; we could never come between them. That's probably why they have been so happily married for forty-five years. I never knew my mother to take a bath without my father washing her back. He'd be out in the yard, and she'd say, "Go get your daddy. Esau, come here." And he'd always come. She had him wrapped around her little finger.

My mother took us everywhere. Most Black kids stayed at home, but we'd get dressed up and we'd go. We got exposed to Jim Crowism because we were always going out. And of course Mama would say, "Go to the bathroom before we leave.... Eat before we leave," because we couldn't do either until we got back. She almost jerked my arm off one time because I saw one of the White women she cleaned for and said, "Mama, there's Mrs. Coates." You didn't talk to those people in the streets. Mama was always clean and dressed up with her hair done. She wasn't going to stop going because of us, and she'd be damned if we were going to hold her up being children. So we learned manners early on, how to act in public, how to speak up, how to talk, and how not to make demands. We'd go with her when she went shopping and when she went to the doctors. She'd have to go up the back stairs and we'd learn to sit in the car for three or four hours without fighting or anything. You took a book to read and acted mannerly. There was a lot of control. When I was already in school and knew about gym sets and swings, we parked in front of the Presbyterian Church in Charlotte and I wanted to go play on the swings in the playground. She told me, "Kate, you can't do that." My experience was that my mother exposed me to the world as it was without protection, and she also taught us how to cope with it, so we all learned our place.

My mother worked as a domestic. At one point she made five dollars a week, and then she found by working for different people she could make five dollars a day. My mother also did all these little odd jobs like sell Stanley Products, vanilla flavoring and liniment, and collect burial money. She did all those things to keep us in kindergarten, and she always tithed. She taught us to give 10 percent to the church that we went to every Sunday. Every Sunday. We went to the Presbyterian church and she always had to pick up every kid in the neighborhood. There was never any private space. We were always crowded in our 1957 Chevy station wagon. "Well, you know, they got to go to church too," she'd say.

It was always assumed that we would work. Work was a given in life, almost like breathing and sleeping. I'm always surprised when I hear people talking about somebody taking care of them, because we always knew we were going to work. The first work I did was as a domestic, cleaning people's houses. The interesting thing was that all the White people we worked for were mill workers. Black women were not allowed to work in the mill then, so the only jobs available to Black women were as domestics or teachers, and there was only one Black school in Kannapolis. They only needed about thirty teachers, so that was very limited. All the Black women I knew worked as domestics and all the Black men I knew worked in Cannon Mills in the low-paying menial jobs. My father drove a truck and did whatever dirty work there was to be done. As I said, my grandmother's greatest pride was that she never worked for a White person, and she used to ridicule my mother in a very covert, subtle way for not having a better job. I was never ashamed that my mother was a domestic because everybody else's mother was a domestic, if they worked at all. So I knew I'd grow up to be a domestic.

Part of the training for Black kids to become a domestic was to learn to do that kind of work at home. 'Cause while your mother's taking care of White kids and cleaning up White houses, you got to do that for yourself. There is nothing that would irritate a Black woman more than to clean a White woman's house all day long and then come home to a dirty house. In some kind of way, almost as if by osmosis, Black girls were supposed to know how to do all these things and who was supposed to be teaching us? Mama would leave before sunup and when she got home it would be sundown, and we were not only supposed to know how to keep house but also how to cook perfect meals and not burn food up, and not to eat up all the food because it had to stretch. This wisdom was supposed to be inside of each of us, I mean, we were disciplined if we didn't know it. So that was very frustrating. That's how I learned to be a domestic, by taking care of house at home. My older sister, who was two years older than me, was responsible for teaching me how to do it. How to mop the floors, how to pick the strings up after the mop, how to dust so that you don't break things, how to wash windows and wipe down the blinds, the whole mechanical system of how to clean a house. I knew all that by the time I was eight. If you didn't do it right you got screamed at. You just figured it out so you wouldn't get hit. It was like, "How did you miss this?" And "Why is there a streak here?" "What are these strings doing on the floor?" Or "You missed this corner." It was like a spot check when she got home, especially on Saturdays, because that was when we were supposed to really clean house and get our clothes ready for Sunday.

So I started working for my aunt who cleaned the house down the road and got two dollars for the day. That was my very first job. I was so proud of it too, 'cause that meant that I had learned at home how to do it. Aunt Tot always drank a lot, has all her life, but she always liked me. Whenever she didn't want to go to work she'd let different nieces take over. Well, I was so honored that she'd let me work for her as a domestic. She said, "Kate, you want to make some money?" It was two dollars and in 1962 that was like a lot of money. She told me it was for the Chapmans down the road. She told me to go down there and she didn't have to tell me what to do specifically, she just told me to put the dinner on, that I had to cook, wash the clothes, iron the clothes, take care of the children and make sure nothing happens to them. Most of the time they didn't want you to wash the floors with a mop; they wanted you to get down on your hands and knees and wash all the corners and stuff.

I was told not to do anything that would cause Aunt Tot to lose her job. So I was meticulous in everything I did because — one, I wanted my aunt to be proud of me, and two, my mother's reputation was on the line because she was training me to be a domestic, and three, my aunt's income was on the line because if anything was broken or not up to par then she could lose her job. The fact that she was going to give me the whole two dollars was a real honor. So I'd walk down to Mrs. Chapman's house and clean up her house and take care of her four kids. One of the daughters was as old as I was, maybe twelve, named Blondie. They would sit around and watch TV and play games, and they didn't think anything of the fact that I was cleaning. I was just Tot's niece who would come in whenever she wasn't there. Aunt Tot was probably out drinking or something but I felt real glad that she would let me come in and do it. That was my first job where I got paid. Mrs. Chapman worked in the mill and so did her husband. He would be there when I got there, and he'd just be leaving. She worked first shift and he worked second. In Kannapolis you can't get through the center of town during the changing of shifts, it's so jammed.

I remember their house was tinier than ours, and there were things in their house that were not even as nice as ours. Most of the White people in Kannapolis didn't clean their houses. That was what Black women were for. That was how Black women would get their income, how they survived. So the Chapmans had this old house, it was like four rooms. Our house was small but larger than the house they lived in.

They would pay you two dollars for two hours of work, but you had a list of things to do and if it took you longer than that, that was your business. All the work they wanted you to do, you could never do in two hours. You had to wash the clothes, hang them on the line and iron them, wash the floors, and do things like clean the refrigerator or clean out the cabinets, all these other little things you did to prove you were worthy of the job. You never did just what you were asked. You always did a little extra. I remember you never ate the food. That was just not a sign of a good domestic. They had food like baloney, which was considered White people's food anyway, so you brought your own food. I'd bring potted meat, sardines, or Vienna sausages.

I resented those Chapman kids. I resented the fact that my mother was always gone and didn't have time to take care of her kids and here I was a kid having to take care of kids who were my same age.

Notes

Preface

1. Cheryl J. Sanders, "Womanist Ethics: Contemporary Trends and Themes," *The Annual of the Society of Christian Ethics 1994* (Georgetown University Press, 1994), 299–305.
2. Letty Russell, ed., *Feminist Interpretation of the Bible* (Philadelphia: Westminster Press, 1985), 40.

Introduction

1. Alice Walker, *In Search of My Mother's Garden: Womanist Prose* (New York: Harcourt Brace Jovanovich, 1983), xi–xii.
2. Hortense J. Spillers, "Introduction: Who Cuts the Border? Some Readings on 'America'" in *Comparative American Identities: Race, Sex and Nationality in the Modern Text,* ed. Hortense J. Spillers (New York: Routledge, 1991), 1–25.
3. W. E. B. Du Bois, *The Souls of Black Folk* (New York: New American Library, 1969), xi.

1. Surviving the Blight

1. Sherley Anne Williams, foreword to Zora Neale Hurston, *Their Eyes Were Watching God* (Champaign: University of Illinois Press, 1978), vii–viii.
2. Victoria Byerly, *Hard Times Cotton Mill Girls: Personal Histories of Womanhood and Poverty in the South* (Ithaca, N.Y.: ILR Press, 1986), 143–60.
3. Dorothy Sterling, ed., *We Are Your Sisters: Black Women in the Nineteenth Century* (New York: W. W. Norton & Co., 1984), 42–43.
4. Ibid., 43.
5. George R. Rawick, *From Sundown to Sunup: The Making of the Black Community* (Westport, Conn.: Greenwood Publishing Co., 1972), 57.
6. Testimony of Sarah M. Grimké, abolitionist from South Carolina, in Theodore D. Weld, *American Slavery as It Is: Testimony of a Thousand Witnesses* (American Anti-Slavery Society, 1839), cited in Gerda Lerner, ed., *Black Women in White America: A Documentary History* (New York: Vintage Books, 1972), 18.

7. Cited by Robert E. Hemenway in the introduction to Zora Neale Hurston, *Mules and Men* (Bloomington: Indiana University Press, 1978), xxi.

8. Langston Hughes and Arna Bontemps, eds., *The Book of Negro Folklore* (New York: Dodd, Mead & Co., 1958), xiii.

9. C. Eric Lincoln, *The Black Muslims in America* (Boston: Beacon Press, 1973), 35.

10. Rawick, *From Sundown to Sunup,* 35.

11. Ibid.

2. Slave Ideology and Biblical Interpretation

1. Antonio Gramsci, *Selections from the Prison Notebooks,* ed. and trans. Quinten Hoare and Geoffrey Norwell Smith (London: Lawrence & Wishart, 1971), 5–23; Cornel West, *Prophesy Deliverance! An Afro-American Revolutionary Christianity* (Philadelphia: Westminster, 1982), 9–127.

2. Winthrop D. Jordan *White over Black: American Attitudes toward the Negro, 1550–1812* (Baltimore: Penguin Books, 1969), 3–98; Thomas F. Gossett, *Race: The History of an Idea in America* (Dallas: Southern Methodist University Press, 1963), 3–31.

3. H. Shelton Smith, *In His Image, But...: Racism in Southern Religion, 1780–1910* (Durham, N.C.: Duke University Press, 1972), 23–207.

4. E. S. Morgan, "Slavery and Freedom: The American Paradox," *Journal of American History* 59 (1972): 5–29; Carl N. Degler, "Slavery and the Genesis of American Race Prejudice," *Comparative Studies in Society and History* 2 (1959): 49–66.

5. Angela Y. Davis, *Women, Race and Class* (New York: Random House, 1981), 391–421.

6. J. William Harris, *Plain Folk and Gentry in a Slave Society* (Middletown, Conn.: Wesleyan University Press, 1985), 67.

7. Joseph R. Washington, Jr., *Anti-Blackness in English Religion, 1500–1800* (New York: Edwin Mellen, 1984), 231–320.

8. Josiah Priest, *Bible Defense of Slavery* (Glasgow, Ky.: W. S. Brown, 1851), 393.

9. Davis, *Women, Race and Class,* 3–29.

10. Oliver C. Cox, *Caste, Class, and Race: A Study in Social Dynamics* (New York: Doubleday, 1984), 353–91; Jordan, *White over Black,* 321–25.

11. Frederick A. Ross, *Slavery Ordained of God* (Philadelphia: J. B. Lippincott, 1857), 11–68.

12. William Sumner Jenkins, *Pro-Slavery Thought in the Old South* (Chapel Hill: University of North Carolina Press, 1935), 90–92.

13. L. R. Bradley, "The Curse of Canaan and the American Negro (Gen. 9:25–27)," *Concordia Theological Monthly* 42 (1971): 100–105.

14. Frederick Perry Noble, *The Redemption of Africa* (Chicago: Fleming H. Revell, 1899).

15. Walter Rodney, *How Europe Underdeveloped Africa* (London: Bogie l'Ouverture, 1972), 730.

16. Lester B. Scherer, *Slavery and the Churches in Early America 1619–1819* (Grand Rapids, Mich.: Wm. B. Eerdmans, 1975), 29–81.

17. Davis, *Women, Race and Class,* 165–96.

18. Washington, *Anti-Blackness in English Religion,* 103–39.

19. George Fitzhugh, *Cannibals All! or, Slaves without Masters,* ed. C. Van Woodward (Cambridge: Belknap Press of Harvard University, 1857, 1960).

20. Washington, *Anti-Blackness in English Religion,* 1–35.

21. *White over Black,* 24.

22. Orlando Patterson, *Slavery and Social Death: A Comparative Study* (Cambridge: Harvard University Press, 1982), 1–14.

23. C. Eric Lincoln, *Race, Religion and the Continuing American Dilemma* (New York: Hill and Wang, 1984), 23–31.

24. Samuel Blanchard How, *Slaveholding Not Sinful, the Punishment of Man's Sin, Its Remedy, the Gospel of Jesus Christ* (New Brunswick, N.J.: J. Terhune's Press, 1856), 63–133.

25. Thomas Virgil Peterson, *Ham and Japheth: The Mythic World of Whites in the Antebellum South* (Metuchen, N.J.: Scarecrow Press, 1978), 91–121.

26. Ibid., 12–26, 38–84.

27. Adam Gurowski, *Slavery in History* (New York: A. B. Burdick, 1860), 165–71.

28. Quoted in William A. Smith, *Lectures on the Philosophy and Practice of Slavery, as Exhibited in the Institution of Domestic Slavery in the United States: With the Duties of Masters and Slaves* (Nashville: Stevenson & Evans, 1856), 25.

29. Peterson, *Ham and Japheth,* 17–34.

30. Alfred Conrad and John Meyer, "The Economics of Slavery in the Antebellum South," *Journal of Political Economy* 66 (1958): 95–130, 442–34; Harold Woodman, "The Profitability of Slavery: A Historical Perennial," *Journal of Southern History* 29 (1963): 303–25.

31. Iveson L. Brookes, *A Defense of the South against the Reproaches and Incroachments of the North: in Which Slavery Is Shown to Be an Institution of God Intended to Form the Basis of the Best Social State and the Only Safeguard to the Permanence of a Republican Government* (Hamburg, S.C.: Republican Office, 1850), 45.

3. The Emergence of Black Feminist Consciousness

1. C. Eric Lincoln, in his foreword to William R. Jones, *Is God a White Racist?* (Garden City, N.Y.: Doubleday & Co., Anchor Books, 1973), vii–viii.

2. Howard Thurman, *Deep River and the Negro Spiritual Speaks of Life and Death* (Richmond, Ind.: Friends United Press, 1975), 135.

3. Benjamin Mays, *The Negro's God as Reflected in His Literature* (Boston: Chapman & Grimes, 1938; reprint ed., Westport, Conn.: Greenwood Press, 1969), 26.

4. George P. Rawick, *The American Slave: A Composite Autobiography from Sundown to Sunup* (Westport, Conn.: Greenwood Press, 1972), 51.

5. La Frances Rodgers-Rose, ed., *The Black Woman* (Beverly Hills, Calif.: Sage Publications, 1980), 20.

6. Barbara Christian, *Black Women Novelists: The Development of a Tradition, 1892–1976* (Westport, Conn.: Greenwood Press, 1980), 13.

7. Paul A. David et al., *Reckoning with Slavery: Critical Essays in the Quantitative History of American Negro Slavery* (New York: Oxford University Press, 1976), 59. For a detailed discussion of the internal slave trade, see Frederic Bancroft, *Slave Trading in the Old South* (New York: Frederick Ungar Publishing Co., 1959).

8. A quotation by Fannie Barrier Williams in Bert James Loewenberg and Ruth Bogin, eds., *Black Women in Nineteenth-Century American Life: Their Words, Their Thoughts, Their Feelings* (University Park: Pennsylvania State University Press, 1976), 15.

9. Henry Allen Bullock, *A History of Negro Education in the South from 1619 to the Present* (Cambridge, Mass.: Harvard University Press, 1967), 155–56.

10. Stated by then Chief Justice Taney in the Dred Scott case, March 1857.

11. Jeanne L. Noble, *Beautiful, Also, Are the Souls of My Black Sisters: A History of the Black Woman in America* (Englewood Cliffs, N.J.: Prentice-Hall, 1978), 63.

12. William J. Wilson, *Power, Racism, and Privilege: Rare Relations in Theoretical and Sociohistorical Perspectives* (New York: Macmillan Publishing Co., 1973), 99.

13. According to *Negro Population in the United States 1790–1915,* published by the U.S. Bureau of the Census (1918; reprint, New York: Arno Press, 1968), five Black women migrated out of the South for every four Black men.

14. Sharon Harley and Rosalyn Terborg-Penn, eds., *The Afro-American Woman: Struggle and Images* (Kennikat Press, 1978), 8.

15. Zora Neale Hurston, *Their Eyes Were Watching God* (New York: J. B. Lippincott Co., 1937; reprint ed., Urbana: University of Illinois Press, 1978), 17.

16. Alice Walker, *In Search of Our Mothers' Gardens: Womanist Prose* (New York: Harcourt Brace Jovanovich, 1983), xi–xii. Walker indicates that the term "Womanist" is "from womanish (opposite of 'girlish,' i.e., frivolous, 'irresponsible, not serious'). A black feminist or feminist of color." Among other things she loves women and men, is committed to the survival of her people and their culture, loves herself. "Womanist is to feminist as purple is to lavender."

4. Moral Wisdom in the Black Women's Literary Tradition

1. Pierre L. Van Der Berghe, *Race and Racism: A Comparative Perspective* (New York: Wiley, 1967), 77.

2. W. E. B. Du Bois, *Dusk at Dawn* (New York: Harcourt Brace and Co., 1940).

3. Frances M. Beal, "Slave of a Slave No More: Black Women in Struggle," *The Black Scholar* 12 (November/December 1981): 16–17; reprinted from vol. 6 (March 1975).

4. Toni Morrison, *The Bluest Eye* (New York: Holt, Rinehart and Winston, 1970), 109–10.

5. Dexter Fisher, ed., *The Third Woman: Minority Women Writers of the United States* (Boston: Houghton Mifflin Co., 1980), 148.

6. Quoted in Arna Bontemps, "The Black Contribution to American Letters: Part I," in Mable M. Staythe, ed., *The Black American Reference Book* (Englewood Cliffs, N.J.: Prentice-Hall, 1976), 752.

7. Richard K. Barksdale and Kenneth Kinnamon, eds., *Black Writers in America: A Comprehensive Anthology* (New York: Macmillan Co., 1972), 59.

8. Barbara Christian, *Black Women Novelists: The Development of a Tradition, 1892–1976* (Westport, Conn.: Greenwood Press, 1980), 239.

9. Jeanne Noble, *Beautiful, Also, Are the Souls of My Sisters: A History of the Black Women in America* (Englewood Cliffs, N.J.: Prentice-Hall, 1978), 63.

10. Mary Helen Washington, *Midnight Birds: Stories of Contemporary Black Women Writers* (Garden City, N.Y.: Doubleday & Co., 1979), 95–96.

11. Verta Mae Grosvenor, *Vibration Cooking* (New York: Doubleday & Co., 1970).

12. Marcia Gillespie, Editorial, *Essence Magazine*, May 1975, 39.

13. Ann Petty, *The Street* (Boston: Houghton Mifflin, 1946; reprint, New York: Pyramid Books, 1961), 266.

14. Gwendolyn Brooks, "Maud Martha," in *The World of Gwendolyn Brooks* (New York: Harper and Row, 1971), 178–79.

15. Margaret Walker, *Jubilee* (Boston: Houghton Mifflin Co., 1966; reprint, New York: Bantam Books, 1981), 406.

16. Alice Childress, "The Negro Woman in American Literature," in Pat Crutchfield Exum, ed., *Keeping the Faith: Writings by Contemporary Black Women* (Greenwich, Conn.: Fawcett Publications, 1974), 32.

5. Womanist Perspectival Discourse and Canon Formation

1. Dennis P. McCann gives this definition as one aspect of philosophical conscientization developed by Paulo Freire. See *The Westminster Dictionary of Christian Ethics* (Philadelphia: Westminster Press, 1986), 120.

2. Toni Morrison, ed., *Race-ing Justice, En-gendering Power* (New York: Pantheon Books, 1992), x.

3. Kathy Russell Midge Wilson and Ronald Hall, *The Color Complex* (New York: Harcourt Brace Jovanovich, 1992).

4. Mary Helen Washington, *Black-Eyed Susans* (Garden City, N.Y.: Anchor Press/Doubleday, 1975), xiv. Books that exemplify this point include Maya Angelou, *I Know Why the Caged Bird Sings* (New York: Random House, 1970); Gwendolyn Brooks, *Report from Part One* (Detroit: Broadside Press, 1972); Toni Morrison, *The Bluest Eye* (New York: Holt, Rinehart and Winston, 1970).

5. Washington, *Black-Eyed Susans*, xiv–xvii.

6. Ibid., xvi.

7. Ibid.

8. Ibid.

9. Abby Lincoln, "Who Will Revere the Black Woman?" in Toni Cade,

ed., *The Black Woman: An Anthology* (New York: New American Library, 1970), 84.

10. Alice Walker, *In Search of Our Mothers Gardens: Womanist Prose* (New York: Harcourt Brace Jovanovich, 1983), 373–74.

11. Here I borrow the title phrase from a 1982 anthology, Barbara Smith, Gloria T. Hull, and Patricia Bell Scott, eds., *All the Women Are White, All the Blacks Are Men, But Some of Us Are Brave: Black Women's Studies* (Old Westbury, N.Y.: Feminist Press, 1982).

12. Walker, *In Search of Our Mother's Gardens,* 373–74.

13. Nikki Giovanni, "Woman Poem," in Cade, *The Black Woman,* 13.

14. Mae Henderson, "Toni Morrison's *Beloved:* Re-Membering the Body as Historical Text," in *Comparative American Identities: Race, Sex and Nationalities in the Modern Text,* edited with an introduction by Hortense Spillers (New York: Routledge, 1991), 62–86.

15. Toni Morrison, *Beloved* (New York: Alfred A. Knopf, 1987), 23. Page references for further quotes from *Beloved* will be given parenthetically in the text.

16. Howard Thurman, *For the Inward Journey: The Writings of Howard Thurman* (Richmond, Ind.: Friends United Meeting, 1984), 199.

17. BBC "Toni Morrison Interview," produced and directed by Alan Benson, edited and presented by Melvyn Bragg (Boston: WGBH, February 1990).

18. Morrison, *Beloved,* 79.

19. Henderson, "Toni Morrison's *Beloved:* Re-Membering the Body as Historical Text," 70–71.

20. Marcia Gillespie, "No Woman's Land: The Refugee Crisis," *Ms.* 3, no. 3 (1992).

21. "Toni Morrison Interview."

6. Resources for a Constructive Ethic: The Life and Work of Zora Neale Hurston

1. Zora Neale Hurston, *Dust Tracks on a Road* (Philadelphia: Lippincott, 1942), 177. For Hurston's elaboration of "the Negro farthest down," read chap. 10, "Research," and chap. 12, "My People! My People!"

2. Zora Neale Hurston, "John Redding Goes to Sea," *Opportunity* 4 (January 1926): 17.

3. Zora Neale Hurston to Langston Hughes, April 30, 1929, James Weldon Johnson Memorial Collection of American Literature, Beinecke Rare Book and Manuscript Library, Yale University.

4. Karla F. C. Holloway, "A Critical Investigation of Literary and Linguistic Structures in the Fiction of Zora Neale Hurston" (Ph.D. diss., Michigan State University, 1978).

5. Hurston, *Dust Tracks on a Road,* 21.

6. Ibid.

7. Ibid., 46.

8. Ibid., 89.

9. Zora Neale Hurston, *Jonah's Gourd Vine* (Philadelphia: Lippincott, 1984), 206–7.

10. Robert Hemenway, *Zora Neale Hurston: A Literary Biography* (Urbana: University of Illinois Press, 1977), 5.

11. Joyce O. Jenkins, "To Make a Woman Black: A Critical Analysis of the Women Characters in the Fiction and Folklore of Zora Neale Hurston" (Ph.D. diss., Bowling Green State University, 1979).

12. Hurston, *Dust Tracks on a Road,* 182–83.

13. Zora Neale Hurston, *Mules and Men* (Philadelphia: Lippincott, 1938; reprint ed., New York: Collier, 1970), 18–19.

14. Ibid.

15. Ellease Southerland, "Zora Neale Hurston: The Novelist-Anthropologist's Life/Works," *Black World* 25 (August 1974): 20.

16. Zora Neale Hurston, *Their Eyes Were Watching God* (Philadelphia: Lippincott, 1917; reprint ed., Urbana: University of Illinois Press, 1978), 236.

17. Ibid., 35.

18. Ibid., 31–32.

19. Ibid., 29.

20. Mary Helen Washington, "Black Women Image Makers," *Black World* 25 (August 1974): 16.

21. Zora Neale Hurston, *Moses, Man of the Mountain* (Philadelphia: Lippincott, 1939; reprint ed., Chatham, N.J.: Chatham Bookseller, 1967), 137.

22. Alice Walker, *I Love Myself When I Am Laughing...: A Zora Neale Hurston Reader* (Old Westbury, N.Y.: Feminist Press, 1979), 176.

23. Ibid., 270.

24. Hurston, *Moses,* 840.

25. Washington, "Black Women Image Makers," 21.

26. Zora Neale Hurston, *Seraph on the Suwanee* (New York: Scribner's, 1948; reprint ed., New York: AMS Press, 1974), 22; see also Worth Turtle Hedden, "Turpentine and Moonshine," review of *Seraph on the Suwanee* in *New York Herald Tribune Weekly Book Review,* October 1948, 2.

27. Hurston, *Seraph on the Suwanee,* 238–39.

28. Ibid., 269.

29. Ibid., 23.

30. Ibid., 41.

31. Ibid., 190.

32. Ibid., 230.

33. Walker, *I Love Myself When I Am Laughing,* 151.

34. Ibid.

7. Unctuousness as Virtue—According to the Life of Zora Neale Hurston

1. Pat Crutchfield Exum, ed., *Keeping the Faith: Writings by Contemporary Black Women* (Greenwich, Conn.: Fawcett Publications, 1974), 34–35.

2. Alice Walker, foreword to Robert Hemenway, *Zora Neale Hurston: A Literary Biography* (Urbana: University of Illinois Press, 1977), xvii. The moral

agency of Zora Neale Hurston culminates in a quality that Alice Walker identifies as "unctuousness." On her own from the age of nine and a runaway from the age of fourteen, Hurston repeatedly had to act sincere in the most insincere situations.

3. David L. Lewis, *When Harlem Was in Vogue* (New York: Alfred A. Knopf, 1981), 99.

4. Jeanne Noble, *Beautiful, Also, Are the Souls of My Black Sisters: A History of the Black Woman in America* (Englewood Cliffs, N.J.: Prentice-Hall, 1978), 148.

5. Harold Cruse, *The Crisis of the Negro Intellectual* (New York: William Morrow & Co., 1967), 9–10.

6. Karla F. C. Holloway, "Critical Investigation of Literary and Linguistic Structures in the Fiction of Zora Neale Hurston" (Ph.D. diss., Michigan State University, 1978), 36.

7. Mary Helen Washington, "Zora Neale Hurston: A Woman Half in Shadow," Introduction to *I Love Myself When I Am Laughing...: A Zora Neale Hurston Reader,* ed. Alice Walker (Old Westbury, N.Y.: Feminist Press, 1979), 8: "To a large extent, the attention focused on Zora Hurston's controversial personality and lifestyle have inhibited any objective critical analysis of her work. Few male critics have been able to resist sly innuendos and outright attacks on Hurston's personal life, even when the work in question was not affected by her disposition or her private affairs. But these controversies have loomed so large in the reviews of her work that once again the task of confronting them must precede any reappraisal or reevaluation of her highly neglected work."

8. Robert Hemenway, *Zora Neale Hurston: A Literary Biography* (Urbana: University of Illinois Press, 1977), 218–20.

9. Walker, Foreword to Hemenway, *Zora Neale Hurston,* xv.

10. Hemenway, *Zora Neale Hurston,* 93–94, 308, 314 (first marriage to Herbert Sheen); 273–74, 314 (second marriage to Albert Price III).

11. Alice Walker, Foreword to Hemenway, *Zora Neale Hurston,* xv, writes, "They [Hurston's critics] disliked her apparent sensuality: the way she tended to marry or not marry men, but enjoyed them anyway, while never missing a beat in her work. They hinted slyly that Zora was gay, or at least bi-sexual — how else could they account for her drive? — though there is not a shred of evidence that this was true. The accusation becomes humorous — and, of course, at all times irrelevant — when one considers that what she *did* write was some of the most healthily rendered heterosexual loving in our literature."

12. Carl Van Vechten to Fannie Hunt, July 5, 1960, James Weldon Johnson Memorial Collection of American Literature, Beinecke Rare Book and Manuscript Library, Yale University.

13. Zora Neale Hurston to the *Orlando Sentinel,* August 11, 1955, in response to the Supreme Court desegregation decision in 1954.

14. Hemenway, *Zora Neale Hurston,* 338, points out that Zora Hurston objected to the implied pathological stereotype in the desegregation decision wherein it was thought that Black students could learn only if they were in close proximity with Whites. Black students would be "uplifted" to White standards

and a White way of life. "The Supreme Court ruling," she said, "implied that just like mules being led by a white mare, black students had to be led by white pupils and white teachers."

15. Roy Wilkins, "The Watchtower," *New York Amsterdam News,* February 27, 1943.

16. Lester Granger, *California Eagle,* December 20, 1951.

17. Wallace Thurman, *Infants of the Spring* (New York: Macaulay, 1932), 239–40.

18. Darwin Turner, *In a Minor Chord* (Carbondale: Southern Illinois University Press, 1971), 120.

19. Arna Bontemps, "From Eatonville, Fla. to Harlem," review of *Dust Tracks on a Road,* by Zora Neale Hurston, *New York Herald Tribune,* November 23, 1942.

20. Harold Preece, "The Negro Folk Cult," review of Zora Neale Hurston, *Dust Tracks on a Road,* in *Crisis* 43 (1936): 364.

21. Sterling Brown, "Old Time Tales," review of *Mules and Men* (1936), a clipping in the James Weldon Johnson Memorial Collection of American Literature, Beinecke Rare Book and Manuscript Library, Yale University.

22. Alain Locke, "Dry Fields and Green Pastures," review of Zora Neale Hurston, *Moses, Man of the Mountain* in *Opportunity* 18 (January 1940): 7.

23. Ralph Ellison, "Recent Negro Fiction," review of Zora Neale Hurston, *Moses, Man of the Mountain,* in *New Masses,* August 5, 1941, 211.

24. Robert Bone, *The Negro Novel in America* (New Haven: Yale University Press, 1965), 41.

25. Hemenway, *Zora Neale Hurston,* 241.

26. Zora Neale Hurston's manuscript chapter "Concert," *Dust Tracks on a Road,* James Weldon Johnson Memorial Collection of American Literature, Beinecke Rare Book and Manuscript Library, Yale University.

27. Zora Neale Hurston to Charlotte Osgood Mason, September 25, 1931, and October 15, 1931, Locke Collection, Howard University.

28. Zora Neale Hurston to Carl Van Vechten, October 30, 1948, James Weldon Johnson Memorial Collection of American Literature, Beinecke Rare Book and Manuscript Library, Yale University.

29. Hemenway, *Zora Neale Hurston,* 332.

30. Barbara Christian, *Black Women Novelists: The Development of a Tradition, 1892–1976* (Westport, Conn.: Greenwood Press, 1980), 61.

8. "The Wounds of Jesus": Justification of Goodness in the Face of Manifold Evil

1. The importance of sermons in biblical discourse is discussed in David T. Shannon's essay "An Ante-bellum Sermon: A Resource for an African American Hermeneutic," in Cain Hope Felder, ed., *Stony the Road We Trod: African American Biblical Interpretation* (Minneapolis: Fortress Press, 1991), 98–123.

2. Zilpha Elaw, *Memoirs of the Life, Religious Experience, Ministerial Travels and Labours, of Mrs. Zilpha Elaw, An American Female of Colour* (London: T. Dudley and B. Taylor, 1846); James Walker Hood, *The Negro*

in the Christian Pulpit; or The Two Characters and Two Destinies Delin-
eated in Twenty-one Practical Sermons (Raleigh: Edward Broughton, 1884);
Bishop Lucius Henry Holsey, Autobiography, Sermons, Addresses and Essays
(Atlanta: Franklin Printing and Publishing Co., 1898); William E. Hatcher,
John Jasper: The Unmatched Negro Philosopher and Preacher (New York:
F. H. Revell, 1908); William Henry Furness, The Ministry of Women (n.p.,
1842); and Amanda Berry Smith, An Autobiography: The Story of the Lord's
Dealings with Mrs. Amanda Berry Smith, the Colored Evangelist (Chicago:
Meyer, 1893).

3. William Lloyd Imes, The Black Pastures — An American Pilgrimage
in Two Centuries: Essays and Sermons (Nashville: Hemphill Press, 1957);
Charles A. Tindley, Book of Sermons (Philadelphia: Charles A. Tindley, 1932);
James H. Robinson, Adventurous Preaching (Great Neck, N.Y.: Channel Press,
1956); Samuel Gandy, ed., Human Possibilities: A Vernon Johns Reader
(Washington, D.C.: Hoffman Press, 1977).

4. This sermon, delivered by C. C. Lovelace, was heard by Zora Neale Hurston at Eau Gallie in Florida, May 3, 1929, and originally published in Nancy
Cunard, ed., Negro: An Anthology (London: Wishart, 1934), 35–39.

5. For other instances of sermons in the African American literary tradi-
tion see the following: Paul Lawrence Dunbar, The Uncalled (1898; reprint,
New York: Negro Universities Press, 1969); Joggin' Erlong (New York: Dodd,
Mead & Co., 1906); and Lyrics of Lowly Life (New York: Dodd, Mead &
Co., 1901); James Weldon Johnson, God's Trombones: Seven Negro Sermons
in Verse (New York: Viking Press, 1927); Walter White, The Fire in the Flint
(1924; reprint, New York: New American Library, 1969); Jean Toomer, Cane
(New York: Boniand Liveright, 1923); James Baldwin, Go Tell It on the Moun-
tain (New York: Grosset & Dunlap, 1953), Notes of a Native Son (New York:
Dial Press, 1955), The Fire Next Time (New York: Dial Press, 1963), and Just
Above My Head (New York: Dial Press, 1979).

6. Published as Black Womanist Ethics (Atlanta: Scholars Press, 1988).

7. Henry H. Mitchell, Black Preaching (Philadelphia: J. B. Lippincott Co.,
1970); Ella P. Mitchell, ed., Those Preaching Women (Valley Forge: Judson
Press, 1985); Robert.T. Newbold, Jr., ed., Black Preaching: Selected Sermons
in the Presbyterian Tradition (Philadelphia: Geneva Press, 1977); Mervyn A.
Warren, Black Preaching: Truth and Soul (Washington, D.C.: University Press
of America, 1977); Joseph A. Johnson, Jr., The Soul of the Black Preacher
(Memphis: C. M. E. Publishing House, 1970).

8. See also Hurston's nonfiction, Mules and Men (Philadelphia: Lippincott,
1935); Tell My Horse (1938; reprint, Berkeley: Turtle Island, 1981); and The
Sanctified Church (Berkeley: Turtle Island, 1983).

9. See Zora Neale Hurston to Carl Van Vechten February 28, 1934, James
Weldon Johnson Memorial Collection of American Literature, Beinecke Rare
Book and Manuscript Library, Yale University.

10. The four plays not discussed in this essay are "Spears," now lost, which
won honorable mention in the 1925 Opportunity magazine contest, "Color
Struck," published in Fire! in 1926, "Fast and Furious" (1932), and "The Great
Day" (1932) musical revues.

11. Ruthe T. Shelley, "Zora Hurston and Langston Hughes's 'Mule Bone': An Authentic Folk Comedy and the Compromised Tradition," *The Zora Neale Hurston Forum* 2, no. 1 (Fall, 1987): 49–60: "Rev. Long points out that by the law of the Bible in Judges 15:16 Samson slew a thousand Philistines with the jaw-bone of an ass...a mule is more dangerous the further to the rear one goes, a mule's hock bone must be much more dangerous than the jaw-bone of an ass."

12. W. E. B. Du Bois, *The Gifts of Black Folk: The Negroes in the Making of America* (New York: Washington Square Press, 1970).

13. Zora Neale Hurston to James Weldon Johnson, May 8, 1934, James Weldon Johnson Memorial Collection of American Literature, Beinecke Rare Book and Manuscript Library, Yale University. The review was by John Chamberlain, *New York Times*, May 3, 1934.

14. See Yngve Briolioth, *A Brief History of Preaching* (Philadelphia: Fortress Press, 1945); C. C. Morrison, *The American Pulpit* (Chicago: Christian Century Press, 1925); Robert T. Handy, *A Christian America: Protestant Hopes and Historical Realities*, 2d ed. (New York: Oxford University Press, 1984).

15. bell hooks and Cornel West, *Breaking Bread: Insurgent Black Intellectual Life* (Boston: South End Press, 1991), 131–46.

9. Womanist Interpretation and Preaching in the Black Church

1. The canon of womanist discourse is growing. Among many, see Toinette Eugene, "Moral Values and Black Womanists," *Journal of Religious Thought* 44 (Winter/Spring 1988): 23–34; "Roundtable Discussion: Christian Ethics and Theology in Womanist Perspective," *Journal of Feminist Studies in Religion* 5, no. 2 (Fall 1989): 82–112 (lead essay by Cheryl J. Sanders; responses by Katie G. Cannon, Emilie M. Townes, M. Shawn Copeland, Cheryl Townsend Gilkes, and bell hooks); Delores S. Williams, "Women's Oppression and Lifeline Politics in Black Women's Religious Narratives," *Journal of Feminist Studies in Religion* 2 (Fall 1985): 59–71; Delores S. Williams, "The Color of Feminism: Or Speaking the Black Woman's Tongue," *Journal of Religious Thought* 43 (Spring/Summer 1986): 45–58; and Emilie M. Townes, ed., *A Troubling in My Soul: Womanist Perspectives on Evil and Suffering* (Maryknoll, N.Y.: Orbis Books, 1993).

2. See Joseph A. Johnson, Jr., *The Soul of the Black Preacher* (Memphis: C.M.E. Publishing House, 1970); Charles V. Hamilton, *The Black Preacher in America* (New York: William Morrow and Co., 1972); Henry H. Mitchell, *Black Preaching* (Philadelphia: J. B. Lippincott Co., 1970); Henry H. Mitchell, *Celebration and Experience in Preaching* (Nashville: Abingdon, 1991).

3. See Robyn R. Warhol and Diane Price Herndl, eds., *Feminisms: An Anthology of Literary Theory and Criticism* (New Brunswick, N.J.: Rutgers University Press, 1991).

4. Elisabeth Schüssler Fiorenza, *In Memory of Her: A Feminist Theological Reconstruction of Christian Origins* (New York: Crossroad Publishing Co., 1983).

5. Isaac Rufus Clark, Sr., was an extraordinary homiletician and master

teacher for twenty-seven years at the Interdenominational Theological Center in Atlanta. Throughout this discussion I refer to his lectures and class notes.

6. Elisabeth Schüssler Fiorenza, *Revelation: Vision of a Just World* (Minneapolis: Fortress Press, 1991), 3.

7. This is an essential component in Alice Walker's definition of "womanist" in her collection of essays *In Search of Our Mothers' Gardens: Womanist Prose* (New York: Harcourt Brace Jovanovich, 1983), xi.

8. Schüssler Fiorenza, *Revelation,* 9.

9. See, for example the sermons in the following anthologies: Walter B. Hoard, ed., *Outstanding Black Sermons,* vol. 2 (Valley Forge, Pa.: Judson Press, 1979); Robert T. Newbold, ed., *Black Preaching: Selected Sermons in the Presbyterian Tradition* (Philadelphia: Geneva Press, 1977); Milton E. Owens, Jr., ed., *Outstanding Black Sermons,* vol. 3 (Valley Forge, Pa.: Judson Press, 1982); William M. Philpot, ed., *Best Black Sermons* (Valley Forge, Pa.: Judson Press, 1972); James Henry Young, ed., *Preaching the Gospel* (Philadelphia: Fortress Press, 1976).

10. See Albert J. Raboteau, *Slave Religion: The "Invisible Institution" in the Antebellum South* (New York: Oxford University Press, 1978); and David Charles Dennard, "Religion in the Quarters: A Study of Slave Preachers in the Antebellum South, 1800–1860" (Ph.D. Dissertation, Northwestern University, 1983).

11. See Benjamin E. Mays, *The Negro's Church* (New York: Institute of Social and Religious Research, 1933); Harry V. Richardson, *Dark Glory: A Picture of the Church among Negroes in the Rural South* (New York: Friendship Press, 1947); Carter G. Woodson, *The History of the Negro Church* (Washington, D.C.: Associated Press, 1921).

12. See Gayraud S. Wilmore, *Black Religion and Black Radicalism: An Examination of the Black Experience in Religion* (Garden City, N.Y.: Doubleday & Co., 1972); and Jualynne Dodson, "Nineteenth-Century A.M.E. Preaching Women," in *Woman in New Worlds,* ed. Hilah F. Thomas and Rosemary S. Keller (Nashville: Abingdon, 1981), 276–89.

13. Elisabeth Schüssler Fiorenza, *But She Said: Feminist Practice of Biblical Interpretation* (Boston: Beacon Press, 1992).

14. See Gerald L. Davis, *I Got the Word in Me and I Can Sing It, You Know: A Study of the Performed African American Sermon* (Philadelphia: University of Pennsylvania Press, 1985); James H. Robinson, *Adventurous Preaching* (Great Neck, N.Y.: Channel Press, 1956); and Bruce Rosenberg, *Can These Bones Live?* (Urbana: University of Illinois Press, 1988).

15. James Forbes, *The Holy Spirit and Preaching* (Nashville: Abingdon Press, 1989).

16. See Jacquelyn Grant, "Womanist Theology: Black Women's Experience as a Source for Doing Theology, with Special Reference to Christology," *Journal of the Interdenominational Theological Center* 13, no. 2 (Spring 1986): 195–212; and Kelly D. Brown, "God Is as Christ Does: Toward a Womanist Theology," in *Journal of Religious Thought* 46, no. 1 (Summer/Fall 1989): 7–16.

17. E. L. McCall et al., *Seven Black Preachers Tell: What Jesus Means to Me* (Nashville: Broadman Press, 1971).

18. Cain Hope Felder, ed., *Stony the Road We Trod: African American Biblical Interpretation* (Minneapolis: Fortress Press, 1991).

19. C. L. Franklin, *Give Me This Mountain: Life History and Selected Sermons,* ed. Jeff Todd Titon, Foreword by Jesse Jackson (Urbana: University of Illinois Press, 1989); Samuel Gandy, ed., *Human Possibilities: A Vernon John Reader* (Washington, D.C.: Hoffman Press, 1977); William Lloyd Imes, *The Black Pastures* (Nashville: Hemphill Press, 1957); Sandy Ray, *Journeying through the Jungle* (Nashville: Broadman Press, 1979); Gardner Taylor, *The Scarlet Thread: Nineteen Sermons* (Elgin, Ill.: Progressive Baptist Publishing House, 1981).

20. See Williams E. Hatcher, *John Jasper* (New York: F. H. Revell, 1908); and Ralph H. Jones, *Albert Tindley: Prince of Black Preachers* (Nashville: Abingdon Press, 1982).

21. See Samuel D. Proctor, *Preaching about Crisis in the Community* (Philadelphia: Westminster Press, 1988); and Kelly Miller Smith, *Social Crisis Preaching* (Macon, Ga.: Mercer University Press, 1984).

22. Abbey Lincoln, "Who Will Revere the Black Woman?" *Negro Digest,* September 1966, 18.

23. See, for example, sermons written and published by African American women in the following anthologies: Ella Pearson Mitchell, ed., *Those Preaching Women: Sermons by Black Women Preachers* (Valley Forge, Pa.: Judson Press, 1985); Ella Pearson Mitchell, ed., *Those Preaching Women: More Sermons by Black Women Preachers,* vol. 2 (Valley Forge, Pa.: Judson Press, 1988); Helen Gray Crotwell, ed., *Women and the Word: Sermons* (Philadelphia: Fortress Press, 1977); Justo L. Gonzalez, ed., *Proclaiming the Acceptable Year: Sermons from the Perspective of Liberation Theology* (Valley Forge, Pa.: Judson Press, 1982); David A. Farmer and Edwina Hunter, eds., *And Blessed Is She: Sermons By Women* (San Francisco: Harper & Row, 1990); Annie L. Milhaven, ed. *Sermons Seldom Heard: Women Proclaim Their Lives* (New York: Crossroads, 1991).

24. Elisabeth Schüssler Fiorenza, *But She Said,* 9.

10. Hitting a Straight Lick with a Crooked Stick: The Womanist Dilemma in the Development of a Black Liberation Ethic

1. For a provocative critique of this dilemma, see Vincent Harding, "Responsibilities of the Black Scholar to the Community," in Darlene Clark Hine, ed., *The State of Afro-American History: Past, Present, and Future* (Baton Rouge: Louisiana State University Press, 1986), 277–84; Oliver C. Cox, "The New Crisis in Leadership among Negroes," *Journal of Negro Education* 19, no. 4 (Fall 1950): 459–65; also Oliver C. Cox, "Leadership among Negroes in the United States," in Alvin W. Gouldner, ed., *Studies in Leadership* (New York: Russell & Russell, 1950), 228–71.

2. Robert K. Merton, "Insiders and Outsiders: A Chapter in the Sociology of Knowledge," *American Journal of Sociology* 78 (July 1972).

3. For example, see the essays in Gene H. Outka and Paul Ramsey, eds., *Norm and Context in Christian Ethics* (New York: Charles Scribner's Sons,

1968); also Paul Ramsey, *Basic Christian Ethics* (New York: Charles Scribner's Sons, 1950); and Alasdair MacIntyre, *After Virtue* (Notre Dame: University of Notre Dame Press, 1981).

4. For a selection of early works on this topic from the perspective of the Black male scholar, see John Hope Franklin, "The Dilemma of the American Negro Scholar," in Herbert Hill, ed., *Soon, One Morning: New Writing by American Negroes, 1940–1962* (New York: Knopf, 1963), 64–69, 73–74; Carter G. Woodson, *The Mis-Education of the Negro* (Washington D.C.: Associated Publishers, 1933); W. E. B. Du Bois, *The Education of Black People: Ten Critiques, 1906–1960,* ed. Herbert Aptheker (Amherst: University of Massachusetts Press, 1973).

5. For a comprehensive critique, see Mary Francis Berry, "Blacks in Predominantly White Institutions of Higher Learning," in National Urban League, *The State of Black America 1983* (New York, 1983); Robert Staples, "Racial Ideology and Intellectual Racism: Blacks in Academia," *Black Scholar* 15, no. 2 (March–April 1984): 2–17; and John Wideman, "Publish and Still Perish: The Dilemma of Black Educators on White Campuses," *Black Enterprise* 10 (September 1978): 44–49.

6. This sort of observation has been made in numerous contexts. See, for example, Harold Cruse, *The Crisis of the Negro Intellectual* (New York: William Morrow and Co., 1967); Betty D. Maxwell, *Employment of Minority Ph.D.'s: Changes over Time* (Washington, D.C.: Commission on Human Resources of the National Research Council, 1981); Jeanne Noble, *The Negro College Woman Graduate* (New York: Columbia University Press, 1954); and Oliver C. Cox, "Provisions for Graduate Education among Negroes," *Journal of Negro Education* 11, no. 1 (January 1940): 222–27.

7. Sheila Ruth, "Methodocracy, Misogyny, and Bad Faith: Sexism in the Philosophical Establishment," *Metaphilosophy* 10 (1979): 48–61; Delores Williams, "Women's Oppression and Life-Line Politics in Black Women's Religious Narratives," *Journal of Feminist Studies in Religion* 1, no. 2 (Fall 1985): 59–71.

8. Chanzo Tallamu, Review of *Slipping through the Cracks: The Status of Black Women, Black Scholar* (July/August 1986): 59.

9. Chandra Talpade Mohantz, "On Difference: The Politics of Black Women's Studies," *Women's Studies International Forum* 6 (1983): 243–47; Margaret A. Simons, "Racism and Feminism: A Schism in the Sisterhood," *Feminist Studies* 5 (1979): 384–401; and the MudFlower Collective, *God's Fierce Whimsy: The Implications of Christian Feminism for Theological Education* (New York: Pilgrim Press, 1985).

10. See John E. Fleming, *The Lengthening Shadow of Slavery: A Historical Justification for Affirmative Action for Blacks in Higher Education* (Washington, D.C.: Howard University Press, 1976).

11. Theodore Caplow and R. McGee, *The Academic Marketplace* (New York: Basic Books, 1958); Pierre Van den Berghe, *Academic Gamesmanship: How to Make a Ph.D. Pay* (New York: Abelard-Schuman, 1970); and Alvin W. Gouldner, *The Future of Intellectuals and the Rise of the New Class* (New York: Seabury Press, 1979).

12. Without doubt the most influential womanists who take this approach are Angela Davis, *Women, Race and Class* (New York: Random House, 1981); June Jordan, *On Call: Political Essays* (Boston: South End Press, 1985); Alice Walker, *In Search of Our Mothers' Gardens: Womanist Prose* (New York: Harcourt Brace Jovanovich, 1983); Audre Lorde, *Sister Outsider: Essays and Speeches* (Trumansburg, N.Y.: Crossing Press, 1984).

13. For examples see Bernice Johnson Reagon, "The Borning Struggle: The Civil Rights Movement," in Dick Cluster, ed., *They Should Have Served That Cup of Coffee* (Boston: South End Press, 1979); Barbara Smith, ed., *Home Girls: A Black Feminist Anthology* (Watertown, Mass.: Persephone Press, 1983); bell hooks, *Ain't I a Woman?: Black Women and Feminism* (Boston: South End Press, 1981).

14. This kind of moral reasoning is delineated in Filomina C. Steady, ed., *The Black Woman Cross-Culturally* (Cambridge, Mass.: Schenkman Pub. Co., 1981); Toni Cade, ed., *The Black Woman: An Anthology* (New York: New American Library, 1970); and Gloria T. Hull, Patricia Bell Scott, and Barbara Smith, eds., *All the Women Are White, All the Blacks Are Men, But Some of Us Are Brave* (Old Westbury, N.Y.: Feminist Press, 1982).

15. Coalition on Women and the Budget, *Inequality of Sacrifice: The Impact of the Reagan Budget on Women* (Washington, D.C., 1983).

16. All these works are either implicit or explicit analyses of this position: Dorothy Sterling, *We Are Your Sisters: Black Women in the Nineteenth Century* (New York: Norton Books, 1984); Jacqueline Jones, *Labor of Love, Labor of Sorrow: Black Women, Work and the Family from Slavery to the Present* (New York: Basic Books, 1985); Bert Loewenberg and Ruth Bogin, eds., *Black Women in Nineteenth Century American Life: Their Words, Their Thoughts, Their Feelings* (University Park, Pa.: Pennsylvania State University, 1976); and Rosalyn Terborg-Penn and Sharon Harley, eds., *The Afro-American Woman: Struggles and Images* (New York: Kennikat, 1978).

17. See, in particular, Ellen N. Lawson, "Sarah Woodson Early: Nineteenth-Century Black Nationalist 'Sister,'" *Umoja: A Scholarly Journal of Black Studies* 5 (Summer 1981); Gerda Lerner, ed., *Black Women in White America: Documentary History* (New York: Random House, 1972); and Dorothy Sterling, *Black Foremothers: Three Lives* (Old Westbury, N.Y.: Feminist Press, 1979).

18. Rennie Simson, "The Afro-American Female: The Historical Context of the Construction of Sexual Identity," in Ann Snitow, Sharon Thompson, and Christine Stausa II, eds., *The Powers of Desire: The Politics of Sexuality* (New York: Monthly Review Press, 1983), 229–35.

19. Darlene Clark Hine, "Lifting the Veil, Shattering the Silence: Black Women's History in Slavery and Freedom," in Darlene Clark Hine, ed., *The State of Afro-American History: Past, Present, and Future* (Baton Rouge: Louisiana State University Press, 1986), 223–49.

20. For examples, see Gayraud S. Wilmore and James H. Cone, eds., *Black Theology: A Documentary History, 1966–1979* (Maryknoll, N.Y.: Orbis Books, 1979); and Preston N. Williams, "Impartiality, Racism, and Sexism," *Annual of the Society of Christian Ethics* (1983): 147–59.

21. Ellen Carol DuBois, et al., *Feminist Scholarship: Kindling in the Groves of Academe* (Urbana: University of Illinois Press, 1985); Beverly W. Harrison, *Making the Connections,* ed. Carol Robb (Boston: Beacon Press, 1985); Barbara H. Andolson, Christine E. Gudorf, and Mary D. Pellauer, eds., *Women's Consciousness, Women's Conscience* (New York: Seabury Press, 1985).

22. For historical work see W. E. B. Du Bois, *The Negro Church* (Atlanta: Atlanta University Press, 1903); Benjamin E. Mays, *The Negro's God as Reflected in His Literature* (Boston: Chapman and Grimes, 1958); Benjamin E. Mays and Joseph W. Nicholson, *The Negro's Church* (New York: Institute of Social and Religious Research, 1933); and Carter G. Woodson, *The History of the Negro Church* (Washington, D.C.: Associated Publishing, 1921).

23. Katie G. Cannon, "The Sign of Hope in Three Centuries of Despair: Women in the Black Church Community," in *Human Rights and the Global Mission of the Church,* Boston Theological Institute Annual Series 1 (Cambridge, Mass., 1985), 44–50.

24. For examples, see Edward M. Brawley, ed., *The Negro Baptist Pulpit* (Philadelphia: American Baptist Publication Society, 1890); Charles V. Hamilton, *The Black Preacher in America* (New York: Morrow, 1972); Henry Beecher Hicks, *Images of the Black Preacher* (Valley Forge, Pa.: Judson Press, 1977).

25. Henry H. Mitchell, *Black Preaching* (Philadelphia: Lippincott, 1970); William M. Philpot, ed., *Best Black Sermons* (Valley Forge, Pa.: Judson Press, 1972); Henry J. Young, ed., *Preaching the Gospel* (Philadelphia: Fortress Press, 1976); and Samuel Proctor and William D. Watley, *Sermons from the Black Pulpit* (Valley Forge, Pa.: Judson Press, 1984).

26. Harry V. Richardson, *Dark Glory: A Picture of the Church among Negroes in the Rural South* (New York: Friendship Press, 1947); William L. Banks, *The Black Church in the United States: Its Origin, Growth, Contribution and Outlook* (Chicago: Moody Press, 1972); C. Eric Lincoln, *The Black Experience in Religion* (Garden City, N.Y.: Doubleday, Anchor, 1974); Albert J. Raboteau, *Slave Religion: The "Invisible Institution" in Antebellum South* (New York: Oxford University Press, 1978).

11. Appropriation and Reciprocity in the Doing of Womanist Ethics

1. "Roundtable Discussion: Christian Ethics and Theology in Womanist Perspective" a response to Cheryl Sanders, in *The Journal of Feminist Studies in Religion* 5, no. 2 (1989): 83–112.

2. Cecil Wayne Cone, *The Identity Crisis in Black Theology* (Nashville: African Methodist Episcopal Church, 1975).

3. Cecil Cone also argued that the Black Power slogans and the motif of Black radicals are inappropriate for doing Black Theology, for expounding upon the orderly description of the faith of the Black church.

4. Cone, *The Identity Crises in Black Theology,* 18–19.

5. "Roundtable Discussion," 111.

6. A three-item, open-ended questionnaire (a. What are the origins of your womanist voice? b. What forces-experiences shape the voice you have? and c. Whose interests does your voice serve?) was sent out in the spring of 1992

to fifty African American women who are theologically trained. The sample was interdenominational and included self-identified womanist clergy, faculty, doctoral candidates, and seminarians across the United States of America. There was an 85 percent response rate.

12. Metalogues and Dialogues: Teaching the Womanist Idea

1. See Helmut Richard Niebuhr, Daniel Day Williams, and James M. Gustafson, *The Advancement of Theological Education* (New York: Harper & Row, 1956); Ed Farley, *The Fragility of Knowledge: Theological Education in the Church and University* (Minneapolis: Fortress, 1988); Joseph C. Hough, Jr., and John B. Cobb, Jr., *Christian Identity and Theological Education* (Atlanta: Scholars Press, 1985); The MudFlower Collective, *Gods Fierce Whimsy: Christian Feminism and Theological Education* (New York: Pilgrim Press, 1989); and Barbara G. Wheeler and Edward Farley, eds., *Shifting Boundaries: Contextual Approaches to the Study of Theological Education* (Louisville: Westminster/ John Knox Press, 1992).

2. Toinette M. Eugene, "Under-represented Constituencies: Minorities and Majorities in the Seminary," *Christianity and Crisis* 49, nos. 5 and 6 (April 3–17, 1989): 110–13.

3. Yolanda T. Moses, "Black Women in Academe: Issues and Strategies," paper for the Project on the Status and Education of Women, Association of American Colleges, August 1989).

4. Audre Lorde, *Sister Outsider* (Trumansburg, N.Y.: Crossing Press, 1984).

5. Elisabeth Schüssler Fiorenza, "Feminist Theology as a Critical Theology of Liberation," *Theological Studies* 36, no. 4 (December 1975): 605–26.

6. Zora Neale Hurston, "How It Feels to Be Colored Me," *The World Tomorrow* (May 1928): 17.

7. Delores Williams, "One Black Woman Reflects on Union," *Union Dues* 2, no. 1 (November 8, 1978): 4.

8. Don S. Browning, David Polk, and Ian S. Evison, eds., *The Education of the Practical Theologian: Responses to Joseph Hough and John Cobb's "Christian Identity and Theological Education"* (Atlanta: Scholars Press, 1989).

9. Michelle Russell "An Open Letter to the Academy," *Quest* 3 (1977): 70–80.

10. See Elsa Barkley Brown, "Mothers of Mind," *Sage Magazine: A Scholarly Journal on Black Women–Black Women's Studies* 6, no. 1 (Summer 1989): 4–11.

11. The term was coined by Wynn Legerton in May 1989 to describe the erotic particles emitted into the air whenever we are doing the work our souls must have.

12. Ann E. Berthoff, *Forming/Thinking/Writing: The Composing Imagination* (Rochelle Park, N.Y.: Hayden, 1978).

13. Beverly W. Harrison, "Toward a Christian Feminist Liberation Hermeneutic for De-mystifying Class Reality in Local Congregations," in *Beyond Clericalism*, ed. Joseph C. Hough, Jr., and Barbara G. Wheeler (Atlanta: Scholars Press, 1988), 137–51.

13. Racism and Economics: The Perspective of Oliver C. Cox

1. For discussion see V. P. Franklin, *Black Self-Determination: A Cultural History of the Faith of the Fathers* (Westport, Conn.: Lawrence Hill, 1984); Vincent Harding, *There Is a River: The Black Struggle for Freedom* (New York: Harcourt Brace Jovanovich, 1981); Albert Raboteau, *Slave Religion: The "Invisible Institution" in the Antebellum South* (New York: Oxford University Press, 1978); Mary Frances Berry and John Blassingame, *Long Memory: The Black Experience in America* (New York: Oxford University Press, 1982).

2. Gayraud Wilmore, *Black Religion and Black Radicalism* (Garden City, N.Y. Doubleday. 1972); W. E. B. Du Bois, *The Souls of Black Folk* (Greenwich, Conn.: Fawcett Publications, 1903; reprint ed., 1969); Martin Luther King, Jr., *Why We Can't Wait* (New York: Harper & Row, 1964); Frederick Douglass, *The Life and Times of Frederick Douglass* (London, 1892, reprint ed., New York: Macmillan, 1962); James H. Cone, *Black Theology and Black Power* (New York: Seabury Press, 1969).

3. Several recent studies include Maulana Karenga, *Introduction to Black Studies* (Inglewood, Calif.: Kawaida Publications, 1982); Manning Marable, *How Capitalism Underdeveloped Black America* (Boston: South End Press, 1983); Paula Giddings, *When and Where I Enter: The Impact of Black Women on Race and Sex in America* (New York: William Morrow & Co. 1984); Bell Hooks, *Feminist Theory: From Margin to Center* (Boston: South End Press, 1984); Leslie W. Dunbar, ed., *Minority Report: What Has Happened to Blacks, Hispanics, American Indians and Other Minorities in the Eighties* (New York: Pantheon Books, 1984).

4. Carter G. Woodson, *The Mis-Education of the Negro* (Washington, D.C.: Associated Publishers, 1933); *The Negro in Our History* (Washington, D.C.: Associated Publishers, 1931); *The History of the Negro Church* (Washington, D.C.: Associated Publishers, 1921).

5. Carter G. Woodson, *African Heroes and Heroines* (Washington, D.C.: Associated Publishers, 1939); *Free Negro Heads of Families in the United States in 1830* (Washington, D.C.: Association for the Study of Negro Life and History, 1925); *The Negro Professional Man and the Community* (reprint of 1934 ed., New York: Negro University Press, 1969); *The Story of the Negro Retold* (Washington, D.C.: Associated Publishers, 1935); *The Mind of the Negro as Reflected in Letters Written during the Crisis 1800–1860* (Washington, D.C.: Association for the Study of Negro Life and History, 1926).

6. George D. Kelsey, *Racism and the Christian Understanding of Man* (New York: Charles Scribner's Sons, 1965).

7. For literature on the theological discussion of this issue, see Albert Barnes, *An Inquiry into the Scriptural Views of Slavery* (Philadelphia: Perkins & Purves, 1857); John Henry Hopkins, *A Scriptural, Ecclesiastical, and Historical View of Slavery: From the Days of the Patriarch Abraham to the Nineteenth Century* (New York: Negro University Press, 1969); William Hosmer, *Slavery and the Church* (reprint of 1853 ed., New York: Negro University Press, 1969); Fred A. Ross. *Slavery Ordained of God* (Philadelphia: J. B. Lippincott Co., 1857); Lesler Scherer, *Slavery and the Churches in Early America 1619–1819* (Grand Rapids, Mich.: William B. Eerdmans Pub. Co., 1975).

8. My understanding of Oliver C. Cox's personal life is based on the article by Gordan D. Morgan, "In Memoriam: Oliver C. Cox 1901–1974," *Monthly Review* 28, no. 1 (May 1976): 34–40.

9. Oliver C. Cox, *Caste, Class and Race* (Garden City, N.Y.: Doubleday, 1948).

10. Ibid., xvi.

11. Gunnar Myrdal, *An American Dilemma* (New York: Harper & Row, 1944). E. Franklin Frazier, *The Negro Family in the United States* (Chicago: University of Chicago Press, 1939); E. Franklin Frazier, *The Negro Church in America* (New York: Schocken Books, 1964); St. Clair Drake and Horace Cayton, *Black Metropolis*, 2 vols. (rev. ed., New York: Harper & Row, 1962).

12. Oliver C. Cox, "The Modern Caste School of Race Relations," *Social Forces* 21 (December 1942): 218–26. For a contemporary discussion, see Lloyd Hogan, *Principles of Black Political Economy* (Boston: Routledge & Kegan Paul, 1984); Robert Allen, *Black Awakening in Capitalist America* (Garden City, N.Y.: Doubleday, 1970).

13. Cox, *Caste, Class and Race*, 332, italics added. C. T. Elizabeth Fox-Genovese and Eugene Fox-Genovese, *Fruits of Merchant Capital: Slavery and Bourgeois Property in the Rise and Expansion of Capitalism* (New York: Oxford University Press, 1983); Manning Marable, *Black-water* (Dayton, Ohio: Challenge Press, 1978).

14. Morgan, "In Memoriam," 35.

15. Oliver C. Cox, "Racial Theories of Robert E. Park, et al.," *Journal of Negro Education* 13, no. 4 (Fall 1944): 452–63. See also Stanford Lyman, *The Black American in Sociological Thought* (New York: Putnam Publishing Group, 1972).

16. At the time of his death Cox was working on a book about race relations. The manuscript was revised, edited, and published posthumously by Wayne State University Press in 1976. The title is *Race Relations — Elements and Social Dynamics*.

17. Cox, *Caste, Class and Race*, 333. James Boggs and Grace Boggs, *Racism and the Class Struggle* (New York: Monthly Review Press, 1970).

18. Oliver C. Cox, "Modern Democracy and the Class Struggle," *Journal of Negro Education* 14, no. 2 (Spring 1947): 155–64. See also Elizabeth Drew, *Politics and Money* (New York: Macmillan, 1983); Robert A. Dahl, *Who Governs?* (New Haven, Conn.: Yale University Press, 1961); G. William Domhoff, *The Higher Circle: The Governing Class in America* (New York: Random House, 1970).

19. Especially useful is Oliver C. Cox's "The Political Class," *Bulletin: Society for Social Research* (January 1944). Cf. Donald Harris, *Capital Accumulation and Income Distribution* (Stanford, Calif.: Stanford University Press, 1978); Samuel Huntington, *American Politics, the Politics of Disharmony* (Cambridge, Mass.: Belknap Press, 1981); Ralph Miliband, *The State in Capitalist Society* (New York: Basic Books, 1969); Nicos Poulantzas, *Political Power and Social Classes* (London: Sheed and Ward, 1973).

20. An elaboration of this point may be found in Oliver C. Cox, "Estates, Social Classes and Political Classes," *American Sociologist Review* 10,

no. 4 (August 1945): 464–69. For documentary information, see L. Carlson and G. A. Colburn, eds., *In Their Place: White America Defines Minorities 1850–1960* (New York: John Wiley & Sons, 1972).

21. Oliver C. Cox, *The Foundations of Capitalism* (New York: Philosophical Library, 1959), 92.

22. Ibid., 62. For detailed discussion, see R. H. Tawnay, *Religion and the Rise of Capitalism* (New York: Harcourt, Brace and Co., 1937).

23. Cox, *Foundations of Capitalism*, 106. Especially important is Walter Rodney, *How Europe Underdeveloped Africa* (Washington, D.C.: Howard University Press, 1974); A. G. Hopkins, *An Economic History of West Africa* (New York: Columbia University Press, 1973); Walter L. Goldfrank, ed., *The World System of Capitalism: Past and Present* (Beverly Hills, Calif.: Sage Publications, 1979).

24. Oliver C. Cox. *Capitalism and American Leadership* (New York: Philosophical Library, 1962), 292.

25. Ibid., 102. See Sidney Lens, *The Military-Industrial Complex* (Philadelphia: Pilgrim Press, 1970); Gordon Adams, *The Iron Triangle: The Politics of Defense Contracting* (New Brunswick, N.J.: Transaction Books, 1982).

26. Cox. *Capitalism and American Leadership*, 4. Cf. Richard Barnet and Ronald Muller, *Global Reach: The Power of Multinational Corporations* (New York: Simon & Schuster, 1974); Douglas Dowd, *The Twisted Dream: Capitalist Development in the U.S. Since 1776* (Cambridge, Mass.: Winthrop Publishers, 1977); G. Kolko, *The Roots of American Foreign Policy* (Boston: Beacon Press, 1969).

27. Cox, *Capitalism and American Leadership*, 7. See James Petras and Morris Morley, *The United States and Chile* (New York: Monthly Review Press, 1976); A. G. Frank, *Capitalism and Underdevelopment in Latin America* (New York: Monthly Review Press, 1969).

28. Cox, *Capitalism and American Leadership*, 24. See also Michael Barratt-Brown, *The Economics of Imperialism* (Harmondsworth: Penguin Education, 1974); Charles Wilber, ed., *The Political Economy of Development and Underdevelopment* (New York: Random House, 1973).

29. Cox, *Capitalism and American Leadership*, 74. See Robert Rhodes, ed., *Imperialism and Underdevelopment* (New York: Monthly Review Press, 1970); Harry Magdoff, *The Age of Imperialism* (New York: Monthly Review Press, 1969).

30. Cox, *Capitalism and American Leadership*, 61.

31. Cf. Oliver C. Cox, "Color Prejudice, a World Problem," *The Aryan Path* (Bombay, India) 8 (June 1947). See also "The Nature of the Anti-Asiatic Movement on the Pacific Coast," *Journal of Negro Education* 15, no. 4 (Fall 1946): 603–14.

32. Cox, *Capitalism and American Leadership*, 133. Essential sources are Sterling Spero and Abram Harris, *The Black Worker* (New York: Atheneum, 1968), and Julius Jacobson, ed., *The Negro and the American Labor Movement* (Garden City, N.Y.: Anchor Books, 1968).

33. Cox, *Capitalism and American Leadership*, 141.

34. Ibid., 242. See Harold Baron, "The Demand for Black Labor: Histor-

ical Notes on the Political Economy of Racism," *Radical America* 5 (1971): 2. For a more detailed historical discussion, see Daniel A. Novak, *The Wheel of Servitude: Black Forced Labor after Slavery* (Lexington: University Press of Kentucky, 1978); *The Roots of Black Poverty: The Southern Plantation Economy after the Civil War* (Durham, N.C.: Duke University Press, 1978).

35. Two helpful articles are Oliver C. Cox, "Race Relations," *Journal of Negro Education* 12, no. 2 (Spring 1943): 144–53, and "Lynching and the Status Quo," *Journal of Negro Education* 14, no. 2 (Spring 1945): 576–88. See also Sidney Willhem, *Who Needs the Negro?* (Cambridge, Mass.: Schenkman Publishing Co., 1970); J. D. Williams, ed., *The State of Black America* (New York: Transaction Books, 1984); Mary Frances Berry, *Black Resistance/White Law: A History of Constitutional Racism in America* (New York: Appleton-Century-Crofts, 1971).

36. See Oliver C. Cox, "Race and Caste: A Distinction," *American Journal of Sociology* (March 1945): 360–68. Also Victor Perlo, *The Economics of Racism, U.S.A.: Roots of Black Inequality* (New York: International Publishers, 1975); Benjamin B. Ringer, *"We the People" and Others: Duality and America's Treatment of Racial Minorities* (New York: Tavistock Publications, 1983); Marable, *How Capitalism Underdeveloped Black America.*

37. Cox, *Caste, Class and Race,* 322.

38. Ibid., 345.

39. For a brief, poignant discussion, see Oliver C. Cox, "Race, Prejudice, and Intolerance," *Social Forces* 24, no. 2 (Fall 1945): 216–19. Also A. Leon Higginbotham, Jr., *In the Matter of Color* (New York: Oxford University Press, 1978); Walter E. Williams, *The State against Blacks* (New York: New Press, McGraw-Hill, 1982); Center for the Study of Social Policy, *A Dream Deferred: The Economic Status of Black Americans* (Washington, D.C., 1983); John Ogbee, *Minority Education and Caste* (New York: Academic Press, 1978).

40. Cox, *Capitalism and American Leadership,* 251.